Custom and
Confrontation

Roger M. Keesing

Custom and Confrontation

The Kwaio Struggle for Cultural Autonomy

The University of Chicago Press
Chicago & London

The University of Chicago Press, Chicago 60637
The University of Chicago Press, Ltd., London
© 1992 by The University of Chicago
All rights reserved. Published 1992
Printed in the United States of America
01   00   99   98   5   4   3   2
ISBN (cloth): 0-226-42919-9
ISBN (paper): 0-226-42920-2

Library of Congress Cataloging-in-Publication Data

Keesing, Roger M., 1935–
    Custom and confrontation : the Kwaio struggle for cultural autonomy /
    Roger M. Keesing.
        p.   cm.
    Includes bibliographical references and index.
    1. Kwaoi (Melanesian people)   2. Kwaio (Melanesian people)—Ethnic identity.
    3. Acculturation—Solomon Islands.   I. Title.
DU850.K42   1992
306'.089995—dc20   92-12610
                                                                   CIP

Contents

Preface

My Kwaio research has now spanned almost thirty years. I could scarcely have envisioned, when I arrived in the Solomons in 1962 to begin field-work for my Ph.D., that so much of my life and intellectual energies would be devoted to a small and remote community of diehard cultural conservatives. Indeed, I could scarcely have anticipated, when I first arrived in Kwaio country in disarray (see Keesing 1991), that I would not only be welcomed—by people reputed to be wild, dangerous, and hostile to outsiders—but that I would be incorporated into their lives so positively, and incorporated into their historical project and struggle.

I had no idea of knowing then that my arrival would be construed as the fulfillment of their prayers and prophecy, and that the ethnographic study I intended, which I characterized to them as "writing down their customs," would be articulated with their efforts to codify their customary law and ancestrally imposed taboos so as to demand their recognition by the state. This articulation between their historic project and my professional goals has been both a blessing and a curse: a blessing because a fiercely proud and independent people have welcomed me into their homes and lives and worked with me supportively through the years in what has been a personally rich and rewarding experience and a rare anthropological opportunity; and a curse, because of the wide gulf between their project and mine, and the impossibility of my fulfilling their hopes and expectations. The book they have thought I was writing all these years could only be produced at the cost of a radical oversimplification and formulaic standardization of a rich and flexibly adaptive cultural tradition; and if it were written, it could scarcely achieve the goals—largely mystical—the Kwaio envision.

This, then, is not the book they have been waiting for. The young Kwaio who have acquired literacy in their language will have to write that themselves (and one of my goals in the last decade has been to empower them to do that). The book I have produced does come closer to the mark than the several books and many articles I have produced, describing aspects of their culture, history, and language. What it seeks to do is characterize their long historical engagement with Europeans, their struggle to preserve their ancestral customs, and to defend their right to follow them on their own lands. Where possible, this history is chronicled through Kwaio voices, as recorded directly through the three decades of my work in the Malaita mountains, and as they have survived in the earlier records. I seek to convey their hopes and fears and the value they place on a rich ancestral tradition that has been denigrated, despised, misunderstood, and feared by Europeans and Christian Solomon Islanders.

I have accumulated many debts, intellectual, personal, and institutional, in the course of my Kwaio research, and it would be impossible to make all of them explicit. First of all, my personal and intellectual debt to the late Jonathan Fifi'i (Fifi'i 1989) has been deep beyond measure. We worked together for most of those years, as friends and fellow ethnographers. My debt to him and his family endures, as even since his death in 1989, I have shared the household of his son and grandchildren. His voice will be heard often in the pages that follow.

Other close friends and collaborators from the early years of my fieldwork are mostly gone, too: 'Elota of Ga'enaafou, 'Aika of Kwailala'e, Talaunga'i of Fou'alabusi, Larikeni of Kwaina'afi'a, Alefo of Ngudu, Osika and Kwai'ime of 'Ai'eda, Go'ubisu of Naakogi, Batalamo of 'Elesi, Boori'au of Gosi, Tagi'au of Furisi'ina, Fenaori of Ga'enaafou, Maakona of Arulauni, Fei'a of Bole, Tome Arika of Farisi. Only a few are left—Bui'a and Geleniu of Darilari, Ma'aanamae of 'Ai'eda, Ngiri'a of Ngudu, Folofo'u of A'esuala, Suufiomea of 'Ubuni, Fa'afataa of Bole, Lounga and Riufaa of Kwangafi—and their ranks are thinned each year. Those who have joined the ancestors live on for me, though, not only in their words recorded on my tapes and in my notes and in my understandings of the cultural tradition they tried to teach me, but in their children, who share their homes and lives and knowledge with me still. My debts, personal and professional, to them and to scores of other Kwaio friends, are immense. My special debts in recent years to Maena'adi of Furisi'ina and 'Elota's oldest son Maefanaomea and his family are particularly strong.

In the Solomons, I am further indebted to Lawrence Fo'anaota of the National Museum, John Naitoro of the National Archives, Japhet Solomon of the Ministry of Education and Training, Senda Fifi'i of the Ministry of Foreign Affairs and Trade Relations, A. V. Hughes of the Central Bank, Prime Minister Solomon Mamaloni, Hon. Andrew Nori, Hon. Francis Saemala, Francis Bugotu, the news staff of Solomon Islands Broadcasting Co., the staff of the University of the South Pacific Centre in Honiara, and many others through the years. Others to whom I am indebted in the Solomons include the staff of the Atoifi Adventist Hospital, particularly the late Len Larwood and his family and the McMahon family, then Australian High Commissioner Trevor Sofield, and the Peace Corps Volunteers David Akin and Kate Gillogly, who worked tirelessly with and for the Kwaio and have been generous in sharing with me their insights and experiences through a period when I could not visit Kwaio country for political reasons. I am grateful to T. E. Anstee of Cairns, Australia, for permission to use his photographs from the 1927 punitive expedition, and to the South Sea Evangelical Mission for permission to use an old photograph.

My intellectual debts through the years have been diverse, and I will not try to characterize them all. Those colleagues and friends whose ideas have had a particular impact on this book, especially my thinking about discourses of resistance, include Fredrik Barth, Jonathan Friedman, Ranajit Guha, Margaret Jolly, Stuart Hall, George Lakoff, and Nicholas Thomas. My less direct but substantial intellectual debts to such scholars as Bernard Cohn, Jean Comaroff, James C. Scott, and Ann Stoler will emerge as well. Shorter versions of the argument of the book have been presented in seminars at the Australian National University, Massachusetts Institute of Technology, Philadelphia Anthropological Society, Canadian Anthropology Society, and University of Bergen. I am indebted to many scholars for useful comments and questions, and where possible, have indicated these debts in notes. I am particularly indebted to two anonymous readers for the University of Chicago Press whose incisive comments prompted me to add a chapter and expand a number of sections of the text.

Institutionally, I am grateful to the Australian National University for the opportunity to carry out sustained research and writing in an idyllic intellectual setting and the resources and freedom to make fieldwork trips back to Kwaio country whenever the precarious political situation has allowed. Earlier Kwaio fieldwork was supported by the U.S. National Science Foundation, the National Institute of Mental Health, the Ford Foundation, and the University of California, Santa Cruz; the Wenner-Gren Foundation for Anthropological Research has supported my recent collaboration with Maena'adi. McGill University has provided a supportive intellectual climate and resources for the last phases of writing.

Personally, my fieldwork companion in the 1960s, Zina Keesing Vitcov, and my fieldwork companion in the 1970s, Shelley Schreiner, contributed enormously to my fieldwork and cultural understanding. Schreiner and I continue to collaborate on the work we did in recording and interpreting Kwaio women's self-accounts. In the last decade, Christine Jourdan has been collaborator in Solomons research, anthropological and linguistic, and she has shared the joys and travails of writing and thought through the creation of the book, and provided love, support, and useful criticism.

Royalties earned from this book, like other earnings from my writings about the Kwaio, will go to the Fataia Development Fund, controlled by Kwaio Trustees. The modest income from my Kwaio writings has been used to support community schools where Kwaio teach one another literacy in the vernacular and transmit valued customary knowledge, a craft cooperative, and other community-operated grassroots development projects.

West Berkshire, Vermont

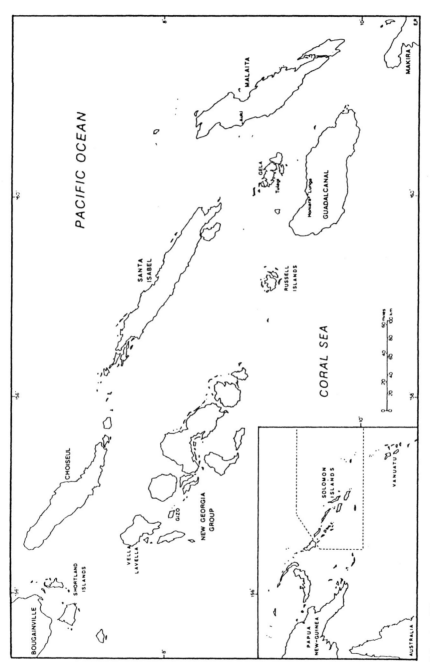

Map 1.   The Solomon Islands

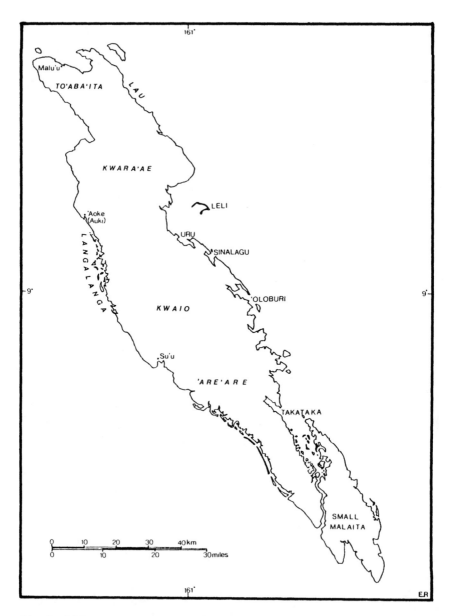

Map 2. Malaita

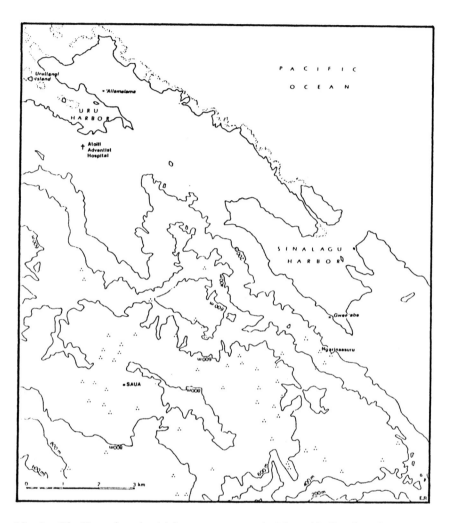

Map 3.   The Kwaio heartland (elevations in meters). Adapted by Eric Ross from
survey maps of Solomon Islands Ministry of Agriculture and Lands. Triangular marks
indicate pagan settlements as of 1964.

A returning Kwaio plantation worker wades ashore at Sinalagu (about 1920). Photo courtesy of South Sea Evangelical Church.

The first ships of the 1927 punitive expedition go ashore to Gwee'abe, from HMAS Adelaide. Photo courtesy of T. E. Anstee.

Desecration. Sailors from HMAS Adelaide pose in Kwaio bush with an ancestral skull. Photo courtesy of T. E. Anstee.

Kwaio prisoners being taken to the coast (1927). Photo courtesy of T. E. Anstee.

Rituals of colonial Tulagi. Anifelo, Basiana's son, is third from left, first row. Photo courtesy of E. Sandars.

Smoke from a sacrifice rises past the skull of Lamotalau of Furi'ilai, killed by the 1927 punitive expedition, as his grandson tends the fire.

Jonathan Fifi'i addresses the Kwaio *kastom* chiefs (1964).

Jonathan Fifi'i addresses the Kwaio *kastom* chiefs in front of Sub-District Committee house, Ngarinaasuru (1963). 'Elota is seated, Folofo'u standing between them.

The Kwaio chiefs discuss a legal case in the Sub-District Committee house, Ngarinaasuru (1963).

Right: Christian and pagan women haggle over fish at the weekly market, Sinalagu (1963).

Folofo'u at Kwaio Cultural Centre opening (1979).

Laefiwane dances at Kwaio Cultural Centre opening (1978).

Within the mountain walls: women of 'Al'eda perform a sacred ritual (1964).

1 Local Eddies in Global Streams

Along nineteenth-century frontiers of colonial expansion, local populations around the tropical world fought as best they could to preserve their ancestral lands and ancestral modes of life in the face of European invasion. But facing overwhelming technological superiority and increasingly efficient firepower, invaded and displaced by white settlers, and subjected to administrative control and the penetration of plantation economies, few tribal peoples[1] were able to resist militarily for long. The exceptional leaders of military resistance—a Zulu Tshaka, a Guinean Samory, a Sioux Crazy Horse—stand out in their singularity; and their eventual defeat was inevitable. Isolation and inhospitable and economically valueless terrain allowed some peoples to preserve their sovereignty well into this century; but even the most remote and conservative peoples were caught up in colonial states and were progressively subjected to their control in the first half of this century. With this process came missionization and the spread of Christianity (and Islam), replacing or being superimposed on local religions.

Since the Second World War, colonies have been transformed into independent nations, oriented toward "development" and in most cases toward Westernization. With the expansion of communications and transportation technology, the isolation of once remote interior areas and islands has progressively diminished. In this process, a kind of creolizing global "Third World" culture has extended its fingers into hinterlands communities; and cultural distinctiveness seems everywhere threatened, by class formation—the emergence of Westernized regional elites and peripheral peasantries—as well as by homogenizing cultural influences.[2] The temptations and pressures to Westernize and commoditize seem irresistible.

The relative powerlessness of marginal peoples to control their destinies has led scholars of various persuasions—conventional development theorists, dependency theorists, World Systems theorists—to view them as passive objects rather than active agents of change. Yet we are

---

1. I use that term in an intentionally broad and general sense to refer to societies anthropologists once called "primitive," with reference to their relatively simple technologies and non-state political organization.

2. For the Pacific, see Hau'ofa 1987.

beginning to get a different view, one that sees peripheral populations as active agents in shaping and controlling their engagement with the outside world, giving local meaning to alien ideas, institutions and things, and in various ways resisting them.

In part this change of perspective has been forced on Western scholars as indigenous peoples—often with allies in the environmental movement—have increasingly been able to make their voices heard internationally. Struggles that were once local and kept under wraps by repressive local authorities or national governments have burst into the media: the Kayapo struggle against environmental destruction and uncontrolled mining, the Yanomami struggle against invasion by miners, the Penan struggle against timber companies. In Third World countries where indigenous minorities were ruthlessly and relentlessly subjected to religious persecution, cultural attack, economic exploitation, and environmental devastation, the veils of silence and secrecy are now, in many places, being lifted.

The assumption that hinterlands peoples have everywhere been complicit in the processes of cultural destruction and Westernization, unable to resist material temptations or value old ways when given new alternatives and exposed to alien forms of power, has had to be reconsidered. The view from the centers of power within the global system still hides and disguises local eddies of creativity, opposition, and counter-hegemonic reformulation and resistance. Yet those who work closely with peoples on the margins or probe local histories close to the ground have come increasingly to see the active, creative, and politically astute side of local engagements with global forces.

In seeing that indigenous peoples have played a more active part as agents locally adapting to and reshaping outside forces, and that resistance in its varying modes has been more common and enduring than we had suspected, it is important for us not to romanticize their cultures or to project onto them our idealizations of primitivity, populism, or political struggle. It is also important to acknowledge the enormous forces that have confronted small and marginal populations with once-distinctive cultural traditions, and to acknowledge and understand accommodation and receptivity to alien cultural forms, as well as resistance. In the Pacific, for instance, Christianity has been an extremely powerful and relentless force of change. Although indigenous peoples have adapted and shaped it to their own cultural forms and values, and in many places and many ways have created syntheses of old and new religious elements, very few peoples exposed to sustained missionary pressures have resisted them and rejected the Christian message. Few peoples with sustained exposure to cash economy and Western material goods have made—and adhered for long periods to—choices that systematically limit their access to cash, in favor of subsistence production and local technologies. There are still culturally conservative peoples in the hinterlands of Papua New Guinea, but few have maintained their commitment to ancestral religions, subsistence orientations, and "traditional" lifestyles for long periods when exposed directly to strong, sustained missionary efforts or opportunities to participate actively in the cash economy. Cultural conservatism has (with some exceptions) primarily been a phenomenon of isolated and remote hinterlands; and as isolation has diminished, so has the traditionalism.

The Kwaio of Malaita, Solomon Islands, are a singular if not totally unique case in contemporary Melanesia. In the mountains above the eastern coast of Malaita, some two thousand Kwaio tribespeople still sacrifice pigs to their ancestors, still carry bows and arrows and clubs, still give mortuary feasts using strung shell valuables, still subsist on food they grow in rain forest swiddens (Keesing 1978b, 1982a). Yet only seventy-five miles away, where the Guadalcanal campaign was fought almost half a century ago, jet planes now bring businessmen,[3] development experts, and tourists to Honiara, the small but bustling capital of the UN's 150th member nation.

While the diehard Kwaio pagans are in some ways relatively isolated at the onset of the 1990s, their traditionalism can in no way be seen as stemming from lack of exposure to Christianity, the outside world, or the cash economy. For 120 years, the Kwaio have been connected to the world economy. The grandfathers of men now in late middle age worked in the cane fields of Queensland and Fiji; their fathers worked on Solomons plantations, and worked with the American military in World War II. Young Kwaio pagan men drift around the growing urban center of Honiara, often getting there by plane. For eighty-five years, the Kwaio have been subjected to sustained pressures of Christian evangelism. While many Kwaio along the coasts have become Christian, those living in the mountains continue defiantly to reject and resist a Christian message they know very well—a message clearly heard and understood in the mountains for half a century.

In the 1920s, the administration of the British Solomon Islands Pro-

---

3. I use the gendered term advisedly, since I have yet to see a foreign businesswoman in Honiara, other than those living in the country.

tectorate forced the Kwaio to submit to the Pax Britannica, a head tax, and an alien legal system. It was not a smooth and easy process: the Kwaio assassinated two British officers and massacred their police patrol in 1927, defending their sovereignty in the face of invasion as forcefully and fiercely as their numbers and technology allowed. Even when overt resistance was smashed, the Kwaio proclaimed their defiance through religious cultism with an unmistakable political message. The struggle by the Kwaio traditionalists for the right to follow customary law, rather than the alien laws brought by the British, has been a theme over decades of resistance and political confrontation. Resistance to Christianity has brought the assassination of two white missionaries, and sustained and sometimes violent confrontation between pagans in the mountains and Christian communities on the coast.

The Kwaio traditionalists follow their ancestral religion and customs, then, not out of isolation but out of struggle. In the postcolonial period, continuing demands for a substantial degree of cultural autonomy—the freedom to follow customary law and the defense of ancestral shrines and taboos against Christian invasion and defilement—has led to sustained confrontation with the governments of Province and nation. They refuse to pay taxes, reject development schemes and logging; they demand massive compensation for past grievances of the colonial period; they reject as best they can an alien legal system, threatening violence against police now afraid to enter their mountains; they demand that they be allowed to live according to "custom" on the land of their ancestors, not Western ways and laws; and they battle the invasive forces of evangelistic Christianity, as represented both by missionaries and by their own Kwaio cousins now living as Christians in coastal villages.

The resistance has continued into the onset of the 1990s. Moreover, by virtue of their stubborn and fierce commitment and the entropy of postcolonial economy and administration, the Kwaio are closer in 1990 to achieving a viable compromise with the outside world, on their own terms, that will allow them to follow their own customs free from governmental interference (but to take part selectively in national economy and polity) than they were in 1940 or 1960.

Kwaio struggle is illuminating with regard to issues about resistance now being debated by scholars in several disciplines. Through the work of such scholars as Ranajit Guha, James Scott, Paul Willis, Jean Comaroff, Lila Abu-Lughod, and Aihwa Ong, we have been learning that for the relatively powerless, resistance may appear in places and in forms that are far from the dramatic, overt confrontations that stand out in historical records and news accounts. For subaltern peoples or classes, resistance may be expressed more or less covertly in hundreds of everyday acts. Resistance may also be expressed indirectly, deflected in "symbolic" and religious forms, when overt political action is impossible. As Guha (1983) shows in analyzing peasant uprisings in colonial India, the construction of counterhegemonic movements as political by those in power is a complex, dialectical process. The colonial or postcolonial state can dismiss resistance cast in religious forms, millenarian or mystical, as superstition or fanaticism, thereby refusing to recognize its political implications.

We find across the decades of Kwaio struggle both armed resistance, and millenarianism, when overt confrontations had been smashed. We find on Solomons plantations resistance by subalterns reminiscent of Scott's Malaysians (Scott 1985); we find now in town predatory class-based resistance reminiscent of Willis's British working class youth (Willis 1977). I show that in different phases of the Kwaio struggle against European invasion and domination, their resistance has taken various forms; yet I show that it would be misleading to characterize one époque of Kwaio resistance as military, another as millenarian, another as political—since the support of the ancestors has been invoked all along the way, in the most "military" and "political" modes of confrontation as well as the most mystical and millenarian.

I show further that there are striking continuities in the Kwaio struggle, in terms of its focal themes and symbols—law, taxation, sovereignty (the power of the King vs. the power of the ancestors)—over half a century. I also uncover striking continuities in the cast of characters. A man we find in his twenties assassinating a missionary turns up thirty-five years later as a Chief in an anticolonial political movement; a man imprisoned for an attack on a government force in 1927 is prepared to attack again in 1947, and is prominent in anticolonial politics in 1967. The son of the leader who assassinated the District Officer in 1927 leads an antigovernment demonstration on the Prime Minister's lawn almost sixty years later—clad in the same mode of warrior regalia his father had worn.

In examining the concept of resistance in chapter 23, I explore a number of conceptual and theoretical problems currently being debated. Can we legitimately speak of resistance when the subordinated subjects do not understand their own actions in these terms—when they see themselves, say, as following the dictates of God rather than opposing earthly domination? Need resistance imply conscious agency? Can we speak of resistance when the subordinate are outwardly passively accepting their situation and powerlessness, yet harboring dreams of liberation and struggle? I argue in the end that although this theoretical field urgently needs conceptual clarification and rethinking, we cannot expect this to come from a refinement in our use of "resistance" as a theoretical concept. Drawing on recent work in cognitive linguistics on the complex internal structures of categories and the pervasively metaphoric nature of semantics, I examine the concept of resistance. I argue that resistance as a concept is prototype-based, iconic-image bound and metaphoric. The metaphoric nature of the concept of resistance, and the various permutations of the prototypic images around which it is built, preclude our defining resistance precisely, or specifying features common to all circumstances that can be characterized through this metaphor. If the concept of resistance is to serve us well, it will have to be through its flexibility and metaphoric richness, not its analytical precision.

One important element that will run through these chapters as a subtext is that "resistance" is often too general a gloss to put on courses of action taken by individuals and groups that had other motives—often diverse, often hidden from one another—in attacking a recruiting vessel or assassinating a missionary or a District Officer, or articulating a message as cult prophet. "Resistance" as a concept smacks of a kind of populist and collectivist motivation: the image, almost irresistibly romanticized, is of comrades standing together at the barricades, ready to give their blood or their lives for a common cause. What we find in Kwaio skirmishes and confrontations with Europeans (or later, fellow Solomon Islanders) is something less dramatic: tangled skeins of personal motivation, hidden schemes, private ambitions, as well as conceptions of collective struggle. (In the Kwaio world as in our own, rhetoric of collective struggle and mutual obligation often serves to disguise the motives and ambitions and strategems of individuals.)

There is another kind of simplification on the other side. It has not been "colonialism" or "Christianity" or "capitalism" or "the world system" the Kwaio have been confronting, but individual District Officer, missionary, plantation manager, Chinese shopkeeper—each with personal motives and private agendas as well as global aims of control, conversion, or profit. We are as prone to reify and oversimplify and essentialize about the other, dominant "side" in struggles for power as to romanticize and spuriously collectivize the subordinate "side" (a point particularly well made by Ann Stoler in her studies of colonial society in Sumatra; see Stoler 1985 and 1989 and Cooper and Stoler 1989). On the other hand, I shall suggest that for the actors as well as the observer, a political interpretation of a situation demands that individuals and their acts be seen as more than that, as representing issues or forces beyond the immediate ones. To resist, in a political sense, is to make such a generalizing interpretation.

There is a further danger in reading "resistance" in historical events which is well illustrated in the Kwaio material. It is all too easy for the interpreter to read events of, say, 1880 in the light of what she knows happened in 1900—or 1980. This danger, on which much metareflection in historiography has dwelt, is compounded when one is working with oral historical sources. Representations of past events, even though they may be encapsulated in "traditional" cultural genres such as epic chants, nonetheless may cast acts long past in the light of subsequent events and contemporary political struggles.

We must, then, situate events and motives in the historical context of their unfolding, and situate representations of them in the historical contexts of their telling. But that itself is not an innocent and transparent process. If it is jarring to represent Basiana, in crushing the skull of District Officer Bell in 1927, as (in some sense) a Freedom Fighter, it is not simply because that would in some ways project contemporary political motives on a man acting in a universe of ancestors and pigs and vengeance. It is partly because conventional premises of colonial discourse and historiography have been so deeply internalized, by academics as well as by Solomon Islanders. Westerners have from childhood onward been deeply conditioned to see European presence around the tropical world as the bringing of civilization rather than as an act of invasion; and Christianized Solomon Islanders have been steeped in these colonial assumptions as well.[4] Whatever intellectual counterinterpretations we may entertain, we are products of an imperialist discourse that irresistibly shapes our language and our perceptions.

Another major theme of the book, running through the substantive chapters and made explicit in chapter 24, concerns the oppositional structure of subaltern discourses of resistance. We find in the counterhegemonic discourses of the Kwaio a logic of opposition and inversion reminiscent of Gramsci's workers (Gramsci 1971) and Ranajit Guha's Indian peasants (Guha 1983, 1984): the categories and semiology of domination are mirrored, inverted, even parodied by the Kwaio. Even where,

---

4. Which is one reason that Keesing and Corris 1980 aroused ire among some Solomon Islanders. See Keesing 1990.

in counterhegemonic struggle, the content and valence of categories is rejected, their structure is characteristically preserved (if "Black is Beautiful," the world is still structured in terms of white and black). This oppositional cast of counterhegemonic discourses raises important theoretical questions. Does it reflect the impress of domination, the hegemonic force of categories and symbols? Or is this oppositional structure itself a mode of resistance, a strategic engagement of the enemy on his own turf? Or does the hegemonic process itself create realities, in terms of political arenas and identifications and symbols?

I examine the ways in which counterhegemonic discourses are inherently oppositional: in which in resisting domination, subaltern peoples invoke and reproduce the categorical and institutional structures of their domination. In resisting domination by the colonial (and now post-colonial) state, the Kwaio have repeatedly produced mirror-images of the political structures used to dominate them, have invoked conceptual entities that were convenient fictions of colonial administration, have mimicked and (often unwittingly) parodied the semiology of colonial rule and white supremacy, and have demanded cultural autonomy by seeking to represent their "custom" in imitation of colonial legal statutes. The logic, I argue in chapter 24, is pervasively oppositional. Yet that in no way invalidates or weakens Kwaio resistance: such an oppositional logic is inherent in subaltern struggles, whether their form is religious or overtly political (see Guha 1983, 1984). Nor should we, in highlighting such oppositional structures, fail to see the instances in which categorical dominations are challenged and rejected—where instead of meeting the enemy on his own turf, the subordinate strategically stake out a different turf, a different battle.

I will argue, too, that the Kwaio accounts throw a kind of sideways light on the assumptions and categories of British colonial discourse, mirroring and even parodying their conceptual structures. To explore the other side of the coin—the nature of colonial discourse and colonial society—would require a different book; but the colonial side lies behind the Kwaio texts and can often be read through them.[5]

If the Kwaio, in confronting and challenging the alien forces that have pacified and attempted to subjugate and convert them, have reproduced the conceptual structures that have been instruments of domination, does this not then itself represent a kind of cultural surrender? Sahlins

---

5. See Keesing and Corris 1980 and Keesing n.d.8 for examinations of colonial discourse and society.

(1981, 1985), in particular, has shown how, in Hawaii, New Zealand, and Fiji, Pacific Islanders incorporated the invaders into their own cultural scheme of things, defining individuals, acts, and symbols in terms of their own categories, symbols, cosmologies, and mythic narratives. This mode of engaging alien beings and their acts by cultural incorporation must obviously characterize first encounters (at least for peoples who had previously been sovereign).[6] The earliest encounters of Malaitans with explorers, whalers, traders, and aspiring labor recruiters must have been constructed through indigenous eyes in terms of cultural categories of "otherness," conceptions of power, and ideas about time and geography: there were no other means to construct them. But once young Kwaio had been taken off to the plantations of Queensland and Fiji by sailing ship, once warriors experienced bullets and cannons, once alien objects such as axes and knives had entered the mountains, the terms of the encounter began to change rapidly. Particularly from the 1920s onward, the engagement of the Kwaio with the forces impinging on them was less one of cultural incorporation or engulfment than one of compartmentalization and containment. For three quarters of a century, the Kwaio have struggled with increasingly powerful outside forces through a strategy not of cultural incorporation but through building boundaries around the ancestral ways and the mountains where they held sway. By compartmentalizing and containing Christians, government, plantations, and cash economy, the Kwaio have struggled to preserve intact a realm where ancestral powers could still prevail, ancestral rules could still be followed, the valued arena of prestige-feasting and exchange could be guarded from alien material objects and the cash economy.

Kwaio anticolonial discourses have a pervasively oppositional character, incorporating categories and symbols of the colonizers, precisely *because* they are articulated in realms separated from those of everyday life. The traditionalists have walled off the economy based on shell valuables from the cash economy, have prevented any women from going to plantations or towns, have prevented Christians from living in the mountains—in short, they have created an invisible wall around "traditional life." (Such a compartmentalization of danger is itself a pattern pervasive in Kwaio cosmology.) Kwaio resistance has consisted not so much in directly challenging alien power as in fighting to defend this in-

6. I have in mind here quite different areas, such as the Malay archipelago (broadly conceived), where indigenous peoples have had centuries of experience of invasion and domination by local princely states or larger expanding empires, and hence where subjugation and incorporation have become, in effect, part of a local cultural tradition.

visible wall. In defending the wall vis-à-vis the alien forces impinging on them, the Kwaio have been able to adopt the categories and symbols of the colonialists without capitulating to symbolic domination *within* the wall. I explore this strategy of compartmentalization and containment in chapter 22.

The struggles by the Kwaio traditionalists, unlike those of some contemporary Third and Fourth World peoples (the Kayapo of Brazil come to mind), are not being played out on the world stage. The stakes are small, the battles are local; the threat to the Kwaio is not one of extinction or massive environmental devastation, but a gradual erosion of valued ways, a final weary capitulation to Christianity. The Kwaio struggle deserves to be taken seriously, although not romanticized or idealized, or generalized as a viable possibility for other peoples. There are lessons to be learned, questions to be pondered, in such a long and sustained effort to preserve valued ancestral ways. Why and how are these ways still valued? Where so many other peoples have seen the technological power and material wealth of Europeans and have opted for the God who ostensibly conveys them, and for the money that is their medium, why and how have the Kwaio resisted this equation and this temptation? Small and local though the battles may be, they illuminate wider issues.

In examining 120 years of Kwaio engagement with the outside world, I have chosen here to let indigenous voices speak wherever possible. For earlier periods, the past is preserved in epic chants and stories; for the period from the 1920s onward, the voices are mainly of men and women who experienced the events themselves. Setting out Kwaio accounts of and commentaries on their history helps to reveal the conceptual structures of anticolonial discourse, which are a central theme of the book.

Weaving a historical narrative out of Kwaio accounts (mainly ones I have recorded over a twenty-eight year period of Solomons research and translated from the Kwaio language) helps to control against excessive projections of my own theoretical biases and interpretive persuasions, and of Western logics, assumptions, motives, and categories, onto Solomon Islanders. There is a danger here of substituting a kind of local storytelling for theoretically grounded analysis—of trying to let a narrative tell itself, in a conversational way, at the expense of analyzing deeper meanings and connections. Such a narrative strategy entails a kind of trade-off, but I hope the benefits outweigh the costs. I have chosen not to encumber the historical account with a running theoretical metacommentary, but rather, to place theoretical and interpretive commentaries in this introductory chapter and the concluding chapters. My motives in

doing so, at the risk of seeming unfashionably atheoretical, have partly to
do with the nature of the material. The force and clarity of the Kwaio
voices that are relied on so heavily in setting out the historical narrative
could easily be buried beneath heavy academic jargon about "discourses"
or "narratives," or other fashionable obscurantisms of our time. The live-
liness of a lively history could easily be rendered both obscure and boring.

A further motive is my hope that the book will be accessible to
nonacademics, particularly to Solomon Islanders, eventually including
Kwaio readers. I will return below to the political mandate that has made
it important that a book about the Kwaio struggle for cultural autonomy
be cast in a form Solomon Islanders can read. It would represent a be-
trayal of a trust long placed in me if the substantive chapters of this book
were cast in such a theoretically obscurantist language that it was inter-
pretable only by scholars who had read Foucault or Bakhtin or Derrida.

That the Kwaio are so often left to tell their own story does not elimi-
nate my inevitably selective and potentially distorting role as interpreter
and intermediary. The dangers of imposing alien logics and categories on
Kwaio experience still hover in the background, since the reader is dependent on my translations. I can illustrate with the language used to
describe the 1927 killing of District Officer Bell and his entourage by
Kwaio warriors. Kwaio accounts usually refer to this as a *mae*. This is a
nominalized sense of the common Kwaio verb 'die, be dead'; in this nominalized form, it can usually be translated as "fight," "battle," "killing,"
etc. Which translation I choose inevitably colors a reading of the Kwaio
text. Similarly, the Kwaio commonly refer to the Christian presence as
sukuru, from the old Queensland Pidgin term for evangelical religious in-
struction. It could be variously translated (depending on the context) as
"Christianity," "mission," "mission village," etc.; and again, the reader is
at the mercy of my translation.

The same problems of course color my own pieces of the narrative. I
have carefully chosen, for example, to refer to some Kwaio killings of outsiders as acts of "assassination," and others as "massacre," "murder," etc.[7]
But do we distort Kwaio motives and meanings by characterizing their
actions using such Western categories? I use "assassination" when the
victim held a publicly recognized *position* and the attack was directed at
that person *as its incumbent* (so that it was an attack on the position, not
merely the individual). (If the Lord Mayor is killed by an angry pen-

7. I am indebted to Don Gardner for querying my use of the term "assassination" in reference to
Kwaio attacks.

sioner, it is an assassination; if he is killed by a jilted lover, it is a murder.)
But obviously, there can be some distortions of meaning and motive
when such distinctions are drawn across boundaries of culture.

In some respects, the narrative strategies I pursue in weaving together
Kwaio voices, and in placing myself squarely in the picture, are ones es-
poused by anthropologists of postmodernist bent, such as Marcus, Tyler,
Fischer, Clifford, Rabinow, Crapanzano, Stoller, and Cushman. The
chapters that follow incorporate indigenous voices wherever possible. I
have tried to weave them together in a quite straightforward way. The
reader will find no self-conscious, experimental, or novelistic style: I
strive here to create clarity, not art. In placing myself in the picture, I
have tried to avoid narcissism or self-aggrandizement, using quoted
Kwaio passages where possible. A further thread in terms of narrative is
that I am unavoidably part of the story politically, as well as in terms of
my own subjectivities. Since 1962, I have been—wittingly and often
unwittingly—caught up in Kwaio political struggles.

Piecing together indigenous voices is only in a limited sense "letting
the 'native' speak for herself"; it is ultimately I, not my Kwaio friends,
doing the representing: weaving and shaping the narrative, deciding
what to include and what to exclude, and doing the translating. Author-
ship is now inescapably ambiguous and problematic; but I cannot lightly
set aside and disclaim my authorial agency or representational responsibility by underlining the many quoted passages.

Whether, in piecing together so many Kwaio voices, I have succeeded
in conveying Kwaio perspectives on their struggles is for the reader to
judge. It is important to emphasize that Kwaio voices are themselves
multi-stranded, multivocal, and perspectival. The Kwaio voices that will
be heard in these chapters represent a collage in terms of time and imme-
diacy. It should scarcely need saying that representations of nineteenth-
century ship attacks or the Bell massacre are squarely situated in the times
and contexts of the telling, not the times and contexts of the event. Ethnographic talk is situated politically as well as temporally and situa-
tionally. Talk about *kastomu* ("custom"), by men or by women, is never
"pure" ethnographic information; it cannot directly answer questions
about "Kwaio social structure" or the "status of women." I have discussed
this microcontextualization and political situatedness in reflecting on the
self-accounts by Kwaio women Shelley Schreiner and I have recorded
(Keesing 1985a).

The voices of men and women, young and old, leaders and led, are
inevitably multiple and perspectival. The cleavages of perspective go

well beyond divisions of gender or status: we cannot speak unambiguously of "women's role in Kwaio society" or "women's perspective [in the singular] on Kwaio society." The situational nature of talk, as well as the singularity of its "authors," needs to be underlined. A senior Kwaio woman who in some contexts will condemn the irresponsibility of young women who menstruate and urinate without proper respect for the boundaries and rules of pollution will emerge as apologist for an errant daughter; the Kwaio man who in one context of litigation will celebrate the rights of patriliny deriving from bridewealth will in another defend the rights of mothers' brothers (see Keesing 1970b). Nor is the ethnographer who records such statements ever the fly on the wall she might pretend to be: we always catalyze and deflect and transform talk in listening and recording (see Keesing 1985a).

Just as the ethnographer can never be an invisible presence, so the author aspiring to let the locals speak for themselves can never do so. As I have argued, it is always we who choose, orchestrate, paste together the pieces for our own rhetorical purposes. And inevitably, as I doubtless have done, we place ourselves in a carefully constructed chiaroscuro of self-justification or self-glorification, however we may proclaim our faiblesse.

A further word about the politics of the situation is needed. As the reader will see, the Kwaio long ago incorporated me—unsuspecting, at first—into their historical-political project. The Kwaio traditionalists with whom I have worked for thirty years have assumed that what I have been working on with them is a codification of their customary law and religious taboos—a sort of customary lawbook. Such a book could not be written, at least from the critical standpoint of an anthropologist (not least of all because Kwaio customary law is extremely flexible, both to the particularities of particular cases and casts of characters and to the politics of confrontation and negotiation); if it is to be produced, it will have to be by the Kwaio themselves. If such a cultural lawbook *were* set to paper, it would not have the decisive political effects in their struggle for the right to practice their customs at the margins of the state that many Kwaio traditionalists anticipate. This account of the historical struggle of the Kwaio is the closest I can come to fulfilling the mandate that has been our common covenant in collective work over three decades. I do not expect that it will have any magical political effects (it may well rekindle the anger of politicians who would prefer that the Kwaio side of this history not be told). But if it can neither be afforded nor understood by Solomon Islanders, it will have no effect at all.

I have tried to remain conscious of a double responsibility, both to the Kwaio people and to the country that has permitted me to carry out the research. The views represented here as the Kwaio have articulated them to me and through me are in some instances not views I share, and certainly not views I have encouraged. (Extremist demands for secession or cultural autonomy or billions of dollars in compensation are, in my own judgment, neither politically realistic nor strategically useful.) However, I believe that such views, as strands in decades of Kwaio resistance, deserve to be heard—and need to be recognized and understood by those with political power in the Solomons, even when they cannot be accepted. I hope that in setting out Kwaio views and quoting Kwaio voices, extremist as well as moderate, I am helping to fulfil in some measure the mandate long laid upon me, even if the hopes held by traditionalists of the benefits that would flow from our common project are unrealistic. The book they have hoped for is a book I do not know how to write; but I have tried to write another kind of book that will convey their political aspirations and struggles to the world outside their mountains.

There is a thin line between acting as a *conduit* through which views can be heard and political *advocacy*; but I have tried carefully to preserve this line. I can only emphasize that statements quoted in these chapters reflect the views of those who made them, and not necessarily the views of the outsider who has woven the narrative together.

In setting out Kwaio history, I follow the boringly iconic convention of putting first things first. So do the Kwaio, by and large, so this is not mere cultural imperialism or mindlessly conventional historiography. I begin with the Kwaio mountains I experienced most recently, in 1989 and 1990, before going back into the pre-European past, far beyond the span of living memory, but vividly preserved in epic chants sung around smoky fires.

2 The Past in the Present

The mists cling to the dense rain-forested slopes around Saua, the air chilled after the night rains. As dawn nears, the dark bodies huddled in the thatched open-sided shelters and around small fires stay warm as best they can. The panpipers are still playing complex contrapuntal melodies; the women and boys, swaying to keep time, thump their leaf bundles.

The pipers joke between tunes, stirring and stretching to keep warm, stroking thighs almost raw from slapping. And then the beautiful pipes weave their designs again, drowning out the frogs in the swamp below: two rows of four, face to face, men of Ngudu and Naala'e and Furisi'ina, with four sets of matched instruments, each playing a melodic line, with Maena'adi in the lead.

It is the new ghost whose presence is most closely felt: the shade[1] of Tagi'au, Maena'adi's father. His death in March 1989, a year and a half earlier, and the death of old Ri'ika across the mountain, had brought an era in this Kwaio heartland to an end. The others who had played a part in the attack on Gafamanu—the colonial government, in the person of District Officer Bell and his police patrol—sixty-two years before had all passed on to ancestorhood.[2] They, too, were there with the feastgivers, as presences felt, voices read through signs and divination; and as links to those ancient ancestors, Amadia and Muno and La'aka and the others, who created and still sustain the ways and powers of Kwaio life.

The tiny settlement of Saua, with its two thatched houses, pigpens under the downhill eaves, its men's house above, its menstrual hut below, looks the same in 1990 as it had eighty years before when Tagi'au was born there. (He had died there as well; most of the Kwaio of the interior move every few years, although they circulate around old settlement sites where they have lived before; a few, like Tagi'au, spend most of their lives in the same clearing, rooted by protective magic and sustaining ancestors.)

Some of the dark-skinned Melanesians clustered for shelter from the night rain look very much as their grandparents and great grandparents had looked when Tagi'au was a young child: unmarried girls and women nude, though wearing ornaments of shell and dolphin teeth; married women wearing little pubic aprons (in Tagi'au's boyhood, blue cotton had replaced barkcloth). Some of the men are naked or wearing fighting belts, as they had been then; many have bows and arrows and killing clubs, as well as the long machetes that by Tagi'au's boyhood were widely

---

1. *Nunui'ola*, lit. "shadow-thing." In different contexts, the shades of the dead are spoken of either with the term *nunu* 'shadow, shade' (which is also used for the soul of a living person, which wanders at night in dream) or with the term *adalo* 'ancestral spirit'. 'Shade' is used to refer to the ghost in terms of its form or state (as an invisible, disembodied presence) and *adalo* is used to describe a dead person as a social actor or agent. See Keesing 1982a.

2. Ri'ika (pictured in Keesing and Corris 1980:142), who died several months after Tagi'au, was a prominent leader whose role in the Bell massacre had been to help save a policeman from West Kwaio who was related to his group. See Keesing and Corris 1980:143.

used. But for decades there have been no Snider rifles, obsolete surplus of Britain's imperial wars that by a century ago had become ubiquitous symbols and instruments of warrior aggression in these Malaita mountains. Bell had been trying to confiscate the rifles when he was killed. The punitive expedition that followed, bringing devastation and massive desecration, had put an end to warrior weapons and deeds.

Most of the men at this mortuary feast—almost all of the younger ones—look strikingly different from the warriors at a similar feast in the year of Tagi'au's birth, the year the Government station was first established on Malaita. They wear shorts, or laplaps (a fathom of cloth wrapped around the waist) if they are older; the younger ones wear T-shirts, emblazoned in the pop culture semiotic styles of Honiara, eighty miles away, with its rock bands and Kung Fu videos and taxis. The older men keep themselves warm if they can with grimy laplaps, wrapped around their shoulders. Some of the women, too, wear more than their grandmothers had: cloth skirts pulled up around their shoulders for warmth against the night chill, and sometimes the stained and ragged dresses which are creeping into the Kwaio mountains because of Seventh Day Adventist–induced ideas of modesty and covered breasts emanating from the hospital on the coast eight miles away and 2200 feet below.

The juxtapositions of the old and the new strike and trouble the anthropological eye, with its cultivated romanticisms about "traditional culture" and the authenticities of the past. When I had first stayed with the Kwaio twenty-eight years ago and had first gone to mortuary feasts, I had been jarred by the intrusive elements. (There would have been some jarring elements along with the rifles in Tagi'au's father's childhood too: some of the younger men had by then worked in the cane fields of Queensland and Fiji, bringing back hats and coats and mirrors as well as weapons.) I had seen my Kwaio neighbors in their everyday work lives barechested, wearing only laplaps casually wrapped around the hips and often shed during work tasks. Why, then, when they were at a mortuary feast or marriage feast, when they were so obviously following ancestral ways in sacrificing pigs and exchanging strung-shell valuables—and when I wanted to photograph them—did they put on their new shorts and T-shirts? 'Elota, the great feastgiver whose autobiography I later edited, was wearing a new yellow T-shirt emblazoned with "US Navy" when I contributed a major valuable to his son's bridewealth in 1963.[3]

3. Keesing 1978b; see photograph p. 106 in 1983 edition.

(I remind myself that young Wa'i, who has been solicitously helping to carry my pack on my way to Saua, is doing so because my contribution to his father-in-law's bridewealth payment twenty-seven years ago entitled me to a share in the bridewealth he himself paid for 'Elota's granddaughter; but because the Government of the now-independent Solomon Islands had kept me out of the Kwaio mountains for almost a decade, I had missed out on my share of the marriage payment. He knows that if I pressed the point, I could set a date, and lay out an appropriate pile of foodstuffs, taro and fish and pork; and he would have to give me a large valuable.) The connections to the past are everywhere for me as well, then, in these mountains where I have spent five years of my life, mainly more than twenty years ago. The children I once bounced on my knees are married now, with children of their own; my knees are less resilient than they used to be. I feel strongly the close presence of 'Elota and so many others, including my old friend Tagi'au; he had died only a few days before I was allowed back at last to Kwaio country, and I had spent a night at nearby 'Aisi'ina communing with Maena'adi and with him, the living and the dead.)

As dawn nears, the weary musicians pipe on. Maena'adi, wise beyond his thirty-five years and an incredible repository of knowledge about the Kwaio past as preserved in its epics and genealogies, often sings at such occasions 'ai'imae epic chants of old intrigues, old battles, ancient feuds. The world Maena'adi evokes in these epics is the world into which Tagi'au had been born—or that into which Tagi'au's father had been born, before the rifles and the ships. We find in these 'ai'imae few deeds that challenge an anthropologist's credibility sufficiently that he wants to call them myths. The epics take for granted a world of pigs and taro and mortuary feasts and blood feuds and punitive ancestors. In other settings, the elder men—and a few younger men like Maena'adi—recount genealogies that extend back fifteen or twenty generations, to the powerful ancestors who brought or created sacred powers, magic and ritual, and passed them on to their descendants. When sacrifices are made, pigs consecrated to these ancestors are raised up in purification of violations of the taboos and rules they impose (most often, of taboos[4] that confine menstruation and women's other bodily functions), the names of the ancestors must be called off, from one generation to the next. Magic works only if the spell is validated by reciting a line of ancestors connecting the human user back to the originating ancestor. So remembering genealo-

4. The Kwaio term is abu, a word cognate with Oceanic tapu.

gies is vital, a linking of the living to the unseen presences on whom their lives and powers depend.

Kwaio seldom talk about the more ancient past, about the origin of humans and their environment, or about the origin of the ways and customs humans follow. Most people, if pressed about the beginnings of things, will say that humans and their ways *eta mai i wado* 'came from the earth': more a way of deflecting irrelevant questioning than a cosmogenic theory.[5] Or they will say that in the olden days people used to know about those things, but now they don't. Sometimes, though, Kwaio savants like Maena'adi will unveil mythic accounts of more ancient and primordial origins. Sitting on a hillside behind a house in Honiara's Melanesian suburbia in 1989, on a Sunday morning with radio-broadcast hymns wafting in the background, Maena'adi recounted to me the story of the ancestral snake 'Oi'oifi'ona, who gave birth to the first humans. These beginnings were not in a mythical far-away land: they took place at Iofana, just across the mountains from where Maena'adi was leading the panpipers at his dead father's mortuary feast.

The past, ancient and recent, is visible, tangible, everywhere in these mountains; every hill has an old settlement site, a shrine, a remembered history; every path and watering place and rocky outcropping is the remembered site of old confrontations, plots, battles, curses, seductions.

The living look back on this time from different angles. Most often—as in the talk I had with Tagi'au and the other elders at Saua a decade before his death—the past is celebrated as a time of autonomy, a time of ancestral powers undiminished and unchallenged, a time of proud warrior deeds. It is portrayed as an era of virtue, particularly for women and the young: strict rules of chastity were followed, the young were unquestioningly obedient, girls and women followed punctiliously the regimens of the isolated latrine and the menstrual area. In the olden days, Kwaio have told me, a settlement often included five generations of the living; the ancients, in a time when ancestral rules were punctiliously followed and ancestral powers were undiminished, lived until their skins were like parchment, so that they faded into ancestorhood. Now, men die in the prime of life. The customary legal system worked better than the alien one: an aggrieved party received compensation, and once matters were settled to the mutual satisfaction of the parties (including the ancestors), amicable social life could be resumed.

5. See Keesing 1987a regarding *wado* as a key symbol of autochthonous origins, and regarding the diversity of religious knowledge, and Keesing n.d.1 for the symbolism and semantics of *wado* 'land, ground, earth'.

Seldom are the costs of the threat and terror that sustained virtue examined; seldom are the cruelties and violence of blood feuding, the death of scores of men in the prime of life, the killing of women and even children to avenge the deeds of warrior menfolk reflectively considered. Maena'adi, though, wise philosopher, has no illusions about the dark side of Kwaio violence and destructiveness. There are other voices, sometimes heard—the voices of women, of children, of those subjected to terror and violent death. We will hear these dissenting voices, too, though most of the time they will be fragmentary, muted, and ambivalent.

The past lives in the present, then, both as practice—as in the mortuary feast for Tagi'au's death, the pigs sacrificed, the rituals performed, the valuables exchanged—and as political symbol.

3 A Reconstructed Past

An anthropologist's ethnographic representations of social life and culture in a contemporary community are problematic enough. Much has been written in recent years about the processes of objectification and representational sleight of hand through which a conventional ethnography comes to be produced. Particular experiences with particular people, inevitably colored by the cultural assumptions, the personality, and the theoretical expectations of the anthropologist, are elevated into rules, roles, and structures. Partly and often poorly understood nuances of meaning in a local language lead to inevitable and sometimes disastrous distortions and mistranslations, particularly as we seek consciously or unconsciously to find cultural exoticism in alien ways of thought (see Keesing 1989a). Even for those who have lived their lives in a community, have grown up speaking its language and following its cultural guidelines, there are multiple realities, divergent meanings and experiences. "The culture" as we have characterized it has too often represented the perspectives of men, usually the most senior or knowledgeable ones, so that the voices and experiences of women, the young, the marginal, the pragmatically unconcerned, remain submerged. The political processes and interpretive negotiations through which the ethnographer and members of the community fashion partial understandings of one another together remain hidden in the objectifying conventions of ethnographic writing.

If it is so hazardous, so subjective, and so presumptuous to write an ethnography of a social world one has observed and participated in (at least around the edges, as a bungling alien), what point can there be in trying to reconstruct the social world that might have existed in the same place a century earlier? I invite the reader to suspend disbelief, to share my guesses—educated ones—about what lies beyond possible view, in the mists of the past.

The task is not as daunting or as presumptuous as it would be in most corners of the Pacific. The Kwaio pagans with whom I have lived are still sacrificing to the *adalo,* still exchanging shell valuables, still practicing elaborate rituals and daily magic; still following ancestral rules separating women from men, observing the invisible lines that divide social space; still subsisting mainly on foods they produce themselves, including those used in pre-European times; still using many elements of pre-European technology. The older men and women insist that the ancestors have not changed their rules, and that in most respects they have not changed their customs (some wax eloquent and indignant about those that *have* changed, such as the prohibition and virtual impossibility of marriage be-tween close relatives—inevitably deploring moralistically the contem-porary decline of ancient virtues). So in reconstructing the Kwaio world of 1850, there are many clues and guidelines in my own fieldnotes and culture-learning.

To extrapolate from the observed present, I draw on the fragmentary glimpses of the past preserved in the *'ai'imae* epics, and on the memories of old people who experienced the early years of this century, when blood feuding was intense. Ironically, the Bell massacre and the disasters that followed provide indirect benefits to the anthropological detective: in 1969–70, I was able to reconstruct in great detail (and with striking con-sistency) who was living where on October 4, 1927—when Kwaio had to flee in one direction or another.[1] Through such extrapolation, I can re-construct with a measure of confidence the general outlines of precolo-nial Kwaio life. But on some matters, the evidence is thin, ambiguous, and hard to read.

A case in point is the nature of settlement patterns. In the period of my fieldwork, Kwaio settlements have been tiny and scattered, homestead clusters of ten or so people (on average), at most two or three or four families. Most settlements are moved every several years, although a few

1. See Keesing 1987c and 1989d for examples of the reconstructions of continuities in social structure.

of the old men I knew, like Tagi'au and the old wizard Fuamae, spent most of their lives in the same clearing. In 1927 the settlements were slightly larger, but similarly mainly occupied for only a few years. Yet there are some fragments of evidence of more stable settlement in an earlier period; sites either defensible or with adjacent fortified refuges, perhaps accommodating most members of a kin group in a cluster of connected clearings. In central Malaita, in the mountains of Kwara'ae as well as Kwaio country, old and now-abandoned mountaintop settlement sites often have stonework platforms where men's houses used to stand. Could the introduction of firearms have led to a centrifugal process, where concentrated defenses and fortifications—effective against bows and arrows and spears—now became maladaptive? I suspect that the centrifugal tendencies in Kwaio sociopolitical life had led to increasing fragmentation and dispersion and mobility, a scattering away from the old nuclear settlements, in the centuries before Europeans intruded; but the archaeology that could tell us has yet to be done. As turned out to be the case when serious archaeology was done in Samoa, it would be dangerous to infer the long-range past from what can be reconstructed of the "ethnographic present." These were, when whites arrived, societies in process and change, not structures statically reproducing themselves.

Another case in point is the scale and frequency of warfare, as opposed to armed confrontation leading to combat and clandestine assassination. Kwaio epics recount assaults on fortified *labu* refuges by massed warriors led by a shield-carrying champion; modes of attack and defense are still a lively part of oral tradition. Yet did such massed assaults (the "masses" would have been small in any event, perhaps two dozen men) take place every year in the Kwaio mountains? Once in a decade? Once in a generation? As with similar episodes of warrior prowess in European sagas, the focusing, selective and dramatizing character of oral narrative makes it difficult to be sure. These uncertainties bracketed (and there will be others), let me assay a brief word picture of pre-European "Kwaio society" as I reconstruct it.

First, the Kwaio speakers mainly lived away from the coast. There is virtually no coastal strip on this precipitous coast, where the steep slopes rise to 2000 feet and more. Settlements were tiny homestead clusters (at least in the latter nineteenth century, as in the twentieth), scattered along the upper slopes and in the rugged, broken interior. Early European accounts mention the absence of canoes on the vast, almost landlocked harbor now known as Sinalagu, and noted that the settlements were high above the coast. Thus, Jock Cromar, writing of an 1886 visit (1935:234), commented that the "local natives were all bushmen—there being no people living on the coast at Sinarango." The Captain of a British warship, writing of an 1886 visit assessing the possibility of a punitive raid, observed that

I do not think a man-of-war has the least chance of getting to the guilty people or their property, even the cocoanut groves being high up the hills, and no canoes visible. In this part of Malayta there do not appear to be any large villages, single houses and clusters of two or three being scattered about the mountains, which here rise to about 2,000 feet.[2]

The interior is a land of sticky red clay, mudstone and limestone, laced with streams; mantled in dense forest, most of it secondary and long cultivated. Rainfall is heavy year-round. Taro was the primary subsistence crop in the mountains, grown in swiddens in a continuous year-round cycle of planting and harvest, a process accompanied by elaborate magical-ritual procedures. Yams, planted in a seasonal cycle, were a secondary staple, but also one marked by first-fruits ceremonies and other special rituals. Individual families were (and are) the primary units of production and consumption, but closely related and co-resident families often pooled the labor of reclearing secondary forest and fencing contiguous gardens. The daily diet also included greens, most often taro leaves and *Hibiscus manihot,* and such morsels of protein—grubs, grasshoppers, prawns, birds, cuscus opossums—as came to hand. Pig-rearing was (and is) a focus of productive and ritual concern; the pigs are mainly consecrated to ancestors or offered up in purification of offenses. They are presented and consumed mainly in contexts of feasting and sacrifice. Pigs were fed partly on tubers, but more regularly on the pith of the boles of sago and fishtail palms and tree ferns (the latter also used for human food).

The technology of production relied heavily on fire. The main felling and chopping tools were smallish adzes crudely chipped from chert, mined in the form of nodules in a few places in the interior. Some groups apparently specialized in the production of adze blades for barter, but otherwise there was little trade within the mountains. The peoples of the interior obtained fish, salt, and other marine products from colonies of "saltwater people" (*ta'a i asi*) along the coast, through barter and purchase (using strung shell valuables, of which more shortly); regular mar-

2. Capt. F. S. Clayton, HMS *Diamond,* in British Colonial Office, *Papers Relating to the Recent Operations of HMS Opal Against Natives of the Solomon Islands* (London, Henry Hansard and Sons 1887), 22.

kets were apparently held for such trade, and fishermen contracted to provide packets of fish for feasts in the mountains. Kwaio technology relied heavily on forest fibers (used to make ropes and cords, nets for trapping birds and fishing, bags, and lashings). It also relied heavily on giant bamboo (used for water and cooking containers, and in tongs, torches and knives, and building construction). Forest hardwoods and palm cores provided the materials for bows, clubs, and spears. Bivalve shells were used as scraping and plucking tools.

Then as now, settlements were small and scattered, islands of red scraped bare to avoid breaches of symbolic boundaries. Thatch buildings mapped out a cosmological design: dwelling houses, built on bare earth, with pigpens under the eaves; men's house (sometimes two, one sacred and one secular) in the upper clearing—like the dwelling houses, with tiny raised doors for defensive purposes; menstrual hut (sometimes two or more) in the lower clearing, symbolically a mirror-image of the men's house. Only men (and boys) can enter the men's houses and shrines; only women (and infant boys) can enter the *kaakaba* (menstrual area) and *bisi* (menstrual hut). (My changing of tenses here is deliberate, to highlight elements that still prevail and elements that have changed.)

Clearings were more tightly clustered then, within easy shouting range should a confrontation or danger demand collective action. The spatial layout provides a kind of vivid sociometric index of social relations. To live in the same clearing is to place lives mutually in mortal danger, since a pollution violation in one household can bring disaster on another;[3] usually only those who grew up together take such mutual risks. But a narrow strip of vegetation, even one a few inches wide, insulates one clearing from another in terms of pollution danger; so a single settlement may consist of two or three subclearings, separated by a few yards or a few hundred. How far is a question of social distance as well as topography.

The landscape is divided into named land tracts, each with a remembered history, over which particular people have rights. Clearing primary forest with crude chert adzes and fire represented a vast investment of time and labor; once cleared for cultivation, the land could be recleared after fifteen or twenty years with much less time, difficulty, and danger. It was secondary growth, then, over which descendants of the pioneer cultivators exercised rights; children inherited these rights collectively,

3. 'Pollution' is a misleading gloss here, but it avoids the need for circumlocution. See Keesing 1982a:60–70; Keesing 1987b; and Keesing 1989c.

but with women marrying out, primary rights were held by and transmitted through men. A land tract, usually between three and ten hectares, represented a single complex of cultivation (in Kwaio taro cultivation, prototypically a kind of amphitheatre progressively cleared and planted) and a contiguous settlement site. Through the progressive cultivation of adjoining areas in the process of pioneer settlement (or so Kwaio theory goes), and the passage of generations, a patchwork of contiguous land tracts came to be collectively held by the descendants of these pioneer settlers. These contiguous tracts constitute a *fanua*, an estate or territory held corporately by the co-descendants of its founders.[4]

For any land tract, and any *fanua*, there is a cluster of descendants in the male line (*futaaniwane*, 'born of men') who hold primary rights, with a senior man acting as steward and spokesman; and other descendants, through one or more female links (*futaanigeni*, 'born of women') who hold seondary rights. (They can live and garden on the land, but need to ask permission from the steward.) These land-owning corporations, with what we may call primary members and secondary members, look like "descent groups," but it is important to remember that they are (and I think this is more generally true of Austronesian-speaking peoples among whom title to secondary forest constitutes property) artifacts of the inheritance rules. Here as in other realms of "Kwaio culture," we find both flexibility and alternative interpretation. Many "descent groups," in the sense of the primary owners of the *fanua* domiciled there, include some men who are *futaanigeni*; through past circumstance, they or their fathers or their grandfathers grew up in their mother's place, not their father's place; parental residence can and often does outweigh agnatic dogma, as long as it is translated into a primary commitment in one's adult life. There is also a countervailing cognatic ideology, voiced in some contexts, that insists that ties through mother and maternal uncle are as strong and binding as those through father, and confer the same rights. In practice, it is a primary commitment to a place, its ancestors, rituals, and special rules and history that determines rights.

The descendants of the original founders of a *fanua* have in many cases died out or dispersed, so that primary title has come to be held by non-agnatically related descendants (there are a few accounts in the epics of succession by what amounts to extermination and usurpation). These non-agnatic descendants who have become primary owners preserve

---

4. The territories are not always neat, since outsiders may have rights (either prior rights or ones acquired through gift, compensation or purchase) over individual tracts within them.

linkages to the founding ancestors of the *fanua* through sacrifice. Indeed, by Kwaio logic it is still those who originally cleared the land who own it: the living are simply acting as custodians and occupants on their behalf, and it is they, the ancestral ghosts, who partake of first fruits.

The descendants of the founding ancestors of a *fanua* constitute a ritual community as well as a property-holding corporation. In many contexts, this ritual community includes its out-married women and entails the lesser participation of cognatic descendants with primary attachments in other places). Each "descent group" has a religious officiant (*wane naa ba'e*, lit. "shrine man") who sacrifices pigs, plays the key part in rituals, and maintains genealogical knowledge. He in turn is backed by a secondary officiant (often a potential successor) who sacrifices the pigs that women eat at feasts and conducts some phases of collective rituals. A *fanua* had a primary shrine used for propitiatory sacrifices and often a separate one used for the crematory sacrifices that plunge the group into liminal sacralization; other specialized shrines for burial and particular forms of ritual are scattered around, usually on hilltops. The founders of *fanua*, mainly nine to twelve generations back by Kwaio reckoning, were themselves linked genealogically, and sacrificed to their ancestors; and these linkages above the level of landholding corporations are recognized both in the common propitiation of the same powerful ancestors and by ritual linkages between the priesthoods.[5]

In fact, the anthropologist's conventional ways of talking about descent and kinship in terms of "corporate groups" and "structures" do unfortunate violence to the way such a system looks to those who live within it. We are taught to think about ancestors as triangles and circles on lineage diagrams: once human beings, but now conceptual entities in terms of which people trace their relationship to one another according to cultural rules. But the experienced world for the Kwaio is very different, I think. The ancestors are *there*, all around; they are still part of the group. What looks to the anthropologically trained outsider as a "descent group" is to those who live in it simply the visible component of a local social universe that it includes the living and the dead. And it is the dead who really define the boundaries of the group, maintain its stability whatever the living do and wherever they go. What the anthropologist analyzes as "sacrifice" is in fact a communion, a collective meal in a context of sanctity and intensified power and danger. It is also a *transaction*, a

5. See Keesing 1967a, 1968b, 1970a, 1970b, 1971, 1987c for accounts of the Kwaio "descent system."

prestation not different in kind from the presentation of a pig from one man to another, except for the hierarchical relationship of power that prevails when the living give to the dead, and the dead give to the living. We also distort the world of Kwaio experience, I have intimated, by talking about "territories" as if they existed in space but not in time; when we cut them off from the histories embodied in and inscribed on them.

The ghosts of the dead are everyday participants in Kwaio life (Keesing 1982; in what follows, I use the present tense, in describing religious practice still followed by contemporary traditionalists in the mountains). Although Kwaio theology is inconsistent and partial, with regard to eschatology as with other matters, the most coherent accounts (Keesing 1987a) are of two soul components, one of which goes off to the Land of the Dead, Anogwa'u;[6] and the other of which hovers around the living, in a constant vigil. The ancestral ghosts police the living, punishing them for violations of strict rules compartmentalizing the blood of menstruation and childbirth and the sanctity of shrines and men's houses and for mistakes in ritual. The mistakes and violations must be purified (literally, "washed"), most often by sacrifice of purificatory pigs. When the *adalo*, the ancestral ghosts, are pleased with the living—for punctiliously following the rules of sanctity and pollution and for raising pigs consecrated in the names of their ancestors—they support their efforts (*nanama* for them, a term cognate with Oceanic *mana*, but used in verbal form) and protect them from malevolent spirits and dangers. The ancestors visit death or disaster on their descendants either by directly "joining" a misfortune (such as a venomous snake or a fall from a tree) to them, or by abandoning them to hostile and malevolent beings and forces. When illnesses, deaths, or disasters occur, Kwaio consult diviners, who learn (usually through breaking knotted cordyline leaves as questions are put to the test) which ancestor is causing problems, and why. In the event of a death, or a failed attack or similar disaster, retrospective interpretations attributing ancestral agency are fashioned through divination.

Magic is performed as an accompaniment of human effort, in feastgiving, in taro cultivation, in fighting, in stealing, in curing, in achieving prosperity and stable living, in securing protection from malevolent forces. Although magic is individually known and held as property (Keesing n.d.2), some forms of magic—for prosperity and stable living, in particular—are open to the community and publicly performed.

The separation of men and women cuts across all realms of social life. The invisible lines that divide the clearing and restrict access to parts of it

6. Conventionally associated with an islet off the northern tip of Malaita.

according to gender are extended within the houses to sleeping and sitting arrangments, and into everyday life regimens as well. Women's
water and men's must be kept separate; men and women eat from separate
containers. Although there is no developed ideology about the power
and danger emanating from women's bodies, its center is in the organs of
reproduction; the blood of menstruation and childbirth, but also feces
and urine, are highly dangerous to men—when they cross the category
boundaries. Yet there is a positive as well as dangerous side to the *abu*-
ness of women and their bodies; and there is no evidence of negative feel-
ings and senses of dirt in the talk of women about their bodies (or, indeed, in the talk of men, which focuses on categorical danger but not
"pollution"). The cosmological scheme in which men's house and the
shrine above are symbolic mirror-images of menstrual hut and childbirth
area below uses what has come to be called "pseudoprocreative" imagery:
men give birth to ancestral spirits through rituals that are *abu* (Oceanic
tapu or *tabu*) and inimical to women as women give birth to humans
through rituals that are *abu* and inimical to men (Keesing 1982a, 1987b).

Senior women who characterize women's responsibilities in Kwaio society, in talk with Shelley Schreiner and me (Keesing 1985a, 1987b),
stressed the crucial part women play in reproducing social order and
maintaining the category separations and virtues on which prosperity
and life itself depend:

> A woman is in charge of the living in her clearing, the territory where she
> lives. She's in charge. She's the "big-woman" there. She is responsible for the
> menstrual area, . . . the food . . . the way people live there (Lamana).

> If I have good sense, if I am responsible, then it's as though I'm the owner of
> the house. . . . I'm the one who is responsible for our living (Fa'afataa).

Such pronouncements, like those of their male contemporaries, are politically charged, and colored by ideologies of writing down and 'straightening out' *kastomu* 'custom'—ideologies which, as we will see, have been
part of the Kwaio struggle for political autonomy in the face of colonialism. They cannot be taken as timeless and decontextualized representations of "women's status."

Women play important parts in rituals, especially those following crematory sacrifice and death of a priest; they are excluded from shrines.
However, some women command extensive esoteric knowledge of magic,
especially curing magic. A senior woman, especially postmenopausally,
may acquire special *abu*-ness that requires her partial separation from
women's realms.

Marriage, serially monogamous, was negotiated by the payment of bridewealth from groom's kindred to bride's kindred. (see Keesing 1967a). Here and in other prestations, the medium of exchange was, and still is, *bata*, strung shell valuables made of beads of ground and polished cone shell. (Kwaio themselves produce the white *bata* that is the main constituent of valuables, but they obtain by trade the red shell beads used to ornament major valuables.) A first marriage usually brought a girl still in her teens to a husband typically in his mid-thirties or even forties, although a younger man might be financed in marrying a sweetheart courted in chaste dates in the forest. A rigid code of premarital chastity and postmarital fidelity, enforced by threat of death, sharply curtailed sexual adventuring and experience. (As we will see, the sexual revolution that gradually followed after pacification has been a major change in modern Kwaio life, and a major focus of concern for old-fashioned moralists, there as here.)

Bridewealth in principle gives the husband's kin, who financed the marriage, rights over children: that remains a major foundation of agnatic organization. In practice, a young widow or divorcée can in some circumstances manage to keep custody of at least younger children (that is a main source of flexibility and deviation from strict agnatic affiliation [see Keesing 1970b]). In some respects, marriage leaves a woman as a jural minor vis-à-vis her husband and his kin. Yet she remains strongly connected to her own place and its ancestors: the pigs she raises are consecrated to both her husband's powerful ancestors and her own, and her children will propitiate ancestors from both sides. Tracing of kinship rests heavily on connection to ancestors through the groups of one's father's mother, mother's father, mother's mother, and beyond as well as agnatic line; one has potential land use rights and allies in all these places, and a man or boy partakes of sacrifices in all of them. Bridewealth transactions have a further function of creating obligation on the part of a husband dependent on his seniors for marriage financing. One way a leader like 'Elota of Ga'enaafou, whose autobiography I edited (see Keesing 1978b), acquires an obligated following who support his feast-giving and productive enterprises is by making major contributions to their marriages. That has a further consequence of creating rights to *obtain* bridewealth when the daughters of marriages one financed get married themselves (here, recall the return bridewealth for the marriages of 'Elota's granddaughters I was denied by Solomon Island politicians).

Another focus of Kwaio life and arena for entrepreneurial investment and power is mortuary feasting. Every competent Kwaio man, and some women, sponsor one or two mortuary feasts (*omea* or *fonunga*) in the course of a career; but important leaders like 'Elota may sponsor thirty, forty or fifty, and display a largesse and a network of investment far exceeding those of lesser contemporaries. Ostensibly, a mortuary feast rewards those who bury the dead (for simplicity, I will call them "pallbearers") for their act of kinship service. In reality, those who bury the dead are kin of the decedent, but usually boys or young men acting on behalf of their seniors; and in reality, significant mortuary feasts align descent-based groups against one another. Both the rights to bury the dead and the prestations to the pallbearers (which align the feastgiving group vis-à-vis those to which it is tied by cognatic kinship and often some form of political rivalry and/or prestige competition) must in the long run be strictly and exactly reciprocated; but there is a good deal of short-term juggling and maneuvering.[7] While in some sense it is the descent group as a group that gives the feast and is aligned opposite its rivals, each mortuary feast also entails dozens of individual kindred-based investments and accumulations of prestations, again creating obligations of reciprocation. The death of a priest or a senior man or woman creates the setting for a major intensification of production and mobilization of wealth; it further (especially following the death of a priest) sets into motion an elaborate ritual sequence in which the living are plunged into close communion with the dead and the powerful ancient ancestors, and enter a liminality progressively removed by a sequence of desacralizing rituals that span many months. Finally, as in the mortuary feast that put my old friend Tagi'au to final rest at Saua, the last taboos are lifted, the ties of kinship that connect the living are renewed, and normal social life can be resumed.

Kwaio sages like Maena'adi see Kwaio culture as having two contrasting poles. One is a positive pole of production, wealth and stable living; the negative pole is destructive and violent (ngada'olanga, lit. "destroying things"). The latter includes killing and violent aggression, but also theft, rape and seduction (which are conceived of as theft of rights that belong to other men, to husbands and fathers), and sheer vandalism. Stealing, especially of pigs but also of valuables and other property, is positively valued and celebrated (although of course the victims of theft deplore it moralistically). Contrasting complexes of magic, and different ancestors, conferred powers of productivity and powers of destruction (Keesing 1985b). Some descent groups specialized in productivity, others in destruction and warrior aggression; but everyone did some of

7. Here see my introduction to 'Elota's Story, ibid.

each. Those groups with warlike ancestors promoting aggression and destruction were regularly forced into defensive isolation or temporary dispersion, so that the sustained regimens of intensive taro, yam, and pig production were infeasible. Safety from external aggression lay in sheer truculence and fear of ancestral powers that conferred invincibility. Such groups clustered around leading warriors, *lamo,* men of violence and presumed ancestrally conferred powers who led in combat and acquired wealth and reputation as executioners and bounty hunters.

For groups specializing in production, safety lay in the ability to mobilize large and irresistibly tempting blood bounties (*sikwa*) of valuables and pigs. A blood feud prototypically began with a seduction (less often with a curse or insult, a theft, or some other transgression, real or imagined). If a girl was seduced (or even propositioned), she was supposed to report it to her kin and give herself up to be killed by entering the men's house (where she would be strangled by her brothers or other close kin). A blood bounty would then be put up for the death of the seducer (or some acceptable substitute, a close relative).

A killing set into motion a cycle of vengeance that could ramify into long chains of sequential killings. If a seducer or thief was killed himself, matters might end there—especially if his own relatives abandoned him (he might then, though, flee to a maternal uncle or other close relative, who was bound to try to protect him). The entire group against whom vengeance was sought, or a group protecting a fugitive, could retire into fortified refuge, or might simply go about normal life heavily armed and vigilant, with fugitive under heavy protective escort. This then set into motion the processes of magic and counter-magic, stealth and treachery, bravery and cowardly execution, recounted in the *'ai'imae* epics (which often involve twenty or thirty killings, and extend over three or four generations, with a cast of hundreds; Keesing 1978b gives examples of such stories).

Killings were more often executions of victims ambushed on paths or in gardens or clearings than feats of warrior prowess in combat, but there was a good deal of the latter, too. A group with a grievance—accusing another group of the theft of a pig or valuables, or angry over a curse or insult—sometimes marched into the clearing of their adversaries, demanding compensation. An angry squaring off of warrior leaders could lead to mortal combat, and leave several men dead on each side. The death of a homicide victim was treated as a quite separate matter from death through illness or what we would call an accident. (For the Kwaio, a fall from a tree, a snake bite, a drowning, a tree-felling accident—as

well as an illness—all require explanation in terms of ancestral interventions.) Rituals through which the victim demanded vengeance were performed on the body. (This is one reason why cannibalism was the most
dire insult to and vengeance on an enemy group; many men I knew in the
early years of my fieldwork had eaten *lakuia*, human flesh. Eating the body
of a slain enemy or an incestuous couple abandoned by their own kin was
not motivated by a quest for spiritual power, but represented a relegation
to animal status.)

Prior to undertaking a raid or staging a killing, the would-be attackers
divined to ascertain potential outcomes or propitious circumstances, and
they usually sacrificed to their ancestors to purify any violations that had
gone undiscovered but could lead the ancestors to visit death or disaster
on them. A theme that runs through these chapters is that in armed confrontations or other kinds of collective political action vis-à-vis Europeans, Kwaio invoked the power and protection of their ancestors.
Explanations of the outcomes of what we would see as armed struggle or
political confrontation are cast in terms of ancestral support or punishment. In such a world, it is thus both difficult and inappropriate to separate the realm of religion from the realm of politics.

Quite often, homicide victims were women—not only victims of actual or attempted seduction, but women accused of theft, or sisters of
men who had violated the rights or reputations of other groups by curses
or seductions. So women in pre-European Kwaio communities—as in so
many other places where men's violence and aggression were culturally
celebrated—had an ambivalence toward it all. They were powerless to
resist male aggression directly. As I have written elsewhere, "Men's killing clubs, and volatile anger fuelled by greed and notions of honour,
could scarcely be challenged: they defined the spaces within which
women had to live" (Keesing 1987b, 55). Moreover, women as well as
men were caught up in the cultural celebration of aggression—ideologies
of pride, bravery, and honor, and demands for vengeance. On the other
hand, women were direct or indirect victims—as targets of life-
threatening sexual aggression and invasion, as potential innocent victims killed for the acts of their menfolk, as mothers and sisters and wives
of men killed in combat or executed in cold blood. This two-sidedness
comes out eloquently in an account by Fei'a of Bole, who had good reason
for ambivalence. When she was a child, her father had left her mother
and run off with her mother's sister—a quintessential and even incestuous violation of Kwaio sexual codes. A bounty had been put up for
his death, but he and his lover were strongly protected; and they increas-

ingly became a social embarrassment to the groups concerned, and (one might say) an affront to public morality. The inability to kill the husband also was an embarrassment to the leading bounty hunters of the time, chafing in frustration as well as itching for the pigs and valuables waiting for the successful killer. Eventually two of the feared *lamo*, who were soon afterwards to be leaders in the massacre of District Officer Bell and his party, ended the scenario by executing not the seducing husband or his lover, but the deserted wife. She was Fei'a's mother, and she was executed by a rifle shot, dying in Fei'a's arms. It is no wonder that her bitterness about the old days emerges; but so, too, does the way in which women were themselves trapped in cultural codes of honor and vengeance.

Women were often killed for things men did. The men would accuse a woman of stealing taro or greens, or urinating in the house and not reporting it. And so they'd kill her. Or a man would proposition a girl, and then men would say, "Let's kill her." . . . The men . . . would lie about a woman. They'd find some excuse to kill her; but what they were really after was the blood bounty—the money and the pigs. "That woman had an affair with a relative." "That woman urinated in the house." "Let's kill her for purification." . . . The women . . . said to the men: "You have to accept compensation, . . . not kill her." "No, we have to kill her." So they'd kill her and put up a blood bounty to avenge her death. . . . The women mourned the death of their sister or their daughter or their mother. They cried, saying: "They've killed our sister." Then they'd say, "I'm putting up my pig for the bounty to get revenge for her. . . . I'll put it up for the death of the man who caused the death of my sister." Another woman might get killed then. That's the way killings went on and on. (Keesing 1987b)

4 The Labor Trade

Through the first half of the nineteenth century, whaling ships were frequent visitors to Solomons waters. Some anchorages in the Western Solomons, and particularly Makira Bay on Makira (San Cristobal), became regular ports of call, where supplies of fresh foods and water could be replenished and local women could be procured for passing sexual pleasures.

The rugged coast of Malaita was avoided, after early confrontations in which crews were attacked. The eastern coast, where in most areas the mountains rise steeply from the sea, acquired a reputation as particularly wild and dangerous. Although Kwaio of the eastern mountains would probably have seen sailing ships on their horizon, I have found no evidence in Kwaio oral tradition that they were accorded any special significance.[1]

The ships acquired a new and devastating significance when they began kidnapping Malaitans along the coast. Kwaio epics tell of how Toobebe and Afio were taken from their canoe near 'Aioo Island, south of 'Oloburi—it would have been about 1869. But Toobebe and Afio were not dead, though the mortuary feasts had been given and blood bounties put up for vengeance. They returned after three years, bringing steel axes and tomahawks and knives, plane blades, cloth and trinkets; and bringing tales of a land beyond the sea. And by that time, more Kwaio had been taken from along the coast, some of whom would not return.

The first European record of "recruiting" on the east Kwaio coast I have found concerns the *Carl*, a Fiji-based sailing ship that became infamous for kidnapping Islanders and transporting them under appalling conditions. Brewster (1938:231) writes of an 1871 raid on the east coast of Malaita in which Kwaio men from Sinalagu were kidnapped and taken to Fiji: "Further on they found some people belonging to a village called Sinarangu, who paddled off to the ship, ten of them, and were captured. After they were tied up they sailed to the mouth of the bay of an island called Leli."

Soon the kidnappings were transformed into voluntary recruiting, as demands for the new tools—and the Snider rifles that became their "illegal" accompaniment—escalated (Corris 1973). By the mid-1870s, Queensland, Fiji, and Samoa bound vessels began recruiting systematically in the Kwaio anchorages ("passages" in the parlance of the burgeoning Labor Trade). It was the senior men who sent young men off to the sailing ships; they collected the bounty given for each recruit, and took most of what was brought back as well.

But many did not come back. Estimates suggest that a third of the Solomon Islanders recruited to Queensland and the other plantation areas

---

1. For the traces of Mendana's visit in 1569 in 'Are'are oral tradition, see Coppet 1977.

did not return. Although conditions on the recruiting vessels improved somewhat after the early brutal kidnappings,[2] the death toll on the plantations through illness was high, with poor and unfamiliar diets, cold Australian winters, diseases such as dysentery and measles, debilitating work regimens, and appalling medical care (Saunders 1976; Moore 1986). Recruits who did not return were mourned; their deaths called for vengeance as well, and blood bounties were put up. The killing of a European—any European—would suffice to claim these bounties, and that made recruiting a mortally dangerous game. The early accounts of the Labor Trade along the Kwaio coast describe "treacherous" attacks by warriors who lured ships' boats ashore by feigning eagerness to recruit.

There were other incentives as well, but it remained for a Kwaio strongman named Maeasuaa, from the islet of Uruilangi in Uru passage, to exploit them. Killing ships' crews not only could yield blood bounties of pigs and shell valuables; it could potentially yield as plunder the trade goods used in the "beach payments" for recruits—but only if one could capture and loot the ships themselves, rather than attacking crewmembers in the boats or on shore. Lounga of Gaafolo recounts Maeasuaa's exploits, which he learned in the form of an 'ai'imae:

I'll start with the first ship Maeasuaa took. It [the ship] came and came and came and came and arrived at Leri. It stayed out there, and people saw it. Maeasuaa from Uruilangi saw it out there at Leri. Maeasuaa went out to it. He got out to the ship and climbed aboard. The people on the ship saw him come, and heard him call out, but they didn't understand him. The white people didn't understand what he was saying [in Kwaio]. He asked them, "What have you come for? Where do you think you're going? What do you want?" But they couldn't understand him. And they spoke to him, but he couldn't understand either.

Then Maeasuaa went back to Uruilangi and said, "Let's attack that ship out at Leri. I spoke to them and they couldn't understand me; and they spoke to me and I couldn't understand them either." He went up to the shrine with his sacred pig and they sacrificed it to ancestor Lagosula. "Let me take that ship." His ancestor said, "Go and take it. Don't be frightened away." So Maeasuaa got his canoes out. And he got in the canoe, and Fataka got in, and Maamasi got in, and Fuiano got in, and Geua got in and Nori got in—all the fighting

2. Scarr (1970:230) notes that "debilitated as a result [of refusing terrible rations], and battened down in a confined, evil-smelling hold, [the Islanders] fell a prey to virulent epidemic dysentery from which, for instance, in 1879, 57 of 153 recruited by Fiji's *Stanley* died. In 1877 Queensland's *Bobtail Nag* lost 8 of a total of 102 recruits from the disease."

leaders [lamo]. They went out to Leri. They paddled out to where the ship
was, and Maeasuaa boarded and went up to the captain. Maeasuaa talked with
the captain. And while he was talking he instructed each of his men to come
aboard and pick out a crew member and stand near him. "One man stand with
the bosscrew, one man stand with the first mate. . . ." There were forty men
on the ship. Maeasuaa gave the signal to attack by striking down the captain;
and each man killed the crewman he had picked out. They killed them all: not
one survivor was left.

Maeasuaa saw that the last one was killed. Then he took all the rice, and all
the meat, and all the tinned fish, and all the tobacco and all the matches and
all the pipes—they filled up all their bags with cargo. And then they burned
the ship: that was that.

And nothing happened to them. Nobody came to attack them. That was to
come later. They didn't know about those things then. Maeasuaa didn't attack
that ship because blood money had been put up—he just attacked it.

A long time passed. And then a second ship came in our direction. It came
and came and came; and it anchored at Uru, at Maeasuaa's place. Maeasuaa
went out to it. "Where are you going?" he called out. "I've come looking for
boys to come with me. I want boys to come with me." But Maeasuaa couldn't
understand. They didn't speak our language. He spoke to them and they didn't
understand; they spoke to him and he didn't understand. Then Maeasuaa said
to his ancestor, "You, Lagosula, this second one—I want to attack it too." But
he got no answer. The ship stayed at Uru for a whole month, expecting people
to come. But nobody came, nobody would talk with them. People couldn't
speak Pidgin then. None of those people had been recruited then.

Maeasuaa gathered pigs and sacrificed them. "These are your pigs, Lagosula.
I want to take that second ship—to make you powerful. Show how strong you
are, through my deeds." And the ancestor said, "It's mine. I'll give it to you."
So Maeasuaa went to the ship. His men went aboard. And they attacked, and
nobody escaped. Just as they had done, the first time. They took all the cargo
off, then set a torch to the ship.

The men on those ships couldn't call for help on the radio. There were no
radios. Who was there to hear and save them? And there was no engine—only
sails. Those were the two ships Maeasuaa attacked at Uru. Not because he was
angry. He just did it. And nobody knew what had happened, nobody knew
what had happened to the ships. They had just disappeared.

Corris (1973:33) notes that

the islanders planned and executed the assaults upon the *Borealis* [1880] and
the *Janet Stewart* [1882] with great skill, sending parties of men out to the

ships, ostensibly to offer themselves as recruits. Once aboard they took out
concealed weapons and cut down the crew and recruits who had joined the
ship at other places. Five Europeans were killed aboard the *Borealis*, six aboard
the *Janet Stewart* including the government agent.

The attacks on the *Borealis* and the *Janet Stewart* hardly went unnoticed. The recruiting ships *Stanley*, *Dauntless*, and *Flirt* joined to take
punitive action after the *Borealis* attack, razing Maeasuaa's village on
Uruilangi, which lies exposed in Uru Harbor. Capt. W. H. Maxwell visited the area in December of 1880, and his account[3] illuminates the
Kwaio reaction to the attack, and to the punitive action.

I was soon boarded by numbers of natives from Quahquahroo [Kwakwaru],
who were evidently under no apprehension that anything they had done was
wrong. They were all full of the Borealis tragedy, which they informed me took
place at Uru Island and was perpetrated by Uru men. They described it exactly
as in the report, but went on to say that after the other schooners had left the
master of a Queensland labour vessel lying at this anchorage, a man called
Taylor, had assembled a force of Quahquahroo men, in addition to his own
crew, and had attacked the island, driven the natives off, and had burnt the
village, cut down all the cocoanut trees, and ruined it; that the natives of the
island had been obliged to desert it, and were scattered about the mainland. . . .

These Quahquahroo natives were evidently excessively proud of their feats
and of having revenged the white men, who, they said, were their friends. . . .
Some of these people were returned Queensland labourers and spoke English,
and seemed to have an immense respect for "Taylor."

I proceeded . . . to examine the island of Uru, which is situated in Quahquahroo Bay. . . . It is small, but evidently had been prosperous, and had
contained a numerous population. . . . Every habitation was destroyed, . . .
every single cocoanut tree was cut down, . . . and the whole place was a scene
of desolation. One or two small villages on the mainland had been also destroyed and the trees felled: indeed, had I intended to administer chastisement,
there was absolutely nothing left for me to do: not a native could be found, and
the nearest villages were at considerable distances up the mountain side.

The seemingly willing participation of the "Quahquahroo" people in
the punitive action calls for comment. First, as has been noted, Kwaio
descent groups were recurrently polarized as enemies; we can guess that
the local bush people were using the Europeans to further their own

3. Letter from Capt. W. H. Maxwell to Commodore J. C. Wilson, 31 Jan. 1881. Western Pacific High Commission Secretariat, Series 4, Inward Correspondence, General, Reel 3; G14065.

project of vengeance, although I have no direct information on this. Moreover, here as in northern Malaita, there were continuing conflicts and feuds between the 'saltwater people'—here, those of Uruilangi[4]— and their cousins in the mountains. However, Maeasuaa seems scarcely to have been chastened by the destruction of his village, since he launched the attack on the *Janet Stewart* only a year and a half later.

The only testimony we have from Kwaio of the time comes from two men picked up in Uru Harbor by ships involved in the punitive raid, and taken to Fiji. They were identified (probably incorrectly) by the cook of the *Borealis*, who was badly wounded in the attack, as among their assailants. They were held in Suva for several months, until they learned enough Fijian to be interrogated. One, "Tavoi" (Kwaio Taafai?), testified[5] that

I came to the beach and saw the boat of the white ship on board which the white men were killed. Four white men were in the boat. I bought 3 tomahawks, 8 pipes, 7 sticks of tobacco. I went back to my town. After two days I came back to the beach. . . . Three big ships lay at anchor.

My town is Tetepu [Tetefou, in Sinalagu Harbor], a hill town. I heard of the white men being killed . . . so I came to the beach . . . with many men perhaps ten. I went down to the beach to a town Yankavunu [Agafunu]. The people of Yuru Timmy's towns folk "moked" the Borealis ["killed" is written in margin near this line].[6] . . . I came down to the beach after the white men had been "moked"—my father said don't "moke" the ships. I went to Qaita [Ga'eta?] near Yankavunu. I was swimming in the sea when I was taken. . . . When I saw the big ship [the recruiting ship *Stanley*] coming . . . I left my boat and swam—four men were with me.

The testimony of the second, Suri, is hardly more illuminating, although it casts some light on understandings of the trading process by the Kwaio and the recruiters.

I am a "kai-colo" ["bush man" in Fijian]. Malayta is my Island—Ailamalama ['Ailamalama, on Uru Harbor, where a missionary was to be killed thirty years

4. Who speak a somewhat different dialect.
5. As recorded by H. Susan, Acting Agent-General Immigration, Crown Colony of Fiji, 26 January 1882, in Colonial Secretary's Office Minute Papers, 1877–1901, Pacific Manuscripts Bureau M157a, Reel 1, 1877–87.
6. "Yuru Timmy" is presumably Maeasuaa. The place name Uru in Kwaio is usually preceded by a euphonic locative "i." Nowadays Uru is used for the entire "passage" but originally it referred to the islet-settlement in the harbor (the full name of which is Uruilangi). I have no explanation for "moke," but it may be Pidgin Fijian.

later] is the name of my town.[7] . . . I came to buy axes, tobacco and pipes: 4 axes, 10 tobaccos, 10 pipes. I gave nothing in return to the whitemen. I am not a chief I am a [common] man. I took the "yan" [a marginal note identifies this as "property"; this is not a Malaita word] to my town and brought back long strings of beads such as I have now in my arms. The whitemen then threw them into the water and said that was not what they wanted. The ship I got axes from was painted white. Four men were in the boat when I bought the axes. They were white men. . . . The next day . . . I went to the beach to take taro to the beach people in exchange for fish. . . . When I was made prisoner I was out at sea in a Solomon canoe. I saw the European boats coming I jumped into the sea they caught me . . . and threw me into the boat.

Maeasuaa's successes did not go unnoticed among his fellow *lamo* in the mountains and on the coastal margins. Among them was 'Arumae of Tetefou, one of the few Kwaio descent group territories on the margins of the vast, almost landlocked harbor at Sinalagu.[8] One temptation for 'Arumae was a blood bounty put up by a man named Tafa[na]'au to avenge the death of his son Boosui. "A ship from Queensland . . . came and seized Taafana'au's son, at Leri. The son's name was Boosui. Taafana'au was angry because of that. When a ship came from Queensland he said, 'Let's attack that ship—because it took my son and he died at Mosilo. Now a ship has come' (Fa'atalo of Kwaina'afi'a)." Lounga's account is more detailed:

'Arumae from Tetefou heard all about Maeasuaa's deeds. "I'm brave, I've killed lots of people, I've done all there is to do—but now Maeasuaa has taken two ships. I haven't taken a ship. If a ship comes to Sinalagu to investigate those others, or if some other ship comes, it must be mine."

'Arumae reached for an areca nut[9] and said, "Here is your areca nut [ancestor] Lagalaga. Use your true powers—make a Queensland ship come here." And [later] he took a *guru* [a kind of trophy hung up by a feastgiver and taken by an aspiring rival in a reciprocal show of strength] from Maeasuaa: "When a ship comes to Sinalagu, you'll hear at Uruilangi what happens to it. You've taken two ships—it *must* not be hard. I have to try my hand at it." And his ancestor caused him to weep then [a sign of possession].

'Arumae waited and waited. He would stand at the entrance of his men's

7. A marginal note says "seems to be very intelligent, does not know Fijian well."

8. At this end, only a fairly low isthmus, an hour's walk across, separates this harbor from Uru, Maeasuaa's base. It is interesting and perhaps significant that "Tavoi," who was seized and taken to Fiji, was from Tetefou.

9. Used as a medium in communicating with ancestors; see Keesing 1982a:188.

house and look [out over the harbor]. But then one day he saw a sign: a snake [*waa'ulafu*, taken to be a messenger from an ancestral spirit] down on the path to the sea. He watched it come and come and come. And he knew a ship was on its way. "That's the ship I prayed to my ancestor for. It's not to go anywhere else; it must come here to me."

And finally the ship that was on its way appeared at the passage. It didn't go over to Gwee'abe [where District Officer Bell was assassinated forty-one years later]; it went to Gwarigwari. Then it went over to Gee'ana, then to Naabele. Then it went over to Ta'aifala. And then at Naafuu, it stopped. 'Arumae watched the ship out there. By that time people had learned Pidgin. He went out to the ship, went aboard, and talked to the captain. "What have you come for?" "I've come for boys. I want 40 boys to recruit with me." "When will you come back for them?" "I'll stay around for two weeks. I'll go back in two weeks." 'Arumae befriended him. The captain said, "You're my friend. You help me find the boys I need. Here's a case of tobacco for you." And he got out a case of tobacco.

'Arumae went back to Tetefou. He arranged to meet his ally Niulato of 'Ofena. "What do you think of this as the ship we take? You know the *guru* I took from Maeasuaa. Let's attack this one. They told me they'd be leaving in two weeks." "That's good—let's go ahead. This is the one for us. Let's kill them." And word went around to all the villages that 'Arumae was going to take that ship.

'Arumae got pigs together. He gave them to [ancestors] Kole and Kafu from Tetefou, and Fulategwa. He sacrificed them for that ship: "This is for the killing of the captain, for the killing of the first mate, for the killing of the second mate. . . ." But the pig was bloody [i.e., blood flowed from the pig's snout when it was throttled, an omen of impending misfortune, showing that the sacrificial pig has not been accepted by the ancestor to whom it was dedicated]. Then they sacrificed a pig at Takwafo'ea, for Nuto. And that pig was bloody too. Niulato sacrificed a pig at 'Ofena to Fe'enaalamo. And that one was bloody too. And he sacrificed a pig to Garigari—and that one was bloody too. And then a . . . pig to 'Akwaga, and that was bloody too. "All these pigs are giving us bad omens—let's turn back." But Ongeamae swore an oath against any of the young people who had been at the shrine at Tetefou telling others that the sacrificial pigs had issued blood. "If anyone lets out the news, they'll break up the fight. We have to go ahead, even if the pigs were bloody."

They set war plans in motion [lit., "they planted spears for the fight"]. The people from Gaafolo heard the plans. The people from Suriauo heard the plans. . . . The Fofonaile people heard, the La'utolo people heard.

Fi'oi from Kwangafi had come down to Tetefou to buy fish. "I'll come back about the ship later on today." He went back up to Baleobala. His son-in-law 'Aumaku, from Kafusiisigi, met him on the path. "Why are you going back up the hill?" "I'm going home." "What are you doing that for? They're attacking the ship today. There will be rice and meat and fish and tobacco and pipes for us to make off with. You have to come with me to join in the fight. How can you leave a good fight like that without taking part?" So the two of them went back down the hill together. They went down to Ta'aifala, where the men were gathered to go out to where the ship was anchored at Lo'omoori. 'Arumae had his big war canoe, Riuasuaa, ready there. He took a load of his warriors out to the ship. Then he came back to shore.

Maenaa'au and Kwainao called out to him, "Come over here for us!" "Stay where you are—you two are troublemakers. I won't have you two joining in, you might mess things up." But Maenaa'au said, "I won't cause any trouble—come back for me." So they got aboard. And Dii'ai called, "Come over here for me—I have to get in too." "No, you're from Kwangafi, and you're a trouble-maker. You can't join in today—go on home!" But Dii'ai said, "No, not me. Take me. Take me to the ship. You can't leave me behind." "No, you can't come!" 'Arumae pressed his objections, but to no avail. So they turned the canoe around and Dii'ai got aboard too. Then 'Otana called out, "Come here, 'Arumae, bring your canoe back for me!" But 'Arumae said, "No, you stay. You're from the Suriauo people, and Baibono as well, and a troublemaker who gets tangled up in blood feuds. Someone might kill you to avenge the death of [name inaudible], and mess things up" [sometimes, in the midst of an attack, one of the participants might be set upon and killed for motives unrelated to the attack itself, taking advantage of the attendant confusion]. "No, that won't happen. Bring the canoe back and I'll get in."

'Arumae turned the canoe around, and then he took all those people out to the ship. He took Kwaota'i and La'utolo, out to the ship. And he took the 'Ofena people—Maageni, Niulato, O'oka, Laaru, Mo'oita—and discharged them onto the ship.

Meanwhile the ship's boat had gone over to Gwee'abe to pick up recruits. It came back after the fight.

In the end, a hundred men had gathered on the ship. Then 'Arumae picked up an axe. He had brought one axe. Lamoka had a second, Ongeamae had a third. They had only three axes, the whole lot of them. 'Arumae went inside the cabin. Ongeamae went in with him. They didn't know about all the rooms on those ships, where the white men were—they didn't know about those things in those days. They only knew about the main cabin. 'Arumae climbed into the cabin where three white men were. He went up to the captain and stood next to him. He put his bare foot on top of the captain's boot, and the

captain objected angrily. And Lamoka and Ongeamae were beside the two
other white men. They thought there were only three white men on the ship
then. 'Arumae was stepping on the captain's boot, and they were shouting angrily at one another. 'Arumae wasn't intimidated. He hit the white man in the
face with his axe. Ongeamae hit the second white man with his axe. And
Lamoka killed the third one. They killed those three white men—just those
three. Then they went back onto the deck.

But there was another white man aboard they didn't know about: the one
who sewed up the sails. He heard the three white men in the cabin had been
killed. He opened the door of the cabin and snatched a Winchester and a
pouch of cartridges. He dashed out with the gun and scaled a rope to the fore-
yard. By the time the people saw him, he was already climbing up. What were
they to do about it? He climbed up and up. He got up to the masthead and
looked down below. The people were still on the deck below. He put five
cartridges into the Winchester. He loaded and cocked the gun. Ongeamae,
'Arumae's twin brother, was hit in the face by the first bullet, and fell dead beside 'Arumae. Ongeamae was shot down, and the others—seeing him fall—
started to jump into the sea. The white man cocked his gun for a second shot.
"This is yours, Gwalaa." He was from Tetefou, too. He fell dead—the second
one slain, shot in the neck. The *bekaman* loaded a third cartridge. "This is
yours, Talange'enia." And he shot him, another Tetefou man, dead as well.
He loaded a fourth cartridge. "This is yours, Maageni." He was Niulato's relative, from 'Ofena. He was shot dead. And then O'oka, also a man of 'Ofena—
the second man from there to be killed.

That was the first five cartridges. The *bekaman* took five more cartridges
from the pouch. "This one is for you, A'ala, from Fofonaile." And it knocked
him over dead. That was the sixth bullet. He loaded the seventh. "This is for
you, 'Otana, from Suriauo." He died too. He loaded an eighth cartridge. "This
is for you, Kwainaakwa, from Gaafolo." He died too. He loaded the ninth cartridge. Maenaa'au was in the water, swimming away. He swam over to the
end of the reef. His nephew Fi'oi, the son of Maenaa'au's sister, called out to
him. He was caught in the cabin. "Maenaa'au, get away from here! Escape
while you can!" "I'm staying!" "Go back to Kwangafi and tell my father and my
brothers what happened to me! I have to stay behind!" "You'll be all right—I'll
come back and save you. How can I go away and leave you there?" Maenaa'au
swam back to the ship and climbed up to help Fi'oi. The white man was waiting for him, and shot him down with the ninth cartridge. Fi'oi tried to get
away, and he was shot down with the tenth cartridge, shot in the head. Ten
bullets, ten corpses. The white man took five more cartridges. He cocked his
gun again. "Here's your cartridge, 'Aetalobo." He was from 'Aifala. 'Aetalobo

was shot. He cocked again. "Here's yours, Gaefia, from 'Aitolo." He was killed too. And another cartridge went in. And then he shot Afolosi. Thirteen men had been killed. The rest of the men in the water got safely to shore.

Then Lamoka looked around at what had happened to his people. He was thinking about Boosui. Boosui had been taken to Queensland. People had said that he had died there, in Queensland, and his father Tafa'au had put up a blood bounty for vengeance, there at Kwairuu. The bounty was put up against any ship that appeared on the horizon. And any ship that came was to be attacked, to avenge Boosui. It turned out [later] that Boosui hadn't died—he was just working there. People had lied.

Tafa'au had been out on the ship with the rest of them. Lamoka looked at him, reflecting that he, Tafa'au, in his desire to avenge Boosui, was at the base of the fight. He had been trying to avenge his son, Boosui. "And he has caused the death of all the men of my descent group." So he picked up his axe and struck Tafa'au down with a blow to the neck. So that was fourteen men dead. And three white men—17 dead in all. 'Arumae had run away to the shore.

Apart from the rhetorical stylistic elaborations, Lounga's account accords strikingly with eyewitness accounts by the survivors, as recounted in a Queensland courtroom seventeen days after the 1886 attack on the *Young Dick* (Keesing 1986b). Again, retaliation was ineffectual, although the disastrous outcome of 'Arumae's venture deterred his fellow *lamo* from similar attacks. However, a blood bounty was put up for vengeance, and in 1888, Government Agent T. S. Armstrong from the *Ariel* was killed at Maanaoba (on the northern tip of Malaita); Jock Cromar, an early recruiter, describes seeing Armstrong's head being taken in a canoe to Sinalagu to collect the bounty (Cromar 1935).

It is worth pausing to reflect on a problem, raised in the introductory chapter, that will run through the interpretation of historical events in the chapters to follow. In what sense, and with what reservations, can we read as acts of "resistance" these early armed attacks on recruiting ships? Obviously, the motives of leaders like Maeasuaa or 'Arumae were mixed. Their goals centrally included plunder of the vessels and the power and prestige that would come from being able to redistribute European goods. They sought as well the fame and prestige that came from successful warrior deeds, a prestige that was seen as reflecting the support of warlike ancestors, and, in satisfying their bloodthirsty proclivities, as enlisting further support. So much the better if the warrior deeds were directed against the powerful aliens. Those who joined in the attacks set in train by warrior leaders had similar motives, but also private and diverse ones relating to kinship obligation, bravado displayed to rivals or siblings or lovers, or whatever.

Yet through all this was a clear recognition that these *were* aliens, that their presence in these waters was invasive, and that they threatened Kwaio power. Moreover, many of the early attacks were explicitly aimed at securing vengeance for the death of kin on the Queensland or Fiji plantations. In the early attacks, "resistance" as a political struggle against Europeans was a subtext, subordinated to traditional cultural goals. As the European presence progressively became more dominant in the decades to follow, and eventually as confrontation had as its clear outcome either subjugation to or freedom from direct political domination and the enforced payment of tribute, the subtext of resistance was to grow into a more and more central theme.

For another fifteen years, recruiting went on in an orderly fashion, punctuated by occasional attacks on recruiting vessels. Several are recorded from the waters between Kwaio and Kwara'ae country: the *Sybil II* was attacked there in 1891, and again in 1893 and twice in 1894. The *Para* was attacked in 1894 and 1895 (Moore 1986:350–51). Honor demanded that the young men dead on faraway plantations be avenged; but with recruiting conducted under the barrels of the guns and recruiters taking such defensive measures as spreading broken glass on the decks when trouble seemed imminent, the old forms of vengeance and plunder had become more and more difficult and dangerous.

Kwaio oral tradition is expansive with regard to the rifles obtained in Queensland and Fiji and the uses to which they were put, but relatively silent in regard to the experiences of the men who went to Queensland. Suufiomea remembers hearing stories of Queensland told by his elders when he was a boy:

My "fathers" Suuka and 'Otomani told me about being in Queensland, at Fodafaka [Bundaberg], Tanasuwela [Townsville]—those places. . . . They went there on a sailing ship. They'd start from our island and it would take three or four weeks to reach Queensland. They weren't ships with engines, like the ones today—they went in a sailing ship. . . . The captain came and signed men on. The name of the ship that took them was *Olokate*. A sailing ship. I asked them if it was big. "A hundred men could go inside—but it didn't have an engine."

They lived in grass houses there—not ones with metal roofs. They had no sago thatch there, so they used grass. That's what they told us. . . . They brought back all sorts of things people hadn't seen before—knives, axes, pipes.

They brought back cats. It was Idumae from A'ala who brought the first cat
back from Queensland. People didn't know what it was. They were surprised at
the way it was tame and friendly, and at the way it washed its own face and
cleaned itself up. People thought it might be something dangerous that would
attack you. Nowadays we know they're good rat-catchers, but people didn't
know anything about them in those days and recoiled in fright.

When people saw the pipes and the stuff you smoked in them—when
smoke came out of men's mouths, they thought it was a kind of *fele* sorcery. But
when people learned what the pipes and smoke were about, they started smoking too.

. . . They worked on processing sugar cane. . . . I asked them what they
grew the sugar cane for. "It's for the juice, the kind of juice we squeeze out of it
and drink. There was an engine to crush it. The juice would come out in one
place and the pith would come out in another. They used the word "engine"
for that. But in the old days they didn't understand English well—not even
Pidgin.

The Kwaio, many of them remarkable genealogists, do remember the
names of men who went to Queensland and Fiji, and still talk about those
who did not come back. Most of the Kwaio in Queensland were repatriated, although some stayed on.[10] But many of those working in Fiji at the
time of repatriation were left there. In 1990, I heard stories of how the
last ship repatriating Solomon Islanders was filled, leaving dozens of men
who wanted to go home stranded in Fiji. One of them was Kwa'ifanaboo
from 'Ai'eda. Hearing his name in the Kwaio mountains brought back a
vivid memory of my 1984 visit to Wailoku, a settlement of Malaita descendants outside Suva, the Fiji capital. I was talking with a community
leader named Pastor Luke Olu, a man of Kwaio-Kwara'ae background,
and had discovered with great excitement that he had begun to respond
to, and answer, my attempts to converse in Kwaio—a language he had
not heard for forty years. When a young boy—his grandson—arrived at
the house, Luke greeted him: the boy's name was Kwa'ifanaboo.

Some of the stories deal interestingly not only with the experiences
and adventures of the Kwaio recruits but also with the Australian
Aborigines—who became for the Kwaio in later decades a symbol of
what people can be reduced to when they are dispossessed of their land.
Bita Saetana ["Peter Satan"], a pagan priest living close to Christian

10. See Fatnowna 1989 for an account of elderly Thomas Kaumae, a Kwaio man who stayed on
in the Mackay area.

communities on the coast, told me in 1977 of his relatives' experiences and recollections of Queensland:

The ships that were recruiting for Queensland were the *Fela* and the *Lokina* and the *Malakula*. Those ships came from Queensland—from Fodafaka [Bundaberg] and Kubei [?] and Mekei [Mackay] and Anamanatalefo [Herbert River]. They recruited—took people to work on the sugar plantations, for three years. It took a long time just to get there, on the sailing ships.

The native people who lived there were just forced by the white men to live in the bush. They called them *manobusi* ["man-'o-bush," i.e. Australian Aborigines]. My mother's father married one of those *manobusi* and lived there in Queensland for ten years, then came back. His named was Toolatena. My uncle told me that those *manobusi* who had been chased from their homelands into the bush had to live on whatever they could find in the forest—snakes, possums, rats, monitor lizards, birds. They were forced to try to find food in the rubbish piles of the plantations—spoiled food or waste that had been thrown away. The white people had ruined them, forced them from their land.

The white people had tricked and deceived them. They had to live in the bush, sleep anywhere at all, in the scrub, under a store, in a tree. The *manobusi* couldn't live in houses—they'd been forced to flee into the forest.

Suufiomea's 'fathers', too, had told him stories of the *manobusi*. He recalled in 1990 being told:

They saw the *ta'a* [people] *manobusi* too. They saw the way they fought. They saw the shelters they made—they just slept in the bush, like pigs. They didn't have good food to eat. Those *manobusi* used something to hunt and to fight which they called *bumala'e*. A piece of wood they made in a curved shape. They'd throw it and hit you with it. But when it was thrown, it would come back to the person who had thrown it, and he'd pick it up. I asked my "fathers" if the *manobusi* looked like us. "Oh, if we fought with them, they'd beat us. They are big and strong. But they just lived in the bush like feral pigs."

In these latter years of the Labor Trade, Malaitans had developed a strong dependence on the goods imported from overseas by the returning laborers, especially steel tools and the aging Snider rifles.[11] Steel tools

---

11. These were originally .505 muzzle-loading muskets, British army issue, which had been converted to breech-loading by British ordnance so as to delay their obsolescence. When they were finally replaced, the obsolete weapons were sold in bulk and traded for nefarious purposes around the colonial frontiers of the world. Copies of them were still being hand-forged in the Himalayas and Hindukush into the 1970s.

had replaced crudely shipped chert adzes by the 1890s, transforming Kwaio technology. The rifles, smuggled back from Fiji and Samoa and Queensland in the false bottoms of chests, had become ubiquitous, symbols of manhood and honor and agents of execution for the *lamo* in the Kwaio mountains.

A celebrated blood feud in the early years of this century led to the killing of 'Ofanaala by Basiana, the most feared *lamo* of his generation. I recorded an account of this feud in 1974, from Lounga of Gaafolo (see also Keesing 1978a and Keesing and Corris 1980:83–85). An early segment tells of how l'alamo of Ngudu (whom I knew as a blind octogenarian priest named 'Ulasia[12]) spent ten years in Fiji, obtaining Snider rifles for his warrior kin. It was with this rifle that Basiana had killed 'Ofanaala; and it was with its barrel that Basiana was to crush Bell's skull in October 1927.

Foolamo was angry about that tree [which Bakua] had cut down. She swore at Bakua. Bakua was angry, and he took his rifle and shot her dead.

Her people, from Wawasila, put up a *sikwa* (blood bounty) to avenge Foolamo. They sought Bakua's death, or the death of [Bakua's father] 'Ofanaala. The *sikwa* stayed and stayed. No one could claim it. Basiana [of Gounaile] said, "People are hunting Bakua and 'Ofanaala for that *sikwa* down there; but we have no rifle to shoot them."

Na'oni'au said, "I'll go to [a plantation] to get a rifle for us to kill 'Ofanaala." Na'oni'au and l'alamo went to Fiji together, to get guns. They stayed in Fiji for a long time. They were cutting sugar cane there. One section worked here, another worked there. The Fijian girls were good to men from our place, so lots of our men just stayed there. Some of them are still there.

Na'oni'au bought a rifle. They kept it, and then Na'oni'au got sick. When he was close to death, he reached for the rifle and gave it to l'alamo. "This is the rifle I came for—to kill 'Ofanaala for our sikwa. The rifle for Basiana. You, l'alamo, are to take it back to him." Then Na'oni'au died, there in Fiji.

'Ulasia stayed in Fiji for ten years. It seemed as though no ship would come to take them home. "You'll never go home again. You'll just stay in Fiji." l'alamo reached for an areca nut, and bit into it, praying to ancestress La'aka. "Bring a ship for me, so I can go home; otherwise I'll die in Fiji." Two weeks later, their [white] overseer said, "A ship is here ready to take you back. Get your cases ready."

By that time, l'alamo had five rifles. Three he had acquired himself; the

12. Kwaio change names when they reach ritual maturity, and many undergo further changes in the course of a lifetime.

fourth was the one Na'oni'au had given him, to take to Basiana; and the fifth
was given to him by Firiaba'e, to take to 'Uga'au. When I'alamo got back, he
gave the rifle to Basiana and another to 'Uga'au.

The Kwaio strongmen had apparently stepped up the scale of blood
feuding at the end of the nineteenth century and the early years of the
twentieth, partly as a result of the freeing of labor time through the introduction of steel tools, and partly because of the transformation of combat
with firearms. However, 'ai'imae of this period suggest that the old weap-
onry was still as effective—in practice, if not symbolically—as the new.
A fragment of an epic told by Maena'adi, another well-known tale
involving the lamo Bibiasi, will serve to illustrate how firearms and traditional weapons were juxtaposed.

Sa'a and Ge'aa and the Fou'afua people and the Riirifu people exchanged
shots. Sa'a's cartridges were finished, and he reached in his bag, at that fight
there at Fou'afua. Two men from 'Aukwale . . . came up to the entrance to
the clearing and saw Sa'a. They raised their rifles and shot at Sa'a . . . but the
shots missed. Sa'a didn't realize he'd been shot at, because in that fight there
were lots of rifles firing. He couldn't hear. They had fired four shots at him before he realized he'd been shot at. . . .

He looked and saw the two men from 'Aukwale who had shot at him. He
found another cartridge and shot at them with it. They ducked down, and the
shot missed . . . and they ran away, back to their place at 'Aukwale.

In that fight, the ancestors must have withheld support. One of the men
from Naabale escaped into the bush by the path entrance; another's lime container was hit by a spear, while he was holding it. Another man was hammered
in the penis by a spear—they were naked in those days, just wearing fighting
belts. The ancestors must have been withholding support: even when they
threw their spears and they hit, they were just blunt. The fight went badly.

So . . . old Ma'aaniana . . . the father of Bibiasi, the one who had killed
Forifo'oa and 'Asuka, ritually broke open a coconut, up behind the men's
house. He prayed: "Oh, empower my sons, to 'fence in' Forifo'oa's people today." . . . He broke the coconut and prayed to the ancestors at Foo'ibo.

Geni saw him go up there. . . . He said, "Founaaringa—go up there and
look behind the men's house." Founaaringa took a wooden spear and
climbed up above the men's house. He climbed up there and threw his spear at
Ma'aaniana, threw it into his neck. It impaled him, right through his body,
and the old man fell dead.

Fouaaringa jumped over the stone platform and down into the clearing.
Then Osi'au, who was just young, shot him with an arrow. He hit him once in

the breast, and again in the back with a second arrow. Founaaringa broke off the arrow shafts and ran off.

The power of the *lamo,* the autonomy of the Kwaio to follow the ways of the ancestors, remained unchallenged into the early years of the century, even though by then the Kwaio of the mountains knew full well from their skirmishes with the recruiters and warships and from the experience of plantation workers abroad that they were no longer at the center of the world.

5 Sukuru

Florence Young's brothers had acquired Fairymead sugar plantation at Bundaberg, Queensland, in 1882. She first encountered "Kanakas" on the plantation. "We were employing at this time some eighty Kanakas, South Sea Islanders from the New Hebrides and the Solomon Islands" (Young 1926:38). She began conducting Bible classes for the "Boys," and by 1886 the classes had grow to some eighty Islanders every Sunday (ibid., 42). In 1886, the Queensland Kanaka Mission was established.

There is no doubt that many of the Queensland converts were deeply transformed by their experience with Christianity. Yet with the home islands still "wild" and "savage," and with the Christian converts being rapatriated at the end of their indenture, Miss Young and her fellow missionaries agonized over the anticipated backsliding of the Christians once they got back to the islands. The dangers a returning Christian would face doubtless deterred many potential converts. One Islander told Miss Young, in the Pidgin English of the plantations:

> Me no want-'im school. Suppose me come along school, by-and-by me no savee fight. Me go home along Island, man he kill-'im me. Along Island altogether man he row, row ROW all the time. Man he go sleep along bed, he hold'im spear, bow and arrow, gun along hand. Suppose he no got-'im gun, some-fellow man he come, he kill him quick (ibid., 47).[1]

1. I don't want Christianity. If I become Christian, then I won't be able to fight. When I go back to my island, someone will kill me. Back in the islands people are always fighting. When a man goes to bed, he sleeps with his spear, bow and arrow, and gun beside him. If he didn't have a gun, someone would come and kill him straight away.

The form taken by the first missionary efforts in Queensland—Bible classes—was to shape a linguistic usage in the Islands: Christianity, and Christian villages, were to be called *skul,* a usage the missionaries themselves came to perpetuate.

In the first years of this century, recruiting for Queensland was halted by imposition of the White Australia Policy; most of the Islanders who had been in Queensland were repatriated (willingly or unwillingly) in 1905. One consequence was a decision to transform the Queensland Kanaka Mission into the South Sea Evangelical Mission (SSEM), and to concentrate evangelical efforts in the Solomons. In 1904 Florence Young had followed her small but devout band of Christians to the Solomons for a first visit. Converts at Sinalagu had sent word that her presence was needed there: "Christians in Queensland from Sinorango had urged the claims of their 'passage' amongst other possible places" (Young 1926:153). On March 24, 1904, "the 'Daphne' put into Sinorango Harbour and a welcome rest was enjoyed" (ibid., 159).

A year later, Florence Young was back again from Queensland. Visiting passages along the east Malaita coast, she "felt loath to pass Sinorango, a place of which we had heard from so many Boys in Queensland" (ibid., 170). She was particularly on the lookout for "Sam Faralati" (Farulate).

Within an hour Sam was on board. He was, of course, delighted to see us, but he needed help, as we could see from his appearance. His hair was decked with feathers, and he wore many rings and shells in heathen fashion. . . .

When he went home he tried to teach his people, and made a brave stand for two years. He met, however, with great difficulties. His people refused to listen to him. His boat was destroyed . . . and when he was ill the people stole all his clothes (ibid., 170–171).

Later in Young's account (ibid., 198), where she describes a visit to Sinalagu in 1909, we learn that

Four years ago, just at this spot, Sam Faralati, a solitary backslider, had been rescued in this harbour, carried round to One Pusu [the mission headquarters on the southwestern Malaita coast] for a few months, and then brought back to make a fresh start with another Christian to help him. He settled at Taifala at the north end of the harbour, and although his life was in danger and his work interrupted for twelve months, God enabled him to win two of his people, who on that day had been baptized.

"Taifala" is Ta'aifala, 'Arumae's land, and just across the water from Tetefou from which the attack on the *Young Dick* had been launched nineteen years earlier. We learn from the SSEM newsletter *Not in Vain* that the "school" (Kwaio *sukuru*) had been established there under 'Arumae's protection.

Another "school" was established on the mountain inland from the harbor, at Bu'obu'o, run by Diakafu ("Jacob"), a former pagan priest who had become a Christian convert in Queensland, and his wife "Topsy" from Makira (San Cristobal). By 1909, "fifty people were coming regularly to school, and fourteen had decided for Christ" (ibid., 198). Another "school" was established at Kafuni'abe, at the other end of the harbor, led by Fiito'o ("Peter Veto") and Basinaamae ("Philip Pasnamai"). Fiito'o had also established a "school" at 'Oloburi. We find tidbits of information on the embattled Christian communities at the foot of the mountain wall in *Not in Vain*: 1907, "30 [at "Kaffiniambi"] have already accepted Christ"; 1908, "1 baptism," but "thirty at Kaffiniambi [Kafuni'abe] have already accepted Christ as their Saviour"; 1909, "7 baptisms"; 1910–11 "5 baptisms" (but only two "stations" listed, with one "vacant pro-tem").

The tiny *sukuru* villages were under constant threat from the pagans. *Not in Vain* records that in 1907 "the work at Wunfor and Forti [was] a good deal upset by the recent murders of six people, four of whom were coming to school."[2] We learn that later in 1907 the Christians had started another *sukuru* settlement at Takwanaangari "but left for a time on account of some murders."

In 1911 an SSEM missionary named Fred Daniels established a mission station at 'Ailamalama, on the crest of the ridge that separates Uru Harbor from the sea, where he intended to work intermittently. Young (ibid., 214–16) describes how, in June 1911, Daniels was shot by two "bushmen." She recounts how "for many years, blood money had been offered at Uru for a white man in revenge for the death of a labourer on plantation service," and goes to pains to point out that the killers "had no grudge against the missionary, neither had their people." An Anglican missionary who investigated the killing concluded that "the motive centred around the seduction of a Kwaio girl by a mission teacher, and Daniels' intervention in getting the couple away to safety at Onepusu"

---

2. *Not in Vain*, 26 July 1907.

(Keesing and Corris 1980:13). Fortunately, we have a Kwaio account by 'Alakwale'a, one of the two assassins, as recounted to Jonathan Fifi'i:

One of the Maasina Rule chiefs from above Uru was a man named 'Alak-wale'a.[3] I had heard the story about Mr. Daniels of the S.S.E.M., who built a church at 'Ailamalama. 'Alakwale'a and Kwa'iga killed him. I didn't know why they had killed him. One day I was talking to 'Alakwale'a. I said to him, "'Alakwale'a, why did you kill Daniels, the man who had brought the Gospel of the church?"

'Alakwale'a replied, "I killed him for two reasons. The first was that two men came back from Queensland, Farulate and Diakafu. They had been custom priests, who sacrificed at their shrines. When they brought back the "school," we saw what happened. We saw men just mixing freely with women. Worse yet, we saw men—these sacred men—just staying with menstruating women. A man didn't even follow the tabus about [not] going to the menstrual huts. We saw that and we were unhappy about it. I saw that with my own eyes. It looked as though our customs were going to die. The mission people were going to come and destroy our customs: our tabus, the rules of the ancestral spirits. That was one grievance.

"The other reason I was angry was because my mother had cursed me, because of a bamboo of ngali nuts.[4] I went out to meet a girl for a date,[5] with my brother Kwa'iga. We came back and were really hungry. We took some taros and roasted them. Then I asked, 'Whose bamboo of ngali nuts is this?' People said, 'It's your mother 'Angota's bamboo of ngali.' We pounded them up in a mortar and ate them. Then we left. Our mother came back. She saw that her nuts were missing and she uttered a curse. She didn't know that we were the ones who had eaten the nuts. She thought it was some child, or someone from outside. She cursed.

"And then people told her who had eaten the nuts. 'Hey, you've put a curse against your own children.' 'Who?' 'Kwa'iga and 'Alakwale'a.' She heard that and was distraught. Word of what she had done spread around. Then people told us about it. 'You two—your mother cursed you because of her bamboo of ngali.'"

'Alakwale'a went on. "When I heard that, I said, 'Hey, why did our mother curse us? Well, it doesn't matter that she has cursed us. That's all right, even

3. See Chapter 11.

4. Canarium almonds, important and highly valued as a seasonal food on Malaita.

5. In Kwaio custom, courtship involves a couple meeting at an arranged time and place in the forest, chastely, standing shoulder to shoulder, talking, and, sometimes, exchanging small gifts.

though she has cursed us, we won't make an issue of it.' I didn't tell people
what I was really thinking. Even though I said it was all right, Kwa'iga and I
were really upset. We talked about it. I said to Kwa'iga, 'I want us to do something. Something that will make her have to run away, something that will
bring fear. What we should do is kill that white man down there, Mr. Daniels.
So everyone will have to run away, and she'll be afraid.'

"So Kwa'iga and I went down to 'Ailamalama. Daniels was doing his church
service, at dawn. After the service, everyone went outside. Only he was left inside. My brother Kwa'iga and I reached for a cartridge for our rifle. I cocked it
and pointed it at Daniels' forehead. Kwa'iga and I pointed it and the "Samoa"
cartridge burst. That's what we called cartridges in the olden days, because
people had brought them back from Samoa. The cartridge burst. It hit Daniels
in the forehead, and he fell down.

"Then Kwa'iga and I slipped away unseen, like a snake that bites someone
and then vanishes."[6]

Again, it is worth pausing to reflect on the confluence of motives involved. We find in 'Alakwale'a's motives both a clear element of resistance against what was perceived as European invasion and the threat
posed by Christianity to ancestral ways and powers, and a personal
project entailing the purification of a curse by the most spectacular means
available. If we give excessive prominence to the element of resistance,
we distort meanings and motives in the context of the time and circumstances. Yet if we discount this element, we cannot understand the
confrontation between Kwa'iga and District Officer Bell thirteen years
later, or the emergence of 'Alakwale'a as anticolonial political leader
thirty-five years later.

What followed the killing of Daniels is recounted by Keesing and
Corris (1980:14–15):

The Malaita missionaries, knowing that if the killing of Daniels went un-
punished it would mean open season on evangelists, ran to the administration
in Tulagi demanding that the murder be punished with a heavy hand; a protective mantle of naval power, and a stern lesson, were needed to secure their
position.

The missionaries and their Australian backers had a measure of political
influence; and the killing of Europeans—unlike the killing of Solomon
Islanders—was deemed by the administration to be an "outrage" calling for

6. An 'ai'imae on the killing of Daniels recounted to me by Maena'adi in 1989 gives a very similar
account, but a much more detailed one. It was actually Kwa'iga who shot Daniels.

stern retaliation. H.M.S. *Torch*, based in Fiji, was charged with exacting vengeance. After a five-month delay a punitive attack was launched, directed by the High Commissioner from Fiji, Sir Frederick May, and the Resident Commissioner from Tulagi. The *Torch* totally destroyed Uruilangi at May's instigation. May, in error, believed that the killing of Daniels had been instigated by Maeasuaa . . . and he justified the attack on Uruilangi accordingly. In fact, 'Alakwale'a and Kwa'iga had been rowed across the harbour by a kinsman-accomplice from Uruilangi; but Maeasuaa, a bent and crippled old man, had long since passed on the mantle of secular leadership to his successors.

The second devastation of Uruilangi, thirty-one years after the first, went beyond that reported by May. Lounga of Gaafolo recounted to me in 1974 that

the white men destroyed Uruilangi. They violated the women. They raped the women, and killed four or five of the "saltwater people" and took all the valuables. I don't know the names of the men who were killed—the women who were raped were 'Afatabu and Muufuru and Kokosi and Neenemo and Arusu'u.

The Uruilangi people were enraged because their men had been killed, their women had been raped, and their shrines had been desecrated, because of a killing that had been perpetrated by someone else. So they made a curse by all the most sacred things of those people who had done it, 'Alakwale'a and Kwa'iga. The "saltwater" women cursed the people from Farisi, and cursed the ancestors of Farisi and the sacred things of Farisi, and the shrines of Farisi—a curse as wide as the sea. They turned everything at Farisi upside down. "It's the people up there at Farisi, 'Alakwale'a and Kwa'iga, who did the fight. You climb up there and punish them."

Keesing and Corris's account (1980:15) goes on the recount the second phase of the punitive expedition, as portrayed in May's report: "While May was busy burning the huts and fishing nets of Uruilangi, a naval party (guided by a man from across the bay at Ngongosila) climbed the steep slope to Farisi in the night, surrounded the settlement before dawn, and attacked the occupants when they emerged."

In 1989 Maena'adi took me to the site of the dawn massacre, and later recounted the *'ai'aimae* that gives the Kwaio version. A small excerpt serves to complement the one based on May's report.

The "soldiers" came up in the night and surrounded the clearing just at first light. Naa'auala had awakened and gone down to the women's latrine, leaving her two young children inside the house, with a plank across the door.

The "soldiers" set fire to the houses, and shot the people as they came out.

They shot Booiri and 'Audila, and Okota [a woman], and shot Fouta.[7]
Naa'auala, down in the latrine, heard the houses burning, and came up and
hid at the edge of the latrine area. She saw her house burning with two children inside. The flames engulfed them.

Only Gauka got away, with his rifle. He decided to ambush the soldiers
above the precipitous path at Afu'ele—he realized that after they had finished
burning the settlement, they'd have to come back by way of Afu'ele. [He had
gone to where Kwa'iga had taken refuge, and enlisted him as well.] "Let's kill
one of them to take revenge for our older brothers [in a classificatory sense] and
fathers who have all been killed."

Kwa'iga thought to himself: "I killed Daniels, and they have killed all of
Gauka's relatives. I'll bet he's lying to me and he wants to kill me for revenge."
Gauka said, "Let's lie in ambush here with our two guns." But Kwa'iga said,
"No, you lie in wait at the top of the steep place, and I'll lie in wait at the bottom." He was just lying. He went down, and then he just slipped away. He was
afraid because he had been the instigator of the killing.

Gauka lay in wait. The soldiers burned the village and cut down the coconut palms and went into the shrine at Otelagwa and overturned all the sacred
oven stones and scattered the ancestral skulls. They shot all the pigs and killed
the cats—destroyed everything. Only Naa'auala and Gauka had escaped.

The white man Mr. Barton (Misa Baaten), who had brought the "army,"[8]
went down with them—the soldiers were in front, he was in the rear. They
went down and down. Gauka lay in wait. He thought to himself, "If I shoot at
the soldiers in front, they'll shoot me for sure. If I wait and shoot at the last
one, then even if I miss, I'll be able to get away."

Baaten and Kambolo were bringing up the rear. . . . When they got abreast
of Gauka, he shot Baaten, up there at the top of Afu'ele. He shot Baaten, who
fell down dead, at the bottom of the cliff.[9]

The Government was confident that the destruction meted out to
Uruilangi and to the Otelagwa people would deter the bush people along
the eastern coast to respect the new forces of law and order and would
render Europeans safe. Keesing and Corris (1980:15) note that

7. Lounga's parallel account cites ten people killed at Farisi (May's report claims five, including
one child burned in the house), and attributes this to the curse by the Uruilangi people: "The slit
gong they took from Farisi is still in Gizo today."

8. At the beginning of the 'ai'aimae he names Misa Kambolo as well—F. M. Campbell, the
constabulary officer, whose descendants (by a Solomon Islands wife) are prominent in the contemporary Solomons.

9. According to May's report, "one sailor and several (local) carriers were wounded when the
rear of the withdrawing column was ambushed" (Keesing and Corris 1980:15).

Europeans expected Malaitans, at least in the area, to be intimidated into détente for a time; and years later the government looked back on the *Torch* raid as one of the few effective early punitive strikes. Yet only three days after the *Torch*'s dawn raid, and only five miles away across the reef-sheltered bay, the crew of recruiting ship *Ruby* was set upon by several men who had come aboard the previous night, ostensibly to recruit. The mate was killed, the captain wounded. . . . Although there is no evidence that the *Ruby* was attacked in direct retaliation for the *Torch*'s raid, this incident hardly supports the government's optimism about the chastening effect of the punitive operation.

It was to be thirteen years before another European missionary presence was established in Kwaio country, again on the peninsula separating Uru Harbor from the sea, near 'Ailamalama, where Seventh Day Adventist J. D. Anderson and his wife established a "school." In the intervening years, another presence was to become more intrusive.

6 *Gafamanu*

Grizzled old Alefo paused in his story of the events almost fifty years before, as we sat in a men's house at Dari'aitolo, on the rim of the precipice that drops 1500 feet into the Lari'ai river below. In 1970 he was into his seventies, but in our years together I had seen his strength and his continuing defiance. The struggle against colonial invasion had been the main theme of his life, in the attack on Bell and its aftermath, in his fourteen years in prison at Tulagi, and in his warrior participation in Maasina Rule five years after his release. Unrepentant in 1947, twenty years after the massacre at Gwee'abe, Alefo had urged an attack on the government officer and police who had come to arrest their leader.

Alefo, and his old compatriot Kwai'ime beside him, talked bitterly about the destruction of Kwaio sovereignty. Kwai'ime had been with him in the attack on the tax house in 1927 and had spent those years with him in Tulagi.[1] Each had been imprisoned for life, leaving a young wife behind. Each had returned to the mountains, released when the Japanese invaded and prisoners could no longer be protected, to find his wife remarried, his place in the Kwaio social world vacant; and each had rebuilt

1. See Firth (1979) for an account of Kwai'ime's trial in Tulagi in 1927, to which he had been an eyewitness.

a life, defiant though embittered. Each had been prepared, after only five years of freedom, to attack the government again in the cause of autonomy from alien domination.

Alefo's comrade in arms Kwai'ime resumed the story, of how the most feared Kwaio *lamo* of his young manhood—Basiana of Gounaile, Tagailamo (Noru) of Furi'ilai, Alefo's older brother Maenaafo'oa of Ngudu—had responded when the colonial government demanded their submission to alien law and taxation in the early 1920s: "Basiana and Maenaafo'oa were angry because their relatives had been hanged. And [the people from the coastal slopes] said, 'You are *lamo*, but though you are strong, [the government] is making women of you. . . . You'll be like women. You'll just have to stay at home.' And they were angry. Noru said, 'Let's kill the white man!'"

That was thirteen years after the attack on Uruilangi and Farisi, precipitated by the killing of Daniels. The British Solomon Islands Protectorate had been established in 1893, with its tiny capital on the island of Tulagi, in the Florida (Gela) group. Malaita, as the primary source of Solomons recruits from the early days of the Labor Trade, and with several small enclaves of European missionaries since the first years of this century, was reasonably well known—or at least, the coastal strip was. Yet the island was effectively devoid of administrative control until 1909, when a government post was established at Rarasu on the west coast. (The government promptly misnamed it for a small island in the harbor, 'Aoke, and then misspelled that—as "Auki.")

The initial government presence in "Auki" was less than impressive. A young District Officer, T. E. Edge-Partington, established the post; F. M. Campbell was in charge of the constabulary, some thirty "native" police. With little backing from the Resident Commissioner in Tulagi in seeking to extend a small zone of "law and order," and limited means to do it (including a whale boat), Edge-Partington chafed in frustration. He was under orders to stage no punitive strikes when Malaitans—often Christians on the coast—were killed. He wrote in the station journal in 1911: "Received news from Dr. Deck [SSEM] of another murder, the usual weekly occurrence, at Darra. [and in a later entry, after noting another murder] . . . Above information entered, but is I suppose useless, as usual being prohibited from doing our duty." When news of Daniels's assassination reached him, Edge-Partington requested permission to stage a punitive strike. He soon got his answer back: "Boat returned from Tulagi with answer to official despatch re murder of Mr. Daniels. Prohibited from going on punitive expedition by Acting R.C. Hope some

more get murdered. Shall not budge" (Keesing and Corris 1980:43).[2]
Keesing and Corris (ibid., 42–43) continue:

Even if his superiors had reinforced his police and supported his punitive
strikes, Edge-Partington would have faced a seemingly insurmountable task of
pacification. Some 40,000 Malaitans, politically fragmented and fiercely independent, speaking a dozen languages and dialects, scattered through a hundred
miles of rugged montains, were more than two Europeans and a squad of ill-
trained police with only a whaleboat for transport could have taken on lightly.
The naval force on call from Fiji when the Resident Commissioner needed to
protect or avenge the lives of Europeans was useless as an aid to pacification
and ongoing administration. It was traditional blood feuding and the almost
daily assassination of Malaita Christians that had to be stopped if Malaita was
to be incorporated into Empire.

Sir Frederick May, the High Commissioner of the Western Pacific,
wrote in his report after the punitive strike on Uruilangi and Farisi suggesting that a force of Punjabi Sikhs or Pathans be brought in to "visit the
villages of the Bushmen of Malaita, accompanied by competent inter-
preters, who should explain to the Bushmen that the Government will
punish them if they do not desist from their lawless practices" (ibid., 44).
Keesing and Corris (ibid.) go on to observe: "That the Malaitans were a
free and sovereign people following their own customs in their own land
was apparently never noticed, certainly never acknowledged."

In 1915, with British government officers going off to fight in the
Great War, the Commissioner of Labour, an Australian named W. R.
Bell, was assigned to the Auki Station. It was a choice reluctantly made,
since Bell's sense of justice and the rights of the Malaitans had aroused
the ire of the planters on whom the Protectorate's revenue depended.

A droll Kwaio account, which I recorded from Bita Saetana in 1977,
connects Bell with Florence Young, the founder of the Queensland Kanaka Mission and later the SSEM.

Mr. Bell was the captain of the *Fela*, recruiting people from Malaita [for
Queensland]. Miss Young paid for his recruits. She paid and paid for them.
Then Mr. Bell asked Miss Young, "Let's be sweethearts" [in Kwaio terms, a
sexual invitation that might have presaged a marriage]. Miss Young said, "You
count up your money. When you have as much money as I do, we can be sweethearts. If you can't match my money, you can work as my cook instead of being

2. This account of the Bell massacre sets out the details of early administration on Malaita, so
here I condense the record quite radically.

my sweetheart." Mr. Bell counted up his money. "I don't have a lot of money."
Miss Young said, "If you don't have enough money, you can't be my lover." So
he stopped recruiting for her and took a job with the government here in the
Solomon Islands. So he started in Tulagi, and then the government put him in
Tatamba; and then they put him in Aola; and then they put him in Kirakira;
and then he came to 'Aoke.[3]

Bell, whose story Peter Corris and I have explored in detail (Keesing
and Corris 1980), was a man of great strength of will and character. He
knew and cared more about the Malaitans than any of his predecessors—
or his successors. To him fell the awesome task of pacifying Malaita and
creating a structure of administrative order.

Like Edge-Partington, Bell faced reluctance from his superiors in
Tulagi and had limited resources. Yet by 1920, he had built up a network
of loyal Malaita police and established an administrative framework, particularly effective in the northern third of the island. Even when he was
forced to impose policies he had initially opposed, such as the introduction of a head tax—an old British strategy for forcing "natives" into plantation labor—he did so with great energy and resourcefulness. His style
was a calculated balance of even-handed justice and friendship (inevitably paternalistic, within the structure of the colonial caste system) and
iron-fisted authority; Bell progressively developed an image and aura as a
Malaitan warrior strongman.

By the early 1920s, only the central mountainous zone of Malaita inland from the east coast remained defiantly outside the framework of administrative order and enforced peace. With a mandate to introduce the
head tax, and a formidable constabulary (mostly from the northern language groups of Malaita), he now had the means.

The Kwaio warrior strongmen clearly knew about the governmental
presence in Auki, even though it had not yet intruded directly on their
autonomy. As Lounga of Gaafolo expresses it, "Mr. Bell's words blew like
the smoke from a fire across the island. 'You have killed, but the killing is
over. Even though you have the rifles you have got from Queensland and
Fiji and Samoa, even though you have killed a thousand people with
them, it is over. Now the law has come to forbid it."[4]

In 1923, Bell moved to introduce the head tax along the east Kwaio

3. The places named were the government stations in the pre-1920 Solomons, on Santa Isabel,
Guadalcanal, Makira, and then Malaita. In fact, Bell had been a Government Agent on the Fiji-
based ship *Clansman* and then had taken a job with the BSIP government as Inspector of Labour.
4. Quoted in Keesing and Corris 1980:91.

coast, and to break the cycle of blood feuding. Grizzled old Alefo, younger brother of the feared warriors Maenaafo'oa and I'alamo (who smuggled the Snider rifles back from Fiji), recounted to me in 1970 how the
governmental presence was first felt directly.

> After a long time [since the killing of Daniels in 1911] the government sent
> its talk, for men to be imprisoned. They challenged us. . . . They wanted
> people to be Headmen. . . .
> Then the government waited a while. Then they came again and brought
> the tax. . . . It started at 'Aoke. We heard about it. "Your time for paying the
> tax is coming soon." We said, "What is that? What is it that is coming?" We
> didn't know about it. Then *gafamanu* came and asked for five shillings.

Bell's diary records (7–8 March 1924) this first tax-collection visit to
Gwee'abe, a small headland extending out into Sinalagu Harbor. "Collecting taxes. Natives coming slowly. [the next day] Sent police inland to
bring Noru [one of the feared Kwaio *lamo*, Tagailamo] and his people.
Reported that Noru said that he would not pay the tax and would kill
anyone who came for him. Collecting taxes, mostly Uru natives who said
they had been searching for the money." A Kwaio account illuminates
what happened, as seen through local eyes. Tagailamo and his fellow
Furi'ilai strongman Fuufu'e had killed their own relative (a young boy
who had defecated in a shrine) to collect a bounty that had been put up
against them (a nasty but accepted Kwaio strategy in blood feuding).

> They came after that blood money at Ga'eta, and the same day Mr. Bell ar-
> rived at Gwee'abe. Tagailamo and Fuufu'e collected the pigs and money . . .
> and went back up to Furi'ilai. They gathered the sacred oven stones for Furi'ilai
> shrine and cooked the pigs. The police started at the coast. Mr. Bell just stayed
> there. [Kwaio Village Constable] Sirifa showed them the way and the police
> came up to [the gathering at Tagailamo's settlement of] Namoteu. . . . The
> people who were cooking asked, "What's happening?" "The police are here.
> They're here to stop the killing." The group went down from the shrine. Tag-
> ailamo and Fuufu'e had their guns and were all for killing the police. Basiana
> said, "You two can't shoot them. Just let them go today."
> [When they got down to Namoteu] Makasi [Bell's clerk] spoke. And [police
> Sgt.] Ba'etalua spoke. And Sirifa spoke. "Your killing, Basiana, and your kill-
> ing Tagailamo, and your killing Maenaafo'oa—and all the killing here in
> Kwaio—is finished today. The law of England has come. Mr. Bell has come for
> the tax at Gwee'abe. He has forbidden killing. Eating pigs from blood bounties
> is finished today."

Ba'etalua and Sirifa set a time and place: "You, Basiana, eat your pigs today—and Tagailamo and Fuufu'e. And then tomorrow, you're to come down to Gwee'abe."

Alefo recounted what happened the next day at the coast.

The people from over three clans gathered. We went down at one time for the tax. We paid the tax at Gwee'abe. At that time, we were afraid of the police—and they were afraid too. From our side, one man stood over here, and another over there [in case fighting broke out]. From the hundred men who went down, fifty paid. They paid the tax. Thirty men didn't pay the tax.

The white man said: "You police, arrest all these men who didn't pay." We overheard, and told the men: "You men who didn't pay the tax are going to be arrested." Basiana heard that his people were going to be tied up. He went to Sirifa and Mani'a [the Uru Village Constable] "They haven't any money. How can he arrest them all? If you try, we'll kill all of you." Mani'a and Sirifa told Bell. The government [Bell] said: "Just wait. If the thirty men who didn't pay the tax can find the money, they can come down and pay at 'Oloburi."

Bell's journal entries for these days and the following weeks are laconic:

Police returned with Noru and about 120 natives. About 25 brought native money and said they could not find English money. They were told to have the money ready at Ulimburi in about a month's time (9 March 1924).

At Olomburi collecting taxes. Natives from Sinarango [Sinalagu] came and paid tax (13 May).

Took steps to bring certain inland natives down to pay the tax (May 14).

Bell arrested a Kwaio bushman, Geni'ilefana, for murder, and took him to Uru for trial. He had another confrontation there, regarding construction of a house for government patrols to stay in while collecting taxes. His comments show how attuned he was to local history and politics, and how he played his cards in situations of conflict.

At Uru . . . I was informed that some natives, of whom a native named KWAIGA was the principal, would not assist in the building of the house and said they wanted paying for it. KWAIGA is the native who murdered Mr Daniels in 1911 and was not arrested. I sent a message for KWAIGA and he came to see me and I told him that I knew all about him and explained to him that he should be the last person to make trouble if he expected his past deeds to be forgotten.

Alefo's and Kwai'ime's accounts of how the Kwaio strongmen responded, with which this chapter began, show how the Kwaio *lamo* were faced with the threat of becoming like women—how their power and their manhood were threatened.[5] Kwai'ime raises as well the temptation of blood money that lured the warriors toward confrontation and killing.

The autobiography of Jonathan Fifi'i, who grew up in the shadow of Headman Sirifa and went on to become a Parliamentarian (Fifi'i 1989), illuminates the grievances that had led to blood bounties being put up in the Kwaio mountains for the death of *gafamanu*—blood money and pigs that made the thought of killing Bell doubly tempting to the famed *lamo* who were being threatened with early retirement and the loss of power and cultural autonomy.

Several bounties had been put up for the death of a white man. One of them had been put up to avenge a man named Kwa'italaunga'i, who had been hanged at Tulagi. Another one had been put up to avenge the death of a man named Dangomae, who had been killed when they were loading copra at Baunani.[6] He was swept over by a wave, fell under the ship, and was crushed.[7] The third one was to avenge the death of a man from the bush who had been working for Lever's at Gavutu, and died. The Doctor there, Dr. Benson, had sawed into the head of his corpse to see what he had died from. His relatives were angry about that: the head of a dead man is really sacred.[8] So they had put up blood bounty for vengeance. Basiana brooded about the possibility that he could collect all three lots of blood money—shell money and pigs—if he killed Mr. Bell. He also brooded about that *dafi* (see below) and about that curse Mr. Bell had made, calling him a "bastard." . . . Basiana put all those things together in his mind, and he called the warrior leaders together.

He summoned the warriors from three groups: Ngudu, 'Oibasi [Furi'ilai], and his own group, 'Ai'eda [Gounaile]. There were also the people from Gwagwa'emanu, and some other groups from the bush. They talked about what was to be done about the Government. Basiana told them his plan. "That

5. In my judgment, having talked at length with Alefo and Kwai'ime and many other partici-pants in the massacre and eyewitnesses to the events leading up to it, Firth (1979) is mistaken in his account of the trial testimony, in representing Kwai'ime as having said that it was the Kwaio women who goaded the warriors into the attack. I believe that either his recollection of the testimony was faulty on this point (after the intervening half century) or that the translation into Pidgin (or Firth's understanding of it) was faulty. There is not a hint, anywhere in the Kwaio oral testimony, including that by Kwai'ime, whose trial testimony Firth purports to cite, that the women themselves instigated the massacre or goaded their menfolk to resist colonial subjugation: they certainly had nothing to gain, and much to lose, by an armed confrontation.

6. Baunani Plantation, on the western Kwaio coast, established by investors connected to the SSEM and later to become a focus of land claims.

7. According to Kwaio cultural logic, the employer would be responsible for such a death.

8. After a body has been interred, the skull is later dug up and kept in an ancestral shrine.

white man has come among us, and he treats us like rubbish. When we go and speak in court, he insults us, speaks strongly to us, curses us. Let's kill him! Let's kill him and collect those blood bounties!" So they began to plot to kill Mr. Bell (Fifi'i 1989:8–9).

Bell, despite his sympathies for the Malaitans and deep knowledge of their customs, had moved perceptibly from a stylized role as strongman, Malaita-style, to increasing violence and aggressiveness.[9] And Bell, although in some ways he swam against the tides of European fashion, was still a product of time and place, still enmeshed in European racism and styles of caste superiority. Fifi'i, who saw Bell in his early boyhood, reflects (1989:5–6) that

you have to remember that things were very different between white people and black people—they used to call us "natives"—in those days. Mr. Bell was a European, and in those days they acted as if they were kings and we were just beasts of burden. Whenever Mr. Bell came ashore, he made two men— perhaps the Headmen or some of his crew—carry him so he wouldn't get his boots or his trousers wet. Then when they had lifted him to a dry spot, he would walk. When he came into the clearing where people were waiting, everyone from our side had to stand upright at attention. They couldn't move about—they had to stand perfectly still. They had to take the pipes from their mouths.

Then he'd walk to the place where he was to collect the tax. He would then tell the Headmen to bring their people to pay the tax. He had his own little place to collect the tax, and a big tax house for the police to stay in. If there were any court cases to be heard, Mr. Bell would have the Headmen bring all the parties to wait for him, so all the cases could be heard then and there. He and the two Headmen would hold a court session. Two policemen with bayonets on their rifles would come and stand beside Mr. Bell. The parties to the case would be brought there, to stand in front of him. Then whoever was making the court complaint to Mr. Bell would state his case. He'd have to do that very loudly and clearly. If he didn't set out his case strongly, Mr. Bell would shout at him: "You bloody bastard! You must talk!" That's the way he talked. He was always that way. He wanted someone in court to speak loudly and strongly: if he didn't, Mr. Bell would swear and pound the table. People were bound to be frightened, with a policeman with a fixed bayonet on each side, and with Mr. Bell speaking so roughly.

9. Corris and I speculate that the physical and psychological toll of years in the tropics, lonely isolation, and ill health had led to irascibility and unsteady judgment.

The Kwaio people began to complain: "This man is cursing us, speaking badly to us, calling us 'bastard'! We come to talk about things that have happened to us, things that have gone wrong, and he curses us, he defiles us with his talk.[10] It's not right." That's the way it was every time he came to court. He quarrelled with people, swore at people, all the time. It wasn't that he was worse than other white men. The whites on the plantations treated us much worse than that. But here was someone in our own place, insulting and cursing us in front of our own ancestors.

The events, plots, and plans that led the Kwaio strongmen to assassinate Bell in 1927, and massacre his police patrol, are set out in detail in *Lightning Meets the West Wind*. There was the anger regarding the tax, which the Kwaio saw as tribute. There was anger about alien law—about the hangings for killings that in Kwaio eyes were quite legitimate. There was anger about specific insults and provocation—the humiliation and physical beating of the two aging retired warriors 'Aufana and Maari'ia in 1926 (Keesing and Corris 1980:110–13), Bell's cursing of Basiana as a "bastard" in 1926. There was anger over the taunts and curses by coastal Kwaio—longtime enemies of the bush kin groups—the polluting curse about "*bisi* people," and the taunts about the Kwaio warriors being like women. And there was anger about Bell's efforts to confiscate the aging Snider rifles that were instruments and symbols of warrior power (Keesing and Corris 1980:115–17).

Hostility over the tax justifies special mention because this has was to be a continuing theme in Kwaio resistance over the following sixty years. Adventist Pastor J. D. Anderson, newly established in 1924 in a post near where Daniels had been killed eleven years earlier, recalled in his memoirs (Anderson n.d.) the talk in the area following Bell's initial tax collection. "Many of the old men, on finding they could not buy anything with their [tax] receipt, were disgusted and said: 'What is this government? It's just stealing our money. We're not going to give any more money just for nothing!'" The Kwaio warriors had in fact confronted Resident Commissioner R. R. Kane, who had undertaken the 1925 tax collection while Bell was on leave, over this issue. Kane made vague and pious pronouncements about the benefits—in the form of law and order and health care—they would get from their tax. That only made things worse. Bell wrote in his 1925 annual report that "the imposition of the Native Tax in this District appears to have caused a very pronounced de-

10. To swear at someone—*taafia*—is an extremely serious offense according to Kwaio custom. In the old days before pacification it often led to killing, and nowadays it often still leads to violence.

crease in the faith of the natives in the goodwill of the Government toward them and consequently the confidence of the natives in the
goodwill of the District Officer does not appear to be quite the same as in
former times."

It is worth considering the confrontation over taxation from both cultural and political perspectives. The Kwaio would have initially interpreted the payment as a prestation, which would give them some hold
over Bell as its recipient. The Kwaio would appropriately have expected
either a material return (on the model of their experience with the cash
economy of the plantations) or a counter-prestation; and until reciprocation came, the recipient would be obligated to them. They saw nothing
in return—no obligation, no reciprocation, only an obligation to pay
again the next year. They appropriately and astutely read this one-way
payment in a political light. They saw clearly that, in conjunction with
the demand for a cessation of blood feuding and the imposition of colonial law, the tax amounted to a form of tribute, an expression of surrender and subjugation. Fifty years later, the Kwaio traditionalists were
to confront the government, on the eve of independence, with a refusal
to pay the tax still being demanded of them.

The 1926 confrontation between Basiana and Bell is particularly illuminating both politically (because Basiana, who had motives and plots
of his own [Keesing and Corris 1980:121–24], launched the attack on
Bell when his compatriots were seemingly wavering) and because it vividly reveals a symbolic theme to which we will return. The account of
what happened when Basiana stepped up to pay his tax in 1926 comes
from Jonathan Fifi'i, an eyewitness to the confrontation as a young boy
(Keesing and Corris 1980:114–15):

> Basiana brought four shillings [not the required five] and gave them to Mr.
> Bell. "Mr. Bell, I'm a bush man. European money is hard for me. I haven't
> gone to work overseas. I haven't earned any European money."
>
> "That's not true! You go back to your place and bring me some pigs—bring
> me something for my police, and they'll pay the fifth shilling for you. Go back
> to your place and get something tonight. You can't sleep here!"
>
> Basiana went back up to his place [about four hours' walk]. He got his *dafi* [a
> crescent-shaped goldlip pearl shell chest pendant] consecrated to his ancestor.
> He smashed it into pieces. He took one of the pieces and ground it down. He
> worked and worked, using the four shillings he had as a guide. He worked until
> after midnight, pressing it against a shilling to check. Finally it was just the
> right size. Basiana said to his warriors, "If he'll accept this, then we're all even.
> If he doesn't, what the hell? Here are my five shillings!"

At daybreak, he went down to Mr. Bell: "Mr. Bell—I made the fifth shill-ing out of a *dafi* consecrated to my ancestor. The four shillings have pictures of your King on them. ["Mine has my ancestor on it"; Fifi'i 1989:7.] So here are your five shillings—take them!"

"Bastard," Mr. Bell boomed in Pidgin. "I'll take it now, but don't do it next time! Don't do it! You hear?"

. . . Basiana was mad—you could see the fire in his eyes. You could see the fury in his eyes.

When Bell came to collect the taxes the following year, Basiana smashed his skull with the barrel of the rifle I'alamo had brought back from Fiji.

7 Gwee'abe and After

October 4, 1927. Although Bell and his police had been amply warned of the impending attack—the sacrifice of pigs, the war councils had made secrecy impossible—Bell was confident that he could force the Kwaio strongmen to back down. He had survived so many threats and confron-tations by sheer strength of will and bold bluff that on this occasion he virtually immobilized his constabulary, with their superior striking power conferred by Winchester repeating rifles, by sending them into the tax house with two or three hundred warriors in the clearing.

The attack at Gwee'abe, a tongue of land protruding into Sinalagu Harbor where the tax house had been built, was launched by Basiana, who slipped into the line of men paying their taxes, stepped up, and killed Bell with one blow. Bell's Clerk Makasi shot Maenaafo'oa, the warrior leader of Ngudu, and Bell's Cadet, K. C. Lillies, fired abortively before he was killed. The police and servants in the tax house had no chance to defend themselves, and only one survived, by feigning death. Within three or four minutes, the two white men and thirteen Solomon Islanders lay dead.

To the government—and to the planters and missionaries, on this one occasion when all the Europeans in the Solomons joined ranks—this was a stunning outrage. All of them had Malaitan employees and ser-vants, and they feared a general uprising. European planters, mainly Australians, volunteered for a punitive expedition—what became known as the "Breathless Army." The Australian Government was asked for support, and the cruiser HMAS *Adelaide* was sent from Sydney.

The punitive expedition that followed was at first comical, as the planters and marines struggled up the precipitous 2200-foot mountain that rises above Sinalagu Harbor, cursing and sweating their way into the interior, burning and pillaging the deserted settlements.

The Kwaio had fled, in one direction or the other. Those who had paid their tax, from the Christian villages in the harbor, and from Uru, and from the kin groups of the coastal slopes and the immediate interior area, clung to their receipts and took refuge in the Christian communities along the coast, under protection of the Village Constables. Those from the kin groups of the interior who had not paid their tax, those who had plotted and staged the attacks and those associated with them, had to flee for their lives into the interior bush.

In the weeks that followed, the European forces were debilitated from disease, deterred by the difficult terrain, and (in the case of the planters, liberally supplied with whisky and gin) immobilized by drink. Apart from despoiling and destroying the deserted settlements, poisoning taro gardens with creosote, and occasionally shooting at one another by mistake, they got nowhere near the fugitives, who knew the terrain and how to survive on wild foods.

The danger to the fugitives lay in the north Malaita police (their ranks expanded by ex-police and other volunteers). Some had felt personal loyalty to Bell, but for most, the main motivation was to avenge their own fallen comrades (in a good many cases, their relatives, since Bell had tended to recruit within families and communities where he had close ties). The opportunity to gain vengeance tenfold and at the same time to break forever the ancestrally conferred power of the Kwaio, under the auspices of the colonial government, was too good to miss.

With little effective supervision from the British officers, and mainly after the ineffectual and disease-smitten planters and sailors had been withdrawn, the Malaitan patrols scoured the bush for the fugitives. With guides from the Christian villages and with culturally sharpened skills of tracking and evasion, the police began a bloody game.

Lightning Meets the West Wind (Keesing and Corris, 1980) documents in detail the havoc wrought by the punitive expedition. Since this has become so much a matter of political contention by the Kwaio in the 1980s, and since the account of the punitive expedition given in the book has itself become politically controversial, some fragments of the evidence as given in Kwaio accounts and accounts by surviving members of the police contingent (including some not quoted in the book) will be illuminating.

First, the voices of the police themselves, recorded directly and expressed to other anthropological researchers, will confirm that in the Solomons, and for the generation involved, these were deeds proudly recounted, not hidden or denied. Anthropologist Ian Frazer (personal communication) interviewed Timi Kakalu'ae of Lau, who as Sergeant headed one of the police detachments, in 1975:

The old man . . . recalled with fervour his experience in the Kwaio hills, where, he claimed, his party (of twelve) accounted for a total of thirty-six lives. He justified this by saying that Basiana and his party attacked Bell with the intention of wiping out the whole party and he intended retaliating in kind without any interest in taking people into custody. He mention two "court" cases over his behaviour . . . as a result of which he was confined to base for a week. They didn't deter him, as once he was released on patrol again he continued to shoot on sight. He said that their orders were to detain people and bring them to the base but he was inclined to ignore them.

Anthropologist Harold Ross (1973:190–91) was given further testimony of the killing: "The Northern Malaitan . . . ramo . . . were probably the most relentless hatchet men in what turned out to be an extremely vicious retaliation against the Kwaio. I met two old former ramo who had accompanied the expedition and who still recited, with obvious relish, tales of the Kwaio men, women and children they had murdered." Usuli Tefu'i, a north Malaita policeman who escaped from the massacre and later took part in the punitive expedition, told me in 1983: "If [Kwaio prisoners] were taken to the coast they were tied up. But anyone we found in the bush we killed—all of them. If you went in the bush you couldn't stand the smell, there were bodies everywhere along the sides of the path."

The diary entries by ornithologist Walter Eyerdam of the Whitney South Sea Expedition, who spent several weeks in the Kwaio interior in 1930, recount how the Headman from Su'u (Malarifu, known as "Whiskey") characterized the punitive expedition and his part in it:

Whiskey told us that about a thousand people were killed by the Sinarango punitive expedition, but of course that is an exaggeration; probably less than 100 were killed. Whiskey claims that he killed about 50 people himself. . . . He said he shot every man, woman and child that he could find and that corpses were lying about all over the district (Eyerdam n.d., entry for February 15).

Eyerdam, who investigated the punitive expedition quite carefully, describes it as "wholesale slaughter," and elsewhere, as "the terrible massacre by the punitive expedition" (Jan. 31), noting how "many innocent people were killed by over zealous police boys and vengeful Salt water men" (Mar. 9).

According to Kwaio testimony, it was the north Malaita patrols led by Kakalu'ae, Ba'etalua (of Bita'ama, To'abaita), and Maekali (of Malu'u, To'abaita) that were responsible for most of the killings. They simply shot prisoners, ones who had been captured and ones who had surrendered, in cold blood at the side of the paths. This is amply confirmed by the accounts of the police themselves. Sale Vuza (later to become decorated and knighted as a World War II hero, in the guise of "Sir Jacob Vouza") commanded a detachment of twenty-five non-Malaitans, police from Choiseul, Guadalcanal, the Shortlands, Simbo, and Santa Ana. He told me in 1970:

People surrendered to me—I arrested fifty or sixty at one time. Maekali and Ba'etalua would shoot one for every two or three they brought in—but not me. . . . Ba'etalua and Maekali didn't kill many people in actual fighting. But if they found two or three people, they'd shoot one. If they shot someone, they'd cut off the legs and hands, and put them on top of the body, and call out [taunting] to [the victim's] ancestors.

The Kwaio accounts accord directly with Vuza's testimony. 'Auekwa'a of Furi'ilai recounted how he was arrested with five men from 'Ubuni, none of whom had taken part in the Gwee'abe massacre.

They lined us up. They put a gun against me here, and another. There were two guns pointed at each of us. One of the 'Ubuni men said, "Hey, they're going to shoot us." I said, "We're like pigs being taken to sacrifice—there's nothing we can do." Then twelve shots rang out—but the two men pointing their guns at me just stood there. They pulled me away. [Constable] Fangamae gave me a heavy knapsack, with twenty uniforms inside, to carry. The five men they had shot—they cut up their bodies, cut them here and here and here, hacked off arms and legs—it was as though they were fish.

Arugeni, who took sanctuary with Headman Sale Babaamae at 'Aulola in the remote interior, recalled that even those who surrendered there were not safe.

Some of the people who were arrested were taken down alive as prisoners. . . . They arrested them at 'Aulola and took them to Tulagi. Then Ba'etalua's section shot my uncle Foribata at Kwaimauto. The next day Ba'etalua arrested four men, Ganigeni, Ke'ofa'i, U'udiamae, and 'Ui'o'omauri, at 'Aulola and said he was taking them down to the coast. But instead of taking them down to Gwee'abe they took them down the ridge toward 'Oloburi. And they shot them one by one, at Foumagari.

Basiana's young sons Anifelo and Laefiwane were at the mission village of Sinasuu in the harbour. Laefiwane recounts how "Maeluma's section arrested us and took us up toward the bush. My 'older brother' Ru'ufiamae was with us, and they arrested him too. They shot Ru'ufiamae there on the path. The police pointed their guns at my brother Anifelo and me, ready to shoot us, there at Nunu. 'Uifaria, a policeman from 'Are'are, stopped them." Keesing and Corris (1980:174) record that "Talaunga'i of Fou'alabusi, the only member of his kin group to have taken part in the massacre, was asleep with his family when their lean-to was surrounded before dawn by Vuza's police patrol. When the first of the occupants came out at dawn, the patrol opened fire, shooting down Fiulamo, Ari'oofi, 'Ufarigo'u and two women, 'Asuamae and 'Asuari'i."

Many of those killed, even apart from the women and children, had had no part in the massacre. Some were men who were scheduled to pay their taxes at 'Oloburi, not Sinalagu, and who for that reason did not have the receipts that allowed sanctuary at the coast or 'Aulola. Others were killed indiscriminately, or to settle old scores and grievances on the part of Headmen or those from the coast who acted as guides (Keesing and Corris 1980:176). 'Elota of Ga'enaafou (Keesing 1978b:77) recalled that

> The people from 'Auagama had no part in the [Bell] killing. . . . Those people didn't kill anyone. They [the police] arrested Teeruma; and he died at Tulagi. They shot Suaboo Ri'oilangi. They didn't find his body—he ran off and died in the forest. Kwalata was in his men's house when the patrol arrived. The police shot him, then cut off his head with a bayonet. They stuck a red cordyline [a sacred plant to the Malaitans] down into his severed neck, and left the body in the men's house.

'Elota recalled how he saw Alefo, who was to spend fourteen years in prison in Tulagi and to be a leader in anticolonial struggle after the war, in police custody after he had surrendered to the Headman at Uru. "They took them down to Gwee'abe. When we got there a policeman named Usuli [Tefu'i] threatened to shoot Alefo: 'He shot my older brother' [Constable Magi]. The other police dissuaded him. 'If you'd gone up there [to the bush] and shot him that would have been your business. But now he's in custody [at the coast] you can't just shoot him'" (Keesing 1978b:76).

In the end, most of the fugitives centrally involved in the massacre surrendered to the Headmen themselves, as Alefo did, to end the carnage, the killing of innocent men, women, and children, the raping of women, the desecration of everything sacred. Alefo recalled that "[Basiana] just went down and surrendered. We just came down, I'alamo and I, to the government. Fuufu'e surrendered himself. [Lists a dozen names] all gave themselves up. . . . Only the nobodies got caught."

The raping of women, the destruction of houses, the theft of valuables, the killing of pigs, and the massive desecration of shrines and things sacred, along with the killings, have all become focal issues of modern Kwaio struggle. We need to look briefly at these facets of the punitive expedition. Keesing and Corris (1980:167–68) recount how

Maenaafo'oa's wife, Fuufu'e's sister and a number of other female relatives of the ringleaders were gang-raped by the police. At least thirteen women and girls were shot, one or two by accident, but most in cold blood. Among the latter were the two daughters of Basiana's father's brother, and Maenaafo'oa's daughter. Basiana's niece was gang-raped by the police and later taken to Tulagi. When she returned, finding herself pregnant, she hanged herself in shame and grief.

Being pagan themselves or recently Christianized, the north Malaitan policemen knew exactly how to overturn the Kwaio cosmos. They systematically desecrated shrines and destroyed sacred objects; threw ancestral skulls into the menstrual huts and threw menstrual mats into the shrines.

In 1977, Bita Saetana ["Peter Satan," a pagan priest] gave his retrospective interpretation of the havoc wrought by the punitive expedition:

The police, the native police, came into the mountains and destroyed our homeland. They killed 400 men, women and children. They killed people who weren't mixed up in the fight. They just shot them. The government force that came didn't follow the laws of England. They killed everyone, in secret: men, women, children. They got hold of young children and smashed their skulls on stones. They shot the older children. They destroyed our shrines—dug them up, overturned everything, smashed the ancestral skulls. They burned the houses. They took the things from the menstrual huts and burned them in the dwelling area. A thousand people and more have died from that. That's what they did in the bush, in our homeland.

These acts of desecration, intended to leave the Kwaio bereft of ancestral support and protection for years, even generations, to come, have
become a central issue in modern Kwaio resistance, as we will see. Ruata
(the brother of Talaunga'i), who saw his family wiped out in a dawn attack, observed fifty years later that

since the fight everything has been bad. [The police] seized two bags of shell
money, with thirty valuables. They just took them. If it hadn't been for that,
I'd be a rich man today. But what can we do now? From that time onward,
even though we stay at our old place, all our living goes badly. What could go
well? Twenty of our consecrated pigs were just eaten [by the police]. Our sacred
things and shrines were desecrated. . . . The shrine there at Fou'alabusi is still
defiled, even after forty years. We try to sacrifice there for the taro, but it does
no good, . . . even though we have sacrificed thirty pigs to purify the desecration.

About two hundred Kwaio men, including not only warriors but aged
priests, were arrested and taken to Tulagi, then confined in prison
(classed as "detainees") while legal proceedings were pursued. A dysentery epidemic swept the prison, and thirty-one Kwaio prisoners died in
custody. (The colonial government vigorously denied reports of a "Black
Hole of Tulagi" in the Australian press, and claimed that most who died
were feeble old men; but they never explained why they had arrested
feeble old men, whose "crimes" at most lay in asking the ancestors to support their warrior sons.) Finally six Kwaio warriors were condemned and
hanged, including Basiana, and fourteen were sentenced to long prison
terms.

It is worth pausing to reflect on the interpretation of the assassination
of Bell and the massacre of his party. In their investigations of the circumstances leading to the attack, particularly the report by Lt. Col. Sir
H. E. Moorhouse, an Africa hand sent by the Colonial Office, the British
sought particular grievances and provocations and misunderstandings.
Was it the tax, or the rifles? Not doubting their right to be there as colonizers, or their mission to bring law and order and civilization as well as
plantation economy, the British could not perceive that beneath the particular grievances and provocations, the issues were power and sovereignty. The attack on Bell and his party was above all a political act, a
last, desperate assertion of sovereignty and the right to follow ancestral
customs free from alien rule. In fact, the perception of the Kwaio warrior
leaders that paying the tax amounted to political tribute and a surrender
of sovereignty was precisely apt. It was the British, entangled by the veils

of imperial mythology, who could not see. The phrase written sixteen years earlier by the High Commissioner of the Western Pacific about intimidating the Malaita warriors into forsaking their "lawless ways" comes to mind.

There can be few more dramatic and direct ways to express resistance than to assassinate the agent of political domination while he is in the process of exacting tribute and to massacre his armed force. But, even here, the concept of "resistance" is somewhat clumsy in its romanticization of action directed to a collective cause. Basiana and the other warrior leaders had motives and agendas of their own, were manipulating, withholding information, and scheming. They were bent on self-aggrandizement and personal vengeance as well as liberation[1]

Keesing and Corris (1980:187–88) describe Basiana's death on the scaffold (as his two young sons, one a young teen-ager and the other only seven, were forced to watch):

Basiana's pride and contempt stayed with him to the end. Before he climbed the scaffold, he put an ancestral curse on Tulagi and flung a last challenge to the Resident Commissioner and Commandant of Police: "Even though I'm going to die, even though I'm going to be hanged, this place, Tulagi, where you have your flag, will be torn apart and scattered." This was taken as something of a joke among the Englishmen in their club on the hill. Perhaps no one paused to remember when they fled in disarray before the Japanese invasion fourteen years later.

A plan was formulated to resettle the surviving "detainees" in what amounted to a concentration camp in southeastern Santa Isabel. But in the end, reason prevailed and the "detainees" were repatriated. The world they came back to was in ruins. With the shrines massively desecrated and relations with the ancestors disastrously disrupted, and with so many of the survivors themselves polluted by contact with menstruating women in the Christian villages, many Kwaio pagans opted to stay on the coast.

Those who went back into the mountains faced not only the wrath of the ancestors, but starvation as well. The taro gardens (and hence planting materials as well as food staples) had been destroyed with creosote by the punitive expedition. The government, ironically, had been forced to provide emergency rations of rice to ward off famine. The descent groups

1. Indeed, there is some evidence in the oral testimony that Basiana knew that he would bring ruin on his people and deliberately plotted that course. See Keesing and Corris 1980:122–23.

on the coastal slopes and immediately inland from the mountain rim survived relatively unscathed demographically but were heavily eroded by
shifts to the Christian villages where they had taken refuge from the
punitive expedition. The descent groups of the interior who had (or were
imagined to have) taken part in the massacre were decimated: a whole
generation of warriors, and the elders who controlled ritual knowledge,
had been virtually wiped out. Bitterness and resentment over the slaughter and the desecration hung, with the mist, over the Kwaio mountains.

8 *La'aka* and the Ruin of Tulagi

For a number of years after the massacre and punitive expedition, rumors
spread through the European community in the Solomons that the
Kwaio were sacrificing pigs to enlist ancestral support for another attack.
District Officers were required to file quarterly reports on the state of
Kwaio "unrest."

In fact, resentment mainly smouldered beneath the surface. Some of it
was directed at the groups whose leaders had planned and led the attack
on Bell and his police, since several groups only peripherally involved
had suffered heavy losses in the punitive expedition. Yet Basiana enjoyed
a heroic status as well, as attested by an American expedition that pene-
trated the Kwaio interior in 1930 to collect bird specimens for the
Whitney South Sea Expedition. Walter Eyerdam (1933:438) tells how
he heard Basiana's deeds celebrated: "Bassiano, the great killer now in
the spirit world, had become a mighty hero. His deeds of daring were ex-
tolled in song, and great were the praises sung to the soul of Bassiano as
warriors and young boys sat around the fire recounting his bloody deeds."

Jonathan Fifi'i's autobiography recounts an event that must have
taken place in about 1933 but foreshadows a movement that surfaced several years later. This movement reflects a religious turn to Kwaio anticolonial struggle, in the face of massive power and repression emanating
from Tulagi.

> When I was a boy . . . there was a man named Lauanaafe, from Kafusiisigi.
> He was Lego's father, a priest for La'aka. He was my 'grandfather'. The inci-
> dent I remembered happened when we went to the closing feast in a chain of
> feasts. It was when I was still a pagan, so it must have been in 1933 or 1934.

They set out the food—pigs and taro puddings—and divided them up. Lauanaafe was quite old, but at that feast he started running around like a man possessed, sprinting really quickly for an old man. He dashed back and forth, then dug his heel in and shouted out to us: "You, a hundred warriors and a hundred women, even though we're gathered here at this closing feast at Sin- ato'oana, and even though we know that Tulagi stands, rising to the sky as a a yellow-bibbed lory flies upward, it will all come crashing down and will be fin- ished. Something is coming to destroy it!" He grabbed his spear and ran back and forth.

Everyone laughed. "That's the stronghold of the government. You're just raving on. Nothing's going to happen to Tulagi." People thought he was crazy. He wouldn't stand still: he was possessed. But he had seen something coming that no one else, white or black, had even imagined (Fifi'i 1989:74–75).

La'aka is a powerful ancestress, the *adalo* most widely propitiated by Kwaio pagans of the interior. Celebrated both for her womanly virtues and her warrior exploits in life, La'aka is both a protective maternal force and a source of powers of destruction. She was to become a decisive sym- bolic force in Kwaio resistance against colonial domination.

In the latter 1930s—the exact date is a matter of some debate[1]—a politico-religious movement surfaced in the mountains high above the headwaters of the Kwaiba'ita River, in the Kwaio interior. At its center was ancestress La'aka. Her earthly agents were a priest who sacrificed to her, Noto'i, and his close supporters Bole and Nagwaafi.

Suufiomea of Age'eriufa recounted to me in 1978 how Noto'i had first received his message from La'aka:

Noto'i went to Solomone [Guadalcanal]. He was a young man then. When he was on Guadalcanal, he met two Merika [Americans]. They were shooting pigeons. They had come on a sailing ship. They met Noto'i there. They asked him, "Where are you from?" "I'm a man from Malaita." The two Americans spoke. Noto'i didn't understand. Noto'i spoke. The Americans didn't under- stand. . . . So Noto'i went and prayed to his ancestress [La'aka] and she straightened it out. Noto'i went back and talked to the two Americans. What the Americans said, Noto'i understood. What Noto'i said, the two Americans understood.

The Americans asked, "Where is your place?" "My place is at 'Atobala, at 'Ole'olea." "Go back there and build a house. Its name is to be *bungu 'ifi* [lit. "conch shell village," the term used in Maasina Rule for large meeting vil-

---

1. Cf. Bennett 1987:279. See also Keesing 1980, 1981.

lages]. Noto'i came back from Guadalcanal and went back to his place. He built a *bungu 'ifi* at 'Atobala. They trained *solodia* [the term used by Kwaio for police]. . . . They built a *gete* [Pijin "gate," a palisade]. The ancestress Noto'i had prayed to when he was on Guadalcanal instructed them in what to do. They raised a pig, Siunaafuge [the name given to purificatory pigs consecrated to ancestress La'aka] on behalf of their work.

Suufiomea went on to recount how a second ritual center for La'aka was built at Kwa'ilalamua, at Age'eriufa (another descent group territory high in the Kwaio mountains inland from Uru).

So they raised a pig at Age'eriufa, and built a men's house for [La'aka]. . . . They built a *bungu 'ifi*, built a *gete*, and a *lanenga* ["learning," an alternative Pijin term for "school," with its implications of religious learning]. And the ancestress La'aka came and instructed them. The ancestress spoke thusly: "I met Noto'i and Bole, and the two of them spoke with the Americans. I told them what to do, how to do what the Americans had told them: build a house, build a meeting village, build a palisade around it [*gete*]. A place where people can receive the message. You are to follow the customs the Americans told about, the customs I have given you. Build a palisade, build a flagpole ["thing for a *fulake*"].
RMK: What kind of flag?
Siifulake and Riifulake.[2] . . . The two flags came from different places: Niusisemba and Niusisileni. Siifulake for 'Ole'olea, and Riifulake for Age'eriufa. We built those *bungu 'ifi*, then the government arrested us. . . . Lots of people came to build the *bungu 'ifi*—400 or 500 of them—when Noto'i and Boli gave them the message at 'Ole'olea. And then again at Age'eriufa. But then the government sent their army. Diake Maenagwa came and arrested us. . . .
If it hadn't been for their arrest, their work would have gone on until the Japanese came to Guadalcanal and the fight started. When I [Suufiomea] went to Guadalcanal in the war [as a volunteer in the Solomon Islands Labour Corps] I *saw* the two flags, the Siifulake and the Riifulake. And the Americans *did* come. We were speaking the truth. So why did the government arrest us?
RMK: Did the ancestral spirit say the Americans would come?
She talked about that. She said, "If you hadn't arrested them, the Americans would have come then." But after they had been arrested, Noto'i was afraid to speak to her. . . .
RMK: I want to hear more about those flags.
I lopped the limbs off a pole for that flag. But the leaders were arrested and

2. *Siifulake* is "sea flag"; the other seems to be a parallel label meaningless in English.

taken away. The rest of us were afraid to do anything more. We didn't actually see any flags. They talked about them, then they were arrested. It was as though they had the shades [nununa] of the flags. They said that if we worked well, the [physical manifestations of the] flags would come. That's what the Simbaariti ["spirit"] said. . . .

Lots of people went hungry, because of the work we were doing. People gathered there and didn't work in the gardens. Those people who believed in what we were doing worked at the bungu 'ifi, following the instructions of the men who were telling us what to do. . . .

The spirit 'rose up' [i.e., spoke through a living person] and said, "Even though you are arresting me, you will see for yourselves. You men and women will see for yourselves, see Tulagi being destroyed. Then you'll know that what I say is true." And she was right. I saw it come true myself, when I went to work in the Labour Corps. I saw Tulagi destroyed.[3]

The colonial records help to provide a chronological framework. District Officer Bengough's Malaita Quarterly Report of September 1939 observes that "during August a most extraordinary story begain to circulate freely in Koio [Kwaio]. It was said that one of the more important ancestral spirits, speaking through the mouth of a man otherwise of no account, had announced that American warships and troops would shortly arrive, and would bring about the destruction of the present administration of the Protectorate." It is worth reflecting that this was a year and a half before the bombing of Pearl Harbor, and more than two years before World War II reached the Solomons. Bengough continued:

Further, all natives who did not live within the boundary named by this spirit, and pay tribute to him, would be killed by the invading troops. . . .

This ancestral spirit . . . was . . . unwise enough to announce the day on which warships and troops would arrive at Uru. Their non-arrival and the arrest of the originators of the affair did much to restore a healthy attitude of unbelief, particularly among the older men.

Bengough estimated that at its height the movement had attracted 2,000 people—that was roughly one in three Kwaio speakers, and most of the population in eastern Kwaio (Keesing 1978a:260).

Whereas the government imagined that Noto'i's movement disintegrated with the arrest of the leaders and the supposedly failed prophecy, the cult activities were resumed when the leaders were released. Jonathan Fifi'i visited Noto'i's stronghold in about 1946 with a Maasina

3. See Keesing 1980, 1981.

Rule delegation, and we have his eyewitness testimony of how the priest conveyed La'aka's message. His accounts (1989:73–74) tells us more about what La'aka's message was and how it was communicated.

Noto'i, Bole, and Nagwaafi were still working on their cult movement, with its centre at Uogwari, high in the mountains between Uru and the west coast. They had ordered their followers to stay in the mountains; the ancestress La'aka had told them that her people were not to come down to the coasts, with the rest of us. So I wanted to find out what was going on. "Men, when we go on that patrol, I want us to go by way of Uogwari, and spend the night there. Let's find out what they're doing." . . . In late afternoon, we got to Uogwari. We stayed there with Noto'i, Bole, and Nagwaafi. They were all really friendly with us. They gave us betelnut, and we chewed it with them. They gave us food, and we ate it with them. They had heard we were coming, and they had baked special food in a leaf oven. . . .

After we finished eating, I said, "Noto'i, I want you to speak the way you do, to me. I want that *adalo* who talks to you to do it while we're here, so we can see how it happens. I want you to have the *adalo* speak to me through you." "All right," said Noto'i, "at dawn tomorrow I'll have her speak to you."

The next morning, we all gathered there. Noto'i started. First, he called on that pig Siunaafuge. . . . He said to us, "This is what the Government arrested us for. That's why we served six months in prison. If you want to hear it, just listen." Then he started to speak. But he just babbled—what whites call "speaking in tongues." We couldn't understand what he was saying. "Blah, blah, blah, blah" [here Fifi'i gives a rapid-fire imitation of glossolalic speech]. . . . I asked him, "Friend, what are you saying? What does it mean? It just sounds like babbling to me."

"She is talking about Tulagi," he said. "She told us years ago that Tulagi would fall, and she's saying that now it has fallen. She's saying that she spoke through me telling all about what was going to happen, long before it happened."

"It's true," he went on. "She spoke through me long before the war came, telling us that Tulagi would be destroyed. And it all came true." "How is it true?" I asked. "What she said, through my voice, like this, was this: 'Even though Tulagi stands, rising to the sky as the yellow-bibbed lory flies upward, it will be finished forever, it will be no more, and the British will fall.' And that's what happened. It all came true. Tulagi was flattened to the ground, and the British all ran away."

"Is that really what she said?" "Yes, that's what she said," he told me.

So La'aka had taken the wireless at Tulagi, and the station there at Tulagi, under her power. She was speaking through Noto'i. "I am the ancient one. I am La'aka. Everything will be overturned. The Americans will come."

We have further testimony from Tagi'au of Furisi'ina, as recounted by his son Maena'adi. Tagi'au recalled visiting Uogwari at the height of the cult movement. Years later, he recalled to his son that La'aka, speaking through Noto'i's glossolalia, had told him, "I stayed with all my children at Tulagi when they were hanged. I was there, on the fence, at Tulagi when they called on me when they went to be hanged. I cried and cried. But it happened." The bitterness that pervaded the Kwaio mountains and infused this movement was expressed clearly in Noto'i's challenge to his captors when he was marched off in 1939: "Even though you put us in prison, the things we said will come true. Tulagi will be destroyed, you'll all run away. And the Americans will come."[4]

Recall that this theme of impending vengeance had been expressed by Basiana as he climbed the scaffold in 1928: "Even though I am going to die, even though I am about to be hanged, Tulagi will be pulled down and destroyed."[5]

Smouldering with bitterness at a government that had enforced their subjugation and pushed their resistance into chiliasm, the Kwaio in the bush struggled to repair the shattered relations with their ancestors. But with every death, every misfortune, came the message that the damage was beyond repair, the catastrophic breach of ancestral rules massive beyond possible expiation or purification. Fifty years later, Maena'adi of Furisi'ina sat with me high in the mountains and spoke in despair of the consequences for Kwaio life, the impossibility of purifying such a total violation of everything sacred: "For a hundred years, or two hundred, the dying will go on. That's what I learned from the elders . . . when I was a little boy. And it's true. I know. I've seen the dying. . . ."

Perhaps the only path to survival and sactuary led down the hill to the Christian villages; or even in bringing the power of the Christian God into the ruined mountains. In 1941, a year before World War II descended on the Solomons, the SSEM circular *Not in Vain* saw a change in the fortunes of evangelism in Kwaio country:

In Koio [Kwaio] two new places in the mountains behind Sinorango [Sinalagu] are making a vigourous beginning for the Gospel. I took 50 Christian

4. From an eyewitness account by Ma'aanamae of 'Ai'eda. See Keesing 1978b:261.
5. From eyewitness accounts by Basiana's sons Anifelo and Laefiwane, who were forced to watch their father's execution.

men with me to build the needed houses. . . . PRAISE GOD! There is a healthy stirring among the Koio heathen I have just heard that they have asked for another Christian centre among them. . . .

A great door is opening in Koio but there are many adversities. . . . Three new places are starting in the bush behind Sinorango; one is about two and a half hours; walk inland! . . .

Four heathen villages inland are willing to be taught the way of life. . . .

It is a great joy to see many new faces in mission villages. A big witch doctor has come from the Koio mountains at Gwounsasula. His child was sick unto death. He sacrificed many pigs in vain. Then the mother took the child to Christians, who prayed, and the child was healed. (1942)

For the Christian missionaries and their flocks in the coastal villages, the celebrations were to prove premature.

9 The World of Colonial Caste and Plantations

Through the 1920s and 1930s, young Kwaio men continued to leave their mountains to work on plantations. The need for steel tools and other trade goods, and the head tax, forced their continuing participation in what had become an internal plantation system.

The copra plantations were mainly established and owned by corporate interests, principally Lever's Pacific Islands Plantation Ltd. and Burns Philp, Pty. Ltd. Flat coastal areas of the Western Solomons, the Russell Islands, and parts of Guadalcanal had been alienated and turned into plantation empires in miniature, dependent on Malaitans for cheap labor. Recruiting ships signed the Islanders—in those days, mainly young, single men—and took them to Tulagi and onward to the plantation areas, where they were held under strict indenture.

The Great Depression, which struck the Solomons two years after Bell was killed, was strongly felt even on the margins of the world capitalist system, with copra prices plummeting and plantations individually owned or leased from the large corporations plunged into debt. Yet the rigid colonial caste system, with its unbridgeable separations between white, Chinese, and "natives" and its relentless racism, continued. Jonathan Fifi'i (1989:34–35), who worked as a houseboy in pre-war

Tulagi, recalls the rituals of empire as seen from the bottom of the colonial hierarchy.

Solomon Islanders, the young people nowadays, wouldn't believe what it was like—the colonial caste system, with the white people all segregated up on the hill, with their hotel and their club; and the Chinese down in Chinatown, who weren't allowed to mix with the Europeans. We Solomon Islanders were at the very bottom of the heap. . . .

Let me give you an example of how the British acted, as if they were our lords and rulers. When I was working in Tulagi, I was given a bicycle to use, so I could ride to Chinatown to get bread. One day I was riding my bicycle, and I saw Mr. Masterman. He was the Commissioner of Labour. He was coming in my direction, and I was going toward him. I rode past him. He called out to me: "Boy!" I came back to him. "Get down!" He told me to get off my bicycle. I got down. "When you see a white man, you can't go past him on your bicycle. You get off and stand at attention until he goes past. Then you can get back on your bicycle. Because white people are the rulers here. You natives are nothing. If you see a white man, you have to give him proper respect."

A similar racism of course prevailed on the copra plantations, with working conditions geared to extract maximum profit for minimum cost of human labor. Fifi'i describes this world vividly (1989:132–35):

The white people were just using black people, the way you use knives and axes. We worked and worked for them. When our people went off to plantations, they had to get up when it was still dark; they were wakened up by the bell. Even if someone was sick, and stayed in his bed, the boss would come in with a bucket of water and pour it over him. He was forced to work anyway. If he was really sick, too sick to work, they'd just leave him until he was almost dead before they'd send him to hospital. I remember a man named Wa'e, from 'Oloburi. He was working on a plantation, and he got sick. He was too sick to work, so they just left him in the workers' quarters. They didn't send him to a doctor; they apparently didn't even give him any medicine. Yet he got more and more seriously ill, until in just a few weeks, he was just skin and bones. Finally, they took him to Tulagi. That was when I was a cook there. I went to see him in hospital. I visited him there, and I asked "How are you doing?" "Oh, I'm going to die."

"How long have you been sick?" "I've been sick for a whole month. I haven't been able to eat for that whole time. Nobody has given me any medicine, or treated me. Finally they brought me here, but I know it's too late. I'm going to die." He died that night.

Some people from our place who had gone as indentured labourers ran away. The Malaita workers would escape from the plantations in canoes. They would paddle over to west Guadalcanal.[1] The Guadalcanal people would report it to the Government station at Aola. The runaways would be arrested and taken to Tulagi. Some of them who ran away just disappeared. They hid in the bush, or they just died; or something happened to them. Maybe they were lost at sea. But they ran away because things were so bad on the plantations.

There was a man named Kouburu. He was a big strong man, but he was slow at cutting copra. He cut his copra, four bags full; he had two more bags still to cut. He just brought back two bags empty. The next day, they gave him six bags and he again brought two of them back empty. The white boss said, "You've cut eight bags, but you still have four left to do. Go and cut four more bags full and bring them in." Kouburu went off with the empty bags and thought about it. He said to himself, "It's impossible for a man to cut six bags full in a day." He got angry, and he ran off into the bush. Nobody saw him again. Nobody knows what happened to him. Maybe he hanged himself; maybe someone killed him in the bush and hid his body. They searched for him, but couldn't find any trace of him.

When someone went off to a plantation, for two years, it was as if he had died. People didn't know whether they'd ever see him again. If something happened to him, it happened. If he died, he just died. If a man died on a plantation, he just died and disappeared; the company didn't do anything about it. If someone got sick when he was a plantation worker, he'd just be forced to work. There were no hospitals and no decent medicines anyway. They'd just give him some salts or something and send him to work. Sometimes, if he got sick enough, he'd be taken to hospital in Tulagi or Gavutu.

A plantation recruit had gone away leaving his father and his mother and his homeland. When a person left, it was as though he had died. And all he'd get for that was ten shillings a month. What could you buy for that, even in those days? . . .

If there was something the men needed to do that had to do with their customs, or something that was taboo for them, the whites would tell them they had to just leave it. "Your customs are for your place, not here. You're here working for money. There's no place for your customs here." So they'd have to break the rules of the ancestors, or ignore them. The Government would say, "Your customs are just rubbish. Those are just lies." Or they'd say, "You're just lying about your customs to get out of your work."

If a white man shouted at us and cursed us, it was all right. But if one of us spoke strongly to a white man, he was beaten, or taken to court. If a white man struck a black man, even though he wounded him badly—even if he shot him

1. From the Russell Islands.

and killed him—it would be ignored or covered up. But if a Solomon Islander struck a white man because he had been abused or sworn at or hit by him, the black man would be imprisoned for two years, or three or four. The Government looked after their side, the white people, not us people they called "natives."

A Kwaio man named Sale Toodia told me how he was in a quarrel. The police grabbed him and tied him up. They put him in a big sack and tied it up. He was tied up so only his face was out of the sack. Toodia bit the bag. He chewed on the bag until the sacking tore. He worked his hands free. He pushed his way through the torn sacking and freed himself, and ran off. . . .

The whites on the plantations would beat their workers whenever they thought something was done wrong. A man named Teleina'o had had a quarrel with his white boss on the plantation where he was working. Afterwards, one of the Europeans there lied to him, saying that he wanted him to come do some work in his house. Teleina'o went into the house, and the other white men were there. They locked the door so he couldn't get out. Then they started punching him. Teleina'o was a big, strong man. He fought back. He punched the man who was hitting him, and knocked him down. He turned on a second one and knocked him down, too. A third one grabbed a pick and hit Teleina'o in the head with it. Teleina'o fell down, terribly wounded. The whites took him to the hospital in Tulagi. There, the doctor stitched up the wound in his head. Teleina'o was kept in the hospital, and when he was sufficiently recovered, he was tried in court for assault and sentenced to prison. That was the white man's justice!

Our people told me about how, whenever they fought back, they were tried and sent to prison. Yet the whites could strike them with impunity. The men who told me about those things were the men who had come back from prison. It wasn't just hearsay. I heard about those things, and I started to think about them. "Even though we work hard for the whites, they treat us like animals."

If a white man was angry at a black man, he'd just hit him, right in front of everyone. Even Mr. Bell did that. He didn't look after the people. He insisted that if someone didn't obey the law, his Headmen were to punch him and hit him with their rifle butts; then they'd take him to court and put him in prison. . . .

Sure, we got our own back. Workers who were angry punched white bosses when they got the chance. But they went to prison for it. The whites beat us up and nothing happened to them.[2]

There was supposed to be a Commissioner of Labour protecting the interests

2. This account is substantially correct. See Bennett 1987 for accounts of how the major companies sent employees who had killed plantation laborers to Australia rather than allowing them to stand trial.

of plantation workers. Once in a while someone tried to do the job properly, and actually was concerned with just working conditions. But if anyone did that, he was regarded as a troublemaker, and sent to some other job. Mr. Bell had tried to stand up for the Malaita plantation workers when he was Inspector of Labour before World War I. But most of the people who inspected working conditions were just concerned with supporting white supremacy and the interests of the planters. Remember that Mr. Masterman was Commissioner of Labour when he made me get off my bicycle in Tulagi, to show proper respect for our white rulers.

Fifi'i is not merely being rhetorical. Judith Bennett, who interviewed many older Malaitans in researching her definitive account of the Solomons plantation system (1987), provides a similar picture of the world of plantations, with its brutality, racism, violence, hatred, and resistance.

Planters regularly gave laborers a blow over the ear or a kick in the backside to make them do what they were told. Violence was so much a part of the expected disciplinary methods of the planters that a white man had to prove himself competent in it to be a success. . . .

If . . . the laborers felt they had been wronged they would frequently gang up on an overseer and beat him. This was particularly true of the Malaitans. Many such cases never reached the courts, although the Europeans were often severely injured.

The Kwaio responded with violence when they could, but for them it meant long prison terms at hard labor, or even death. Fifi'i describes two confrontations.

There was one man named Mr. Widdy[3] who was really terrible to the people who were working on the plantations. He'd get angry at even the slightest thing. There was a man named Selengi who got in a fight with Mr. Widdy. They hit one another. Selengi hit Widdy with a club, and Widdy kicked him and knocked him down. Widdy grabbed the club and killed him with it . . . (1989:134).

[They acted] as if they were a superior caste, and as if we were just animals, here in our own country—acting as if they were the rulers and we were the slaves. But we Malaita people held our own, even though the white people treated us like dirt. When we got our chance, we got our own back. I remember another thing that happened when I was at Tulagi. Again, Mr. Masterman was involved. There was a man named Sau Beriboo, a Kwaio man. He was a

---

3. C. V. Widdy, who was the head of Lever's plantation operations before World War II.

real tough character, a big, strong man. He'd done a lot of stealing and fighting. Anyway, Sau was working on a ship's crew, for a man named Dick Leacock.

One day, everyone working in Tulagi was given a holiday. It was a public holiday, so nobody was working. But Dick Leacock made his crew work all day. Sau was incensed, and went to Leacock: "We want to take tomorrow off, to make up for the holiday we didn't get!" Leacock said, "Impossible! If I tell you you have a holiday, you have the day off. If I tell you to work, you work!"

"But everybody had the day off, and we had to work. We're going to take the day off to make up for it!," Sau retorted. So Dick Leacock wrote a letter to Mr. Masterman, as Commissioner of Labour. "Take this letter to him in the Labour Office." Sau gave Masterman the letter, and he read it. Sau wasn't allowed to stand there in the office. He had to hand it to Mr. Masterman and then go outside again. Mr. Masterman, read the letter, called out to him. "Sau!" "Yes, sir." "Come here."

Sau came in. "Sau, why in hell didn't you follow the orders your master gave you? Why did you pay no attention to your master Dick Leacock, and think you could have a holiday?"

"We had to work all day when everyone else had a holiday. So now we're taking a day off to make up for it!" Mr. Masterman raised his right hand and slapped Sau. Sau grabbed his forearm and pulled him forward across the table, and then pushed his face down into the table. "You, Mr. Masterman, aren't half the man I am. I'd like to kill you."

Masterman gasped, with his face flattened onto the table: "It's all right, son. It's all right. Don't tell anyone what's happened between us. I won't tell anyone. Don't tell anyone I hit you, and don't tell anyone you hit me. I can see how strong you are. Let's just keep it between us. You go back." Masterman sat down and wrote a letter to Dick Leacock. Sau took it back. Dick Leacock read and said, "All right, all you men have a holiday today. The Master said you are to have a holiday today." Of course, by nightfall every Solomon Islander in Tulagi knew about it (1989:35–36).

Bita Saetana—"Peter Satan"—spoke to me in 1977 of his plantation experiences:

The *kabani* [the "company," Lever's] came—to Benika, and Feana and Bibisala. The man who was number one before was Mister Widdy. And Mr. Hay[4] And Mr. Birifi [?]. Those were the ones who struck people and killed people. Mr. Widdy had assaulted fully thirty men. He'd killed five men before I

---

4. Kenneth Dalrymple-Hay, who, when I knew him in the 1960s, was the obscenely fat owner of the Mendana Hotel in Honiara, one of the last bastions of extreme colonial racism. In those days, no Solomon Islander was allowed in the door, except as a waiter or menial (always barefoot). Hay spoke with bravado of the fact that there was blood money put up for his death by Kwaio at Sinalagu.

arrived. Five of them were killed when I was there. He said they were working too slowly.

We'd have a quota of copra to cut every day. Some men couldn't work that fast, and by five o'clock they hadn't reached their quota. Some would have to work all night. I worked there sometimes into the night, by the light of pressure lamps they brought. All night sometimes.

When the bell sounded, the whites would come running. If you'd taken a spell, reached into your bag for a smoke, you'd get thumped on the back with a stick. If you were strong and tough and fought him back, he'd pull out a gun and shoot you. That's what they used to do at Lever's.

Mr. Birifi would only warn you once. The second time, he'd shoot you. I, Bita Saetana, I fought with him, at Nigatuu. He hit me with a shovel, on the foot. I hit him back and knocked two of his teeth out: when I was a kid, I was really strong.

The assaults on the workers happened every day. Today four or five workers would get beaten up; tomorrow it would be three or four more. That went on for two years, while we were working for Lever's cutting copra. Nowadays, it's just a fun game, working on the plantations as young men do today. But in those days, we'd get bashed all the time. We'd cut copra day and night, and get beaten up if we didn't get our quota cut. And for that, we got ten shillings a month. Twelve pounds for two years.

Another white man was Mr. Lolengatana.[5] And Mr. Iesi. And Mr. Siri. Those were our bosses, at Lever's. We heard in the afternoon that one of our young Kwaio men, Tiimote, had been assaulted by his overseer. He cut him in the forehead with a machete.

Three of the white men came that afternoon. I said to my friends, "The white men wounded one of us with a knife—let's get them back." So that evening we went to their house. We burst inside and wrestled them to the floor. We were Buani and Fa'afefea and Toomasi—I don't know his other name. We thumped them, wrestled them to the floor, and then rubbed lime—our betel-chewing lime—into their eyes. They were blinded. Then we let them go. Their eyesight was messed up, and so a steamer came and took them back to their place. Each of us got four years in prison for that.

Nowadays it's not bad, working on a plantation. But in the old days, workers had their teeth knocked out, or were blinded, or killed. We fought back when we could, but we went to jail, they didn't. Old Osifo'oa [who was then living as an elderly and crippled Christian], when he was a young man before the war, killed three white men at Yandina—he did it secretly; they never found out who did it.

---

5. I give the Kwaio rendering of the names, which are hard to identify with certainty.

Another Kwaio man who acquired a reputation as strongman and troublemaker in the world of plantations was Simone Maa'eobi. Maa'eobi, as a plantation worker in the 1930s, was famed among his Kwaio comrades, and more widely, for the strength of his punches[6] and his courage in standing up to whites. He recounted to me how, having been sent to company headquarters at Gavutu after a plantation brawl, he had been held by the shoulders by two foremen and beaten ruthlessly by C. V. Widdy. Breaking loose, he had pushed Widdy through the wall, thrown him off the porch, and beaten him senseless. Maa'eobi had then calmly taken the company launch to Tulagi and charged Widdy with assault. According to Maa'eobi's account, at least, Widdy was fined £5 and Maa'eobi went free.

These sporadic acts of retaliation occurred against an everyday background of subjection to the brutal and exhausting regimen of plantation labor (see Bennett 1987, chap. 8). Bennett comments that "the plantation was a 'total institution,' remaking its inmates temporarily into creatures geared to obey and produce by controlling every aspect of their lives. For those whose lot is was to be nothing more than a laborer, life on the plantation was stifling and often brutish" (ibid., 184).

Poor quarters, poor rations, an exhausting work regimen from before first light until long after dark, violence and abuse, simply had to be endured most of the time. To resist by working slowly risked not only violence, but it also meant having meager wages further cut or having to work even longer hours. To resist by escape or violence risked imprisonment or death. Most of the time, most of the men had to keep their thoughts of retaliation or escape to themselves or share them only with close workmates.

Maa'eobi's strategy of using the legal institutions of the colonial state to achieve both protection and redress underlines how astute the Malaita workers had become in applying pressure to the cracks between the planters and the government. Even though the government was beholden to the major corporate interests—principally Lever's and Burns Philp—that controlled the Solomons economy before World War II, there were laws and regulations to be followed. The Malaitans used them strategically when they could (see ibid., 170), and none more acutely than the Kwaio, who had acquired a mystique with Europeans even before the Bell

6. Folofo'u, later to become a leader in Kwaio political confrontations with the postcolonial government, told me that when he was a young man he inadvertently got in the way when Maa'eobi took a swing at a Chinese trader on his ship in the harbor, after an argument over prices. Folofo'u said that Maae'obi hit his shoulder so hard his arm was unusable for a year.

massacre both for their warrior fierceness and courage and for their ma-
nipulations as troublemakers.

The Kwaio have for decades distinguished categorically the three institutional forces that have brought whites to the Solomons, hence the
three capacities in which they have had to deal with *ta'a kwao* 'white
people': *gafamanu*, the government, *kabani*,[7] the plantations, and
sukuru, the missions. The other category of foreigners was the *saenamanu*
('Chinamen'), the Chinese trading community. It is worth pausing here
to examine briefly the structures of colonial society.

The planters and plantation interests and the administration of the
British Solomon Islands Protectorate had a kind of approach-avoidance
relationship. The government was dependent on copra export duty for
much of its revenue, and at home the major corporate interests exerted
considerable political influence that could be applied through the Colonial Office to matters of policy in what was a laughably small, remote,
economically and politically inconsequential corner of the empire[8] As
Bennett (1987:166) observes, "The government had above all to consider the needs of the commercial planters because they and their associated merchants and shippers represented the sources of the protectorate's
revenue." The major plantation interests continually agitated for sources
of cheap labor, instruments to force labor indenture, such as the head
tax, reduction in export duties, and stabilization of low wages. Where the
plantations demanded profit, colonial policy called for at least rituals and
pretenses of justice, requiring that native labor be managed according to
strict law. In this and other matters, conflict was common (ibid.).

In the ludicrously small and remote island capital of Tulagi, the rituals
of empire and hierarchy took on a comical air. Anthropologist Ian Hog-
bin told of how, in Tulagi in the 1920s and 1930s, the air was one of
formal hierarchy and imperial propriety: "It was all very, very pukka. Everybody went around in starched whites, all wearing ties, mostly wearing
jackets. If one went to call on the Resident Commissioner, and one had
neglected to bring a tie or a jacket, the Government Secretary . . . had
both of these ready so that one could slip these on before seeing His
Honour."[9]

Behind the outward displays of European caste solidarity, there were
more subtle and more insidious lines of cleavage within the white community than the ones that divided those in commercial enterprise from

7. Pronounced "kambani" in Kwaio, which prenasalizes *b*, *d*, and *g*.

8. And one whose officers occupied a very low rung on the prestige ladder of the colonies; see
Keesing and Corris 1980, chap. 3 and p. 73, and Huessler 1963.

9. Personal communication, recorded on tape, 1978.

those in government. There were issues of class and nationality at stake as well. Many of the whites managing local copra plantations were dismissed as riff-raff by the British gentlemen who were running the Solomons. The Australians, in particular, were often regarded as rough and boorish colonials. It was the ruffian element that predominated in the daily running of plantations, and it was they who were the most racist and brutal toward the "natives."

Even government employees, whether British or Australian or whatever, were carefully placed on class hierarchies, with mechanics, carpenters, or other tradesmen placed almost as low as planters who had gone native, or worst of all, had married local women or openly taken them as concubines.

Despite their differences of class and origin and conflicts as well as convergences of interest, solid lines of racial supremacy and caste solidarity as well as passions for alcohol and sport kept commercial interests and government together, and whites aligned together against the Chinese and "natives." The Chinese were marginalized; with the "half-castes" who were in the long run to acquire an important place in Solomons commercial life, they were placed between whites and "natives" on the strict ladder of the colonial caste system (Bennett 1987:206–209).

Vis-à-vis the "natives," whites carefully maintained appearances of a united front. Disgust, hate, fear, mockery, condescension, and sometimes paternalism were part of a complex of imperial racism now well documented. Bennett (ibid., 184) notes that "the social distance between master and laborer was . . . reflected in the terms of reference the planters used to speak of their employees. 'Boy' was universal, 'coon' and 'nigger' common." J. C. Barley, as District Officer of Malaita, wrote in 1933:

> Scarcely 10% of the European settlers in the Protectorate regard the native otherwise than a "necessary evil" in the economic life of the community or as being entitled to any sort of sympathetic attention or interest. . . . He is almost universally looked down upon as belonging to a somewhat unclean and definitely inferior order of creation, as one who does not know the meaning of gratitude, loyalty or affection, and who will invariably mistake kindness for weakness and immediately take advantage of any person rash enough to trust him and treat him as a fellow human being (quoted by Bennett ibid., 179).

But there was always something of a mystique, in the British Colonial Service, about adventure and courage in the wilderness and about acquiring a close knowledge of "native" ways and customs. So when they were on tour, some colonial officers cultivated close bonds with police and headmen and sought to learn about local custom. Barley himself had gone on to add, after this characterization of the racist attitudes of his fellow Europeans, that "my personal experience of the native . . . has always been diametrically opposite to this." Yet what is striking in retrospect is how rigidly caste boundaries were maintained even away from government stations. (One British government officer, M. J. Forster, was still famous all over Malaita in the 1960s, although he served for only a few months as District Officer in 1940; wherever I asked Malaitans what he had done that distinguished him from so many others, I was told that it was that he would sit with Malaitans when he ate his rations on tour, and had shared food and tobacco with them.)

I have not, so far, raised questions of gender. There were few white women in the Solomons before World War II. There were a few nurses, a few white wives (of planters and government officers); and occasionally there was a white woman in a higher-status profession—a lawyer, a doctor (though she was the wife of a businessman). Apart from the women missionaries, white women were too much of a rarity in the Solomons to have been accorded a very clear role in colonial society. But in the Solomons as elsewhere in the tropical colonies (Boutilier 1984; Stoler 1989 gives a good bibliography of the extensive literature), women faced particularly difficult problems, as subalterns in their own patriarchal society and part of the ruling white caste in colonial society.

The missionaries, the other main segment of the Solomons white population, were isolated from the planters and government officers in many ways (not least of all, because most of them avoided alcohol and stayed away from Tulagi). The one issue on which they joined ranks with the government officers and planters was in maintaining the strict boundaries of racial separation and supremacy, even in outlying mission stations. The South Sea Evangelical Mission on Malaita, the Methodists in the western Solomons, and the Seventh Day Adventists all emphasized Christian family life as a model, and women played important parts as teachers and healers as well as wives. The planter's or government officer's wife would have been a remote and cloistered presence for Malaitans, other than to the few who worked as houseboys.[10] They were more likely to have had contact with the formidable mission ladies of the SSEM, its founder Florence Young and her sisters and successors.

The missionaries preached of Jesus' message, preached of love and

---

10. See Fifi'i 1989 for the perspective of a houseboy in prewar Tulagi.

brotherhood. But the world they depicted was run by a white God, with a white Jesus as his agent. The white missionaries enjoined obedience to the white man's superiority, a passive acceptance by the "natives" of their place as "boys"—Satan's sinners rescued from his clutches, cleansed of their wild depravity, reborn as innocent children whose proper destiny was to serve Europeans obediently, peacefully, and diligently. In their practice as well as in their precept, the missionaries maintained the caste superiority of the Europeans.

But there was another Christian voice, speaking of a different message, a different Jesus. Jonathan Fifi'i (1989:40–41) recalls:

There was a man named Fallowes, an Anglican priest.[11] When I was in Tulagi, he called the Gela people and the people working at Tulagi together for a meeting. He was living on Gela. We'd heard that he regularly wore a laplap—two yards of cloth—the way we "natives" did. He called a meeting for us, the Gela and Malaita people and others at Tulagi, at Sasabe No. 2. Everyone went to hear what he had to say.

He spoke in Pijin. "I'm an Englishman too. But I see the British Government here treating you badly. I see all sort of wrongs being done to you. The Government only helps their fellow white people. They don't help you black people. You've heard the Government tell you, 'Oh, that white man is crazy!' Well, I'm not crazy. My mind is working perfectly clearly, and I'm a well educated man. I'm not crazy.

"I see the way you live, in poverty. The Government collects lots and lots of money as export duty on the copra you produce with your labour. Why doesn't the Government do anything for you? They haven't brought you any education. I've been teaching people that they should have leaders to represent them. But the Government says, 'No, we won't allow it.'"

He was right. The Government sent word that we were not to believe what that crazy man was preaching to us. Mr. Ashley, the Resident Commissioner, said, "He's crazy. You aren't to believe anything he tells you. I'm the Government, and I have the power here. I treat you well. We're not destroying anything of yours. He's just lying to you." Eventually, the Government deported him.[12] They sent him back to England. They told everyone that he had been sent to the lunatic asylum.[13]

11. See Bennett 1987 for a detailed account of Rev. Richard Fallowes, his work as a priest on Isabel in the early 1930s, and his return to the Solomons in 1938–39.

12. He was deported by the High Commissioner, Sir Harry Luke, with the support of conservative Anglican Archbishop Baddeley, who found Fallowes's version of Christianity rather too revolutionarily Christian.

13. Rev. Fallowes continued to serve as a missionary, and was alive and working in Swaziland, in southern Africa, into the late 1970s.

Rev. Richard Fallowes was sane enough—too sane for this world in miniature where the British paraded with plumes and swords, where whites drank themselves silly, where missionaries preached of brotherhood and enacted local tyrannies, where Solomon Islanders suffered pain and humiliation, sweated and died, in the land of their ancestors.

Beyond the Solomons, the world was being plunged into collective insanity.

10 Ta'a I Marika

When news came in 1942 that the Solomons were under threat of Japanese invasion, many young Kwaio men were working on plantations around the Solomons. Tome Kwalafane'ia remembers how he was at Nolo, in the Shortlands—back to finish his term of indenture after a six-month prison term, for striking his white plantation manager.

The Japanese started getting ready to invade the Solomons. So then our [white] bosses said, "Let's all go into the jungle to build houses, so if the Japanese really come we can hide in them, in the bush. So we built houses in the bush. . . . Then the war started in earnest; it was really coming.

We worked for one month, then we finished our term.[1] Baba'aniaboo and I were ready, and the *Kurumalau* came to take us to Gavutu. We arrived at Gavutu in the middle of the day, and found that everyone had run away. We found two men at the wharf. "Everyone has run into the bush, because a Japanese plane is coming." A Chinaman held the bowline. So we went out again in the ship.

. . . Three of us went off into the bush to look for [ngali] nuts. We heard a noise coming. "Hey, what's that?" But there was an old man, a relative, working there who had come with us. "Hey, that thing that's making a noise sounds like the plane that came last time. That was no good!" We looked and looked. "There it is!" "Oh, that's the one!" "What do we do now?"

We ran to the beach. 'Eriboo and I got our canoe and paddled back toward Gavutu. We saw that plane dive down over Tulagi, and drop a bomb. Then another, at the government wharf at Tulagi. Then he came in our direction. Some of us were in canoes, some in dinghies. The plane dropped one bomb

1. I have recorded a number of accounts of these events from Kwalafane'ia in Pijin and in Kwaio, as linguistic texts, and some fragments have been published (see Keesing 1987d and 1988). This is a new version, recorded in 1989; the previous segment comes from Keesing 1987d.

into the sea, but it didn't hit anyone. The sea just boiled up, and all our canoes capsized. Then we paddled over to Gela and stayed there. Then the white men summoned us back to Gavutu. "You working boys, you come!" They had us come into the store. "Take bags of rice and cases of meat. These are your rations. Then go back into the bush."

The *Kurumalau* and other ships had just left. I think they had gone back to the "big place" [i.e., Australia]. We were just left there. We were like wild pigs in the bush. . . . Finally a couple of ships from 'Aoke came to Siota, on Gela, and picked us up and took us back to Malaita.

When the Japanese invaded the Solomons, capturing Tulagi and the Guadalcanal plains and New Georgia, Malaita was spared direct attack. Malaitans got a peripheral view of the naval and air battles surrounding the American counterattack and landing. Again, their direct role was to be their historic one—as manual laborers, but this time, for the Americans (in Kwaio, "Ta'a i Marika," lit. "the people from America"). It was a role that was to change radically the Malaitan view of whites, the world outside, and their engagement with colonial rule.

Jonathan Fifi'i (1989:48–49) recalls how, after he was sent back home from a school in northern Malaita when the Japanese invaded the Solomons, he was recruited to lead a Kwaio detachment of the Solomon Island Labour Corps.

When I got back to my place, word had come from 'Aoke. Mr. Trench[2] had sent word to Headman Silifa, and Headman 'Adi, and Headman Braun Kwarialaena. "We want three 'sections', one from Sinalagu, one from Uru, and one from 'Oloburi. We need 25 men from each passage, with one man in charge of each section."

Headman Silifa got together 24 men, and he asked me to be the 25th. "I want you to go with our detachment. You've just come from school. The Americans who are in the middle of this war don't understand Pijin, and they don't know our language. So you have to go and be the interpreter for our detachment. This is a bad time. We have to be able to understand one another." I said, "But I'm only a young man." I was only 21 years old. But anyway, I became the interpreter. It was my job to translate for the Americans, but also to lead our detachment: I was made the Sergeant.

We went by land to 'Aoke—there was no ship to take us. We were really hungry along the way: it took us two days to walk to 'Aoke. Some of the men roasted fern pith to eat. I had to be in charge of all that.

2. Sir David Trench, who went on to become High Commissioner of the Western Pacific and later, Governor of Hong Kong.

When we finally got to 'Aoke, we were given a warning by Mr. Trench. "If you are brave enough, you'll volunteer to go to Lunga. There's a war going on—people are getting killed. If you're not prepared to risk your lives, if you're afraid, then you should turn around and go home. But the wages will be good—one pound a month." Mr. Trench told me that I was to get four pounds—I said that was fine. Before the war, the wages on the plantations had been only ten shillings a month. So to us, a pound a month sounded like good pay! And the four pounds for me, as a Sergeant—that was really special. . . . In Tulagi, I'd been getting five shillings a month.

So we went off to Lunga, on the government ship *Mendana*. There were fifty of us on board—two sections. It was only a small ship. When we got near Lunga and could see, it was amazing! Lots of trucks, airplanes, warships. We got there and landed. We slept in tents. They gave us mosquito nets: there were lots of mosquitoes around—big ones that were biting a lot. There were thousands of Americans landed there. There were tents everywhere, and foxholes. We had to dig foxholes for ourselves. The dugout we dug was big enough that a whole "section" of 25 could take cover inside, and deep enough that we could stand neck deep.

The Americans had shot a lot of Japanese, and the bodies had been washed down the Tenaru River. The bodies had started to stink, and we were given the job of burying them. We had the job of carrying cargo, too. And carrying back the bodies of the people shot in the bush. And carrying ammunition up to the front lines in the hills.

The fighting was going on there. The Japanese were along the Mataniko River, and when the shooting started, we had to crouch down while we were working. The fighting was really bad. We were afraid in the daytime, and afraid at night, too. The food was good, and the work was good. So it was being afraid that was the bad part. Sometimes, when we were at Tenaru, the Japanese bombed us. Around five o'clock in the morning, they'd bomb us. One morning a bomb fell very close to us. It fell on the foxhole of the section from West Kwaio, and lots of men were killed. That day, we ran away, because our friends had been killed.

At first, we ran off to the stream at Ngalibeu. The Americans had discussed what to do about us. We had all been staying in the Tenaru Camp. But after that bombing, they scattered us around. Some were sent to be stationed at Lunga Beach. Some to Mataniko no. 3. Some to Ngaribe'u. Some to Tenaru. They divided us up. They sent us back to Lunga Beach, and we stayed there.

For the Kwaio recruits to the Labour Corps this was an awesome and often terrifying experience. 'Asuabe'u recalled that we ate with them. They were kind with us 'boys'. They talked with us, and that was good. We shared the same plates, and the same food. . . . The British hadn't been kind to us—they'd been too strict. But the Americans were kind with us. We saw the Black Merika—the Niguru. Their hair was like ours. Their bodies were like ours.

Suufiomea remembered,

I saw the Americans. They were swarming like ants. They were different from the British. The British had been too strict with us. They wouldn't eat with us, they whipped us, they called us pigs. . . . But the Americans were kind to us. They shared their tables with us. . . . We ate together, shared the same food.

We got two pounds a month. The Americans wanted to give us more, but our British officers wouldn't allow it. . . . I shared food with the Negroes. They were kind to us. Their bodies, their hair, were the same as ours.

Jonathan Fifi'i, as Sergeant in charge of his "section," recalls the strange organization of the Labour Corps, with the Americans working every day with the Solomon Islanders, but the British and Australian plantation bosses, commissioned as officers for the purpose, officially commanding them, and the Solomons' constabulary still imposing pre-war style discipline.

We were in a strange situation. We had signed up for the Solomon Islands Labour Corps. The officers of the Labour Corps were white men who had been our plantation bosses before the war—the men we hated, and the men who despised us. They were put in command of us because they spoke Pijin and because what was left of the British administration imagined that those plantation bosses knew how to control us and make us work. But they weren't the ones we were actually working with. It was the British—some of them were really Australians—who were commanding us and paying us. It was their police who pushed as around. But they weren't the ones we were working for. We worked during the day for the Americans. That put us in a strange situation. During the day we lived in one world, and at night and in the morning, in our Labour Corps camps, we lived in a different world where our officers tried to treat us as if we were plantation labourers.

There, we Solomon Islanders were still being treated like dirt. We weren't being allowed to wear long trousers, or to wear shirts, when we went off to work. We just had to wear our khaki laplaps. Those of us who were Sergeants and Corporals tied torn strips of cloth around our arms, and they painted our chevrons on them. The three stripes of a Sergeant, or the two stripes of a Corporal, were just painted on. We tied them on like the customary armbands we wear. But when the others put their armbands on, with their stripes, I didn't want to wear mine. I'd been given a shirt, and I got a set of chevrons and sewed them on it. But the officer in command of us tore off the chevrons, and then the shirt. Only whites were supposed to wear shirts, not us 'natives'!

With the Americans, it wasn't the same at all. The Americans worked, and we worked too. We did the same work together. They showed us how to use the tools or do the work. That was the first time we'd ever seen white people do physical work. Before the war, the white people we'd seen had just sat down and watched us do the work. They'd just sit in an office, and have some foreman boss us around. We'd never seen white people do any hard work, with their hands, the way the American soldiers were doing.

One of our jobs was to go and pick up the dead bodies—sometimes they'd been in the bush for a few days—and take them to the cemetery. We'd dig graves and bury the dead. Sometimes we'd unload bombs and ammunition from the supply ships. Sometimes we'd unload rations and other cargo. The Americans would work alongside of us. When we'd be digging a hole, or a ditch, the Americans would be next to us with shovels and picks in their hands, too. We saw those American soldiers working, and sweating, and we said, "These white people aren't proud. We get sweaty and dirty, and they get sweaty and dirty too. We carry cargo, and they carry cargo. These white people aren't afraid to work."

When it came to eating, the Americans would ask us to come and eat with them. "Just bring your plates and have some food with us." They weren't disgusted by sharing food with us. When it came time to eat, the American soldiers called us to join them. They'd say, "Here's a plate for you. Here's your spoon." We'd never seen anything like that. White people had never shared their food with us before. They'd never let us eat with them. Why hadn't the British ever shared food with us? Why hadn't they ever treated us like fellow human beings?

Our own "officers," the ones who were supposed to be commanding us, had been planters in the Solomons before the war. They saw that these awful things were happening. When they saw us eating with the Americans, they lined us up at the end of the day. "It's not right for you to eat with those white men. You have to eat by yourselves. You have to take your own saucepan and your own rice, and go off and cook it and eat it by yourselves. You're not supposed to mix with them when they're eating."

Those were our "officers"—our old plantation bosses, Mr. Widdy and Mr. Waters and the rest. They always lectured us like that, trying to "keep us in our place." They told us we were just supposed to work with the Americans, not eat with them or make friends with them. We told the Americans what our orders were: "We've been told we can't eat with you." "Why not?" the soldiers asked.

"Because we're black. We're what they call 'natives'." The Americans got really angry about that, and swore. But from that time on, the men in my section were afraid to go and eat with the Americans. I was the only one who would go and eat with them. My men just went and cooked their rice and ate by themselves.

The Americans we worked with would ask, "What do you think about the people who are running the plantations? How do they treat you? How well do they take care of you?" We told them, and they told us, "Oh, the way you're being treated is wrong. You aren't strong." Some of the Americans said, "Let's talk." So we talked with them. One man was a Lieutenant named Kingsley. They talked to us. What they told us was this. "You have to do something to become strong, in dealing with the British government. We see how you're being treated—it's no good."

We thought about that and talked about it. "Oh, that's what Fallowes was trying to tell us in Tulagi, before the war. That's what he was telling the people of Gela and Isabel. What he was telling them is the same thing these Americans are telling us." We started to think about that. Our minds really started to open up. We started to see things clearly for the first time.

One of the things that really made us start to think about the way we were treated was seeing all the soldiers from around the world with coloured skin. The war brought soldiers from everywhere to the Solomons. Australian soldiers came; New Zealand soldiers came. The American soldiers came. Lots of white soldiers. The Negro soldiers, among the Americans, were black. The Gilbertese and the Ellice Islanders were brown. So were the Maori, and the Filipinos. The Papuans and New Guineans were black, the same as us.

We saw them all and we were surprised that there were so many coloured people from so many different places. "Hey, there are people like us, who've come with the army!" What I had started to reflect on was this. First of all, their uniforms were the same as the white people's. Second, they had the same ranks as everyone else. Some of them were Sergeants. Some of them were Lieutenants. Some of them were even Majors. Third, their salaries were the same as everyone else's. Fourth, their food rations were the same as anyone else's. The fifth thing was that their living was the same as everyone else's. We saw the other black people, and they looked like they were doing well. They were living well, wearing proper clothes, they were well paid.

The Negro soldiers asked us, "Does your government look after you well? What money do you earn?"

"Only ten shillings a month. Now, here in the war, they're giving us one pound a month. Those of us who are Sergeants are getting four pounds a month." We thought that was a lot. But the Negro soldiers said, "They're tricking you. That's nothing, it's no good. It's just a pittance." We thought we were well paid.

We felt shamed in the face of the other dark-skinned people we were mixing up with. They saw us and they felt sorry for us, too. Some of them laughed at us and made fun of us. Some of them were angry about how we were treated. "You're treated like rubbish, they're walking all over you." "What's awful about you, that you get treated that way?"

So this started us thinking; we started to get ideas. We felt angry that we'd been given no power, that we had been treated like rubbish. We had to change all that. Whatever trouble we brought on ourselves, we had to stand up to the government (Fifi'i 1989:49–52).

Fifi'i recalled his old comrades in arms, with whom he was to spend four years as a political prisoner, men from 'Areare, to the southeast of Kwaio country—Nori, brilliant ideologue of political resistance, who was to die of tuberculosis at age thirty, and Aliki Nono'oohimae, who lived into his seventies, long enough to see his country become independent.

Aliki was the Sergeant for the West 'Are'are section, and Nori was the Corporal. Aliki Nono'oohimae's section and my section were working together. We brought the bodies of people who had been killed and buried them. We unloaded cargo. I got to know Nori really well. We became close friends. Nori had no formal education. He had been in Tulagi, and then worked on a plantation. Nori was a strong man, especially for talking. He wasn't afraid of anything or anyone. Even though he was a young man, he wasn't afraid to speak out in front of people. . . .

We were working at what was called "Class Two Warehouse," along the bank of the Lunga River near the shore. We went every day to move cargo in and out. . . . The British who were supposed to be in charge of us paid no attention to us when we were at work. So we Sergeants were in charge of our own sections. The American who supervised our work was named Jackson. He was a black American—a really strong man, a boxer. He was in charge of the cargo. There was another man with him, a white man named Alvin. He was a little short man, but really friendly. When one of the cases we unloaded was broken open, Jackson told us to help ourselves—to open any tins we wanted and eat or drink whatever was inside: pineapple juice or apricots, or whatever it was. "Don't be afraid. Take whatever you want. The case is broken. We're supposed to throw those ones away."

We Sergeants and Corporals weren't supposed to carry cases. We were supposed to sit around and supervise our men. So Jackson and Alvin used to sit
and talk with us while the men worked. Jackson would ask, "How do the British treat you?" We told him. I'd been to school a bit, and could speak some
English. So I'd do the translating. Although Nori spoke Pijin, he kept pressing
Jackson with questions. If there was something in Pijin Jackson and Alvin
didn't understand, I'd turn it into English. "What do they pay you when you
work on plantations?" they asked. "How much does the government pay you
when you work for them?" "Ten shillings a month. A boy who doesn't yet have
hair under his arms gets five shillings. If a man has worked for two years and
signs up for a second time, he gets one pound. If he's worked five or six years or
more, he'll get one pound five shillings," we said. "We have to pay five shillings a year in tax." "Oh, that's no good. Do you get on well with the whites?
Is your standard of living on the plantations all right?" "No, not at all. The
whites don't allow us to go into their houses or offices. We just have to stand
outside and the white man stands on the step and talks to us. If it's a Headman
or a foreman, he's allowed to come inside the office, but he has to stand at attention across the table from the European. He can never sit down: he just
makes his report or gets his orders, says 'Yes, sir,' and turns around and leaves
straight away."

"Don't you have any way or any place where you can have meetings with
the whites?" "What do you mean?" we asked. "I mean sitting down across a
table from one another and having a meeting." "Impossible!" we said. "We
don't have anything like that."

"Do you demand your rights from the Europeans? Do you talk strongly with
them when you have to?" "Talk to them how?" we asked. We couldn't imagine
such a thing. "Complain to them, make demands to them, tell them what
you're unhappy about."

We'd talk like that while the others worked. When Jackson would see that
the men were sweating and were hot and tired, he'd call them over. "Hey,
come and sit in the shade and have a rest. You've been working hard; you're
sweating." So they'd take a break.

Then he'd ask us, "Is that the way it is on the plantations? When you get
hot and tired from working in the sun, does the boss tell you to take a rest in
the shade?" "Impossible," we said. "We have to keep working. When it rains,
we have to keep working without a break. When the sun is hot, we have to
keep working without a break. They never let us take a break like that. A man
isn't even allowed to fill his pipe and light it, and have a smoke. He has to lie
and say he has to go and relieve himself, and then go off and fill his pipe."
Jackson listened to all this. "That's really bad. With us black Americans, if we

have some disagreement with the whites, or some grievance, we sit down at the table and settle it. We argue out our grievances and demands, our two sides. Then when our dispute has been resolved, we all get up from the table and things are straightened out." Alvin, the white man, agreed with him that that's the way things were sorted out. "That's how we black people in America pressed for education, and better working conditions. You see that nowadays, we black people and the white people get on all right together. We have equal rights. We just mix up with one another."[3]

"There's one thing I want you to listen to carefully. Don't be afraid when you hear what I have to say." He started using a word that was new to us: "struggle." "You have to struggle against the government. If you confront them strongly, the government will have to pay attention. If you make your demands strongly, the government will be forced to listen. Once they agree to sit down with you and discuss your grievances, then you can start moving ahead, the way we black people did in America."

We listened to what he had to say. Nori and Aliki Nono'oohimae and I discussed it. "How are we going to do that?" We talked again with Jackson. "What demands does the government make of you?" he asked. "They demand taxes. Five shillings for each man every year." "And the government takes it?" We told him the government collected it, and that we never saw any benefit from it. "You have to refuse to pay it," he told us. "Whatever they do, refuse to pay taxes. When they confront you about it, make your demands. Tell them, 'You, the government, treat us like rubbish. We do all the hard work, and you treat us like dirt.'

"If you press strongly enough, and refuse to pay taxes and work on plantations, your situation will get better. If you don't, after the war things will be really bad for you. You see how all the plantations all over the Solomons have been destroyed in the war. If you don't do something to lift up your side, you'll end up working just the way you did before, like animals. But you'll have to start all over again, clearing the ruined plantations and planting new coconut palms. It will be terrible for you. You'll be like slaves.

"After the war you have to organize. You have to make your demands. You have to struggle. You have to refuse to do the kinds of things you used to do, and refuse to accept the conditions you suffered before the war. Don't be

3. That was hardly literally true in 1942, although it was to become true (in most parts of the U.S.) in the subsequent forty years, through a continuation of the confrontationist politics Jackson was advocating. It took Martin Luther King and a decade of the civil rights movement to break the back of racist extremism in the U.S. However, even though in 1942 black soldiers served in segregated units and were kept out of combat, they were certainly more equal to whites than their Solomons counterparts.

afraid. They may arrest you. They may put you in prison. But they won't kill you. It will be like demanding your rights from your father. He may slap you, he may hit you, but he won't kill you. Don't be afraid.

"What you're doing, if you start a political struggle, needs a name. But you should give it a name from your language. If you give it a name from the white man's language, they'll think it is something someone else started for you. You have to give it your own name and make it your own struggle. Don't tell anyone that we played a part in teaching you. You have to raise yourselves up, and do it by yourselves. If you say that it was us Americans who taught you these ideas, they'll dismiss it and will tell you that we just lied to you. You have to take what we've told you and make your own movement out of it. You have to give it your own name, and follow your own ideas. You have to lift yourselves up. We can't do it for you."

Nori and I talked about it. "Even if they hit us, or even kill us, we have to go ahead strongly. If we give it up when they start threatening us and putting pressure on us, the whites will just laugh at us."

We agreed that we had to keep quiet about what the Americans had taught us about struggle. If anyone pressed us about that, and asked us where we'd got those ideas, we agreed to say just that it was "Captain Joe War." The Americans were all "Joe" to us. If the government forced us to tell them where we'd got some of those ideas, it was just to be "Captain Joe War"—not Jackson or Alvin or Lieutenant Kingsley or any of the others who had talked to us and given us ideas. . . .

Aliki and Nori and I kept talking about what we could do to be certain that after the war things wouldn't be the same as they had been before—even if our officers, our old plantation bosses, were trying hard to make certain we would go back to be their slaves, the way we were before.

Those "officers" were trying to keep us "natives" in our proper place, so they and their companies could go back to making money from our work. They tried their best to keep us from getting any ideas or acquiring any possessions that would make us think we were human beings, not "natives" whose place was to serve and work for white people. There was one thing that made us really angry. Older men on Malaita are still angry about that, to this very day.

During the fighting, the Americans gave us trousers and shirts and soap, and razor blades and mattress covers. We put those aside to be sewn into skirts for our womenfolk. Because in those days, cloth was really scarce. We had all these things we'd been given in our tents. One day, when we had gone off to work, the British who were in charge of us got the police and went into our tents. They took all of the things we'd been given. They separated them into piles. The old clothes went in one pile, the new clothes and good stuff went

into another. The old clothes and worn things were put in a pile. They poured
kerosine on them, and they burned them all. The good things just vanished—
they must have kept them, or given them back to the Americans. So when we
came back, we found that all of our things had disappeared. The same thing
happened in every Labour Corps camp.

The next morning, we refused to work. The American soldiers eventually
came and talked to us. "Oh, they did a really rotten thing to you. But come
and work, and we'll give you more things." After that, the Army and Marines
gave us lots of stuff—trousers, shirts—all that kind of stuff. The stuff that had
been burned and confiscated wasn't just items we'd been given for nothing,
Army property the Americans were giving away. Many of those were things
that had been given to us in exchange for our doing extra work in our off-duty
time—doing people's laundry, or climbing coconuts, and things.

Three months after our things had been burned the first time, while we were
out at work, the British came into our tents a second time and took all our
things. They separated the old things out, and burned them. This time we
found out what they did with the new things. They set up a store, and tried
to sell them back to us. Captain Moore and Captain Axin were the ones who
did it.

We were angry about that, and wanted to stop the work we were doing.
They did that twice. Finally, they allowed us each to make a box 2'6" by 2'6".
We were told that when we were to go home, we'd have to set out the things
we had. All those things we were authorized to keep that would fit into a man's
box, he'd be able to take back home. "Otherwise you might take rifles back,
and the government prohibits those. The Americans who are befriending you
are giving you things you shouldn't have." . . .

We were angry about that, but our anger just smouldered for a long time. . . .
So Aliki and Nori and I went on talking. We'd talk and think about what we
could do about it. We decided that the important thing was not to be afraid.
After the war was over, things had to be different. The Solomons would be a
different place then. Everything had opened up. People from all over the place
would be coming here, the way they had during the war. But we knew someone
had to fight to make our world change. If we didn't stand strongly, nothing
would happen (Fifi'i 1989:52–55).

The name given to the movement has been much discussed in the literature. The versions Europeans conjured up at the time—"Marching
Rule" and even "Marxian Rule"—reflect both government linguistic in-
eptitude and an inability to comprehend a political challenge to colonial
domination in its prewar racist style. Fifi'i's recollections about the nam-

ing of the movement (1989:60–61) leave no doubt as to the intentions of the leaders.

We talked about a name for our political struggle. Nori wanted us to use the 'Are'are word *maasina*. I have to explain that name, because the Europeans have said so many silly things about it. Said it was "Marching," or even "Marxian." Because the whites called it "Marching Rule," lots of Solomon Islanders used that. But that's not the way it started. That wasn't the name we gave it.

That word Nori proposed is used for a relationship between siblings and for a set of siblings. In 'Are'are, the word is *ma-asi-na*. *Asi-*[4] is the word for a younger brother, in the Malaita languages. The *ma-* is used for the relationship between people related in that particular way: here, a set of brothers, or "brotherhood." In our Kwaio language, it is *waasina*. In north Malaita languages in is *ngwaasina, saasina, thaasina*. We used that name because our program was to join all the Malaita people together as brothers: Christians and pagans, 'Are'are and Kwaio and Kwara'ae and Langalanga and Lau and Baegu and Baelelea and To'aba'ita and Maramasike. We were all to be united as brothers and sisters, in our struggle. . . .

At the very end of 1943, I took another section of 24 men from our place and I brought them back to Lunga. We worked there until the war was almost over. Nori and Aliki Nono'oohimae had gone back to Malaita in 1944.

Two or three months after they got back to Kiu, Nori had gone to Sinalagu, while I was still on Guadalcanal. He called a meeting, to go on for three days.

'Elota of Ga'enaafou, a young man who by then was becoming prominent as a Kwaio feastgiver, recalled that first meeting (Keesing 1978:96).

I went down myself to the meeting at the government tax house at Gwee'abe. We talked for two days solidly—nobody slept, not even children. When the leaders from 'Are'are were pressing us and urging us so strongly, who could sleep? When we heard their plans, they sounded good. "If we work strongly we will free ourselves from the government. When we are free other kinds of people will come here to work with us. If American companies come, they will pay us well; and they will also fill up your boxes." We heard all that and were glad—even the old men.

Then they said that the Americans were our brothers. But before the war the King had not let them come to us. But now the Japanese had chased the British out, and the Americans had chased the Japanese out, they could help us. "If you do this work strongly, if you organize yourselves, the government will leave."

4. The hyphen indicates that a pronoun suffix is attached: *asi-gu*, 'my younger brother'; *asi-na*, 'his younger brother'.

Fifi'i had tried to organize the Kwaio when he had gone home in 1943, but he had been prevented from taking the lead by his senior relatives, Silifa, the government Headman, and Kwarialaena (Fifi'i's father's brother), his deputy. But they too were won over by Nori's rhetoric. Fifi'i (1989:62) remembered that

when the Americans were getting ready to leave, I went back to Sinalagu with my 24 men. When I got home, people told me, "A man named Nori came here. They came here on patrol and called a meeting; and we gathered for it. We decided to join the work they are doing. We're going to join, as though we were all close relatives, to work together and take care of one another."

I had to find out whether the Headmen were still opposed to my joining in. I found that Silifa and Kwarialaena had understood what Nori was saying, and they supported him. Silifa talked to me about it. "I was wrong about that work you tried to start, when I told you to drop it. Nori came and talked to us. I support what he's doing. I want you to go ahead and do it now. Lead the people the way I lead them as Headman, by treating them with kindness. If there's trouble sometime, let it come. But you have to be close to the people."

The Rule of Brotherhood had come.

11 Maasina Rule

Fifi'i led a Kwaio delegation to 'Are'are, to visit Nori and Aliki and the Headman, Hoasihau; and then to Small Malaita, where a man named Timothy George, who had grown up and been well educated in Queensland, had taken up local leadership. It was time to organize a political structure in Kwaio and other districts. (In building their political framework, the Malaitans used the structure of districts, "passages," and "tax lines" created by the government for their administrative purposes. This reactive nature of political resistance will be examined in more general and theoretical terms when Kwaio resistance has been followed into the onset of the 1990s.) Fifi'i's account (1989:62–66) continues:

When we got to Sinalagu, we held meetings there. Then we went to Uru and held another meeting. Then we went back to 'Oloburi and held meetings in the bush and on the coast. The people chose me to be the Head Chief, for all of Kwaio District. There were to be ten Head Chiefs, responsible over the chiefs in the subdistricts. The leaders were called Chiefs or Araha (our Kwaio word is *alafa*). We were the Araha Ba'ita, the Head Chiefs.

The people chose chiefs to represent each area. Geniria represented 'Oloburi. Nunumae, Sinalagu, along with 'Elota. Farage represented Uru, along with Maesubaa. We chiefs spoke about land. We talked about how, if we just stayed quiet, the government would come in and take our land away. They'd lie to us, and they'd give the land to outsiders. We had seen the big area of West Kwaio from Su'u to Kwa'a that had been taken by white people, who were making money from it.[1] The land belonged to the West Kwaio people. They had been tricked when the whites got title to it. We had seen what happened in the Russell Islands, where the local people had had all their land taken away. That's what we were worried about. So we went ahead with our work.

Before I got back from Guadalcanal, Nori had held a meeting in which he had talked about what he called the "pound head." It was Nori's and Aliki's own idea, not something Jackson or the other Americans had told us to do. The idea behind the "pound head" was this. If we collected a pound from every man, and put it aside in a fund, then if the government arrested us, we'd be able to use the money to hire a lawyer. We'd be able to fight our case, whatever happened.

Everyone contributed his pound. It wasn't like a tax: people only gave it once, and they kept track of who had contributed. People in each district kept the money. 'Elota and Nunumae kept the money for east Kwaio.

After I started to organize our people as their chief, Nori and about a hundred men went on a big tour. They came to Sinalagu and we met there. Nori talked with us about how we were going to put our plans into action. We decided that we needed a way to communicate our plans and interests to the government. "The government doesn't know what's in our minds, and we don't know what's in theirs. We have to ask for a meeting area where we can meet with them. If we have a place to meet, when the government makes its plans and intentions clear to us, we can reply to them."

Nori and I talked about the progress we had already made. "Even though the British government may do bad things to us, our message has been spread now. Our people have listened to our ideas and supported them. Even though they may kill us, even though they may do bad things to us, what we are demanding will come to pass. We can't be afraid."

Nori told the Kwaio chiefs, "All your people have to come down to the coast, so the government can see us, all joining together. We have to be joined

1. This area was known as Baunani Plantation, acquired by the Malaita Company and closely connected to the South Sea Evangelical Mission, which had its headquarters down the coast at Onepusu.

together, as if we were close relatives. Because if you all stay scattered through the mountains, the government won't see us. The government will think that we are just talking nonsense in making pronouncements about Maasina— 'brotherhood'—if we are all scattered in our separate places. We have to join together, and think as one mind, so the government will know it. Otherwise the government won't pay any attention to us.

"The second thing—nobody is to go and work on plantations. Plantations are there so Europeans can make money from our work. But we have to resist that. The government and the plantation companies work together against us. If we hit a white man there, we go to prison. But if a white man hits us, nothing happens to him. They live in good quarters, we are treated like dirt.

"The third thing is that we have to refuse to pay taxes to them. When they satisfy our conditions, when they agree to give us some power and do the things we are asking for, then we'll pay the tax.

"The fourth thing is the census. The government wants the census for their own purposes. But we won't allow them to take our names, and count us.

"Whatever work the government tells us to do, we have to refuse to do it. We don't get paid for it. We built the big 'road' around Malaita with our hands, our knives and our axes. But we didn't get paid for it. We just had to do it for nothing. We had to do it so the District Officers and District Commissioners could tour around. But they didn't pay us for our labour. We've had to unload their cargo, build rest houses for them. We've had enough of it.

"They just deceived us. So now, whatever they tell us, we won't believe them any more. If they arrest us, they arrest us. If they kill us, they kill us. And all of us—women and children as well as men—have to stand together.

"If they let us have our own council to represent our interests, and if they let us have chiefs representing our side, then we can work with the government. If our representatives agree that something the government proposes is all right for their people, then it can go ahead. But the way it is now, the government just parades its power, and our side never gets heard.

"To show them we are strong, you have to come down to the coasts and make big buildings there where you can stay and hold meetings. Then when the government and the police come around, they can see all of you joined together, and they can see how strong we are. Don't be afraid. The government will hear our side if they see us standing strongly together."

'Elota (Keesing 1978b:96–98) recalls:

We started to do that work. We built communal villages for people to gather. We built one on the coast, and one in the mountains. We made lots of things. . . . We built our communal village at Fanuariri; all of us Waariu people were there. We worked hard to feed everybody. That cost us a lot of [shell] money. We decided to make a big pig farm at Waariu. We made fences and gathered all our pigs together. . . . We built a village down at the seacoast at Gelebasi, and made a big communal farm of sweet potatoes and pineapples. We had another big communal garden at 'Osi, another at Fanuariri. We built palisades and watchtowers in the village at Gelebasi: people said the government might come and invade us.

Fifi'i (1989:66) explains the rationale for these communal farms.

The projects we started there—farms for pineapples, and things—were for business. We organized the planting of pineapples and coconuts, so we could sell them. We expected that we could sell them to Europeans, as well as to one another. People made the farms in big collective work groups, so they belonged to everyone, not just to individuals. We wanted to have big, impressive projects partly so the government could see that we were working hard to get things done, not just sitting around talking. The farm we made at Gelebasi was for pineapples: acres and acres of them. . . . Lots of people bought the pineapples. The money was saved with the other Maasina Rule money that had been collected. That was for business.

Fifi'i's recollections, recounted in 1983 after a long career as parliamentarian, note the irony in the Protectorate Government's condemnation of these Maasina Rule projects: "Nowadays everyone is talking about 'development.' They forget the work we did back then to develop ourselves, all working together. Nowadays, everyone is greedy, trying to make money himself at the expense of his own brothers and his own people. Things were different in the days of real Brotherhood" (1989, 66).

Kwaio organization during Maasina Rule calls for closer examination. The local lineages that are the independent corporate groups and political units among the Kwaio are tiny and fragmented; there are dozens of them. Because of deviations from the ideal agnatic pattern and their fragmentation, membership is often overlapping or ambiguous. This fragmented social structure was hardly suited to a coherent new political order. Indeed, it had not suited the purposes of Bell and his administrative clerk Makasi when they had extended the tax to the Kwaio. In northern Malaita, small local descent-based groups are tied together (although not necessarily very neatly) into segmentary hierarchies, organized in ritual, that culminate in eight clans. The higher, more inclusive levels, articulated with an administrative classification of "passages" (i.e., anchorages, as conceptualized and named in the days of the nineteenth-century Labour Trade), had provided the "lines" according to which tax collection was organized. When they got to the east Kwaio "passages" of Uru, Sinalagu ["Sinarango"] and 'Oloburi, Bell's To'abaita (north Malaita) clerk Makasi had looked for the equivalent of the eight north Malaita clans. Instead he found only the dozens of Kwaio descent groups, too cumbersome for organizing the tax rolls according to "lines." The Kwaio Headmen were left to invent for Makasi a vastly reduced and agglomerated set of "lines." They did so by taking clusters of descent groups within a local area, tied together by skeins of intermarriage, cognatic kinship, and exchange, and arbitrarily assigning a name to each. Thus "Waariu" was used to label a cluster of a dozen descent groups at the top of the mountain wall above Sinalagu and inland from it—Bole, Darilari, Fouafoafo'a, Ga'enaafou, Kwaina'afi'a, Kwaini, 'Ola'o, etc.

When the Kwaio constructed an overarching political counterstructure in Maasina Rule, it followed this pattern that had been created by the administration. The Kwaio District had a Head Chief. Each "passage"—Uru, Sinalagu, 'Oloburi—had a Full Chief. Each "line"—Waariu, Kwangafi, Kwailala'e—had a Chief. The same scheme, fraught with ambiguities and contradictions in its actual application, was being used in anticolonial "custom" activities during my early fieldwork in the 1960s.

If we look at the roster of Kwaio Chiefs in the Maasina Rule period, we find some names that had emerged in earlier Kwaio confrontations with Europeans and their power. Some, like Alefo of Ngudu, were among the warriors in the attack on Bell's police twenty years earlier. They included as well 'Alakwale'a, one of the two assassins of Fred Daniels in 1911.

Another figure who became prominent as a Chief in Maasina Rule was the older son of Bell's assassin Basiana, 'Abaiata ["Abiathar"] Anifelo. He had been fourteen when his father killed Bell, and fifteen when he was forced to watch him die on the scaffold. In Tulagi, he was kept by the police, and trained as their bugler. He was "rescued" by women of the South Sea Evangelical Mission, and taken to their Bible school at Onepusu on the west Malaita coast. There, he was taught in Pijin to be a catechist. Although he has remained a dedicated Christian in the years since,[2] like many of the SSEM teachers he rebelled during Maasina Rule against the racism and paternalism of the mission and the way the knowledge made available to Malaitans was limited to the Bible and Pijin

2. Wavering at least once, at the end of the 1960s, when he set into motion the rituals to return to the mountains as a pagan. His brother Laefiwane remained a pagan throughout his life, and was a firebrand extremist in separatist antigovernment politics in the late 1970s and early 1980s.

rather than English. As a Maasina Rule Chief, he spoke bitterly about the government and about the missions.

Although a solid political unity had been built up in the southern half of Malaita, the situation in the north was more precarious. It was in To'aba'ita and Lau and around the government station at 'Aoke ("Auki") that the administration had extended patronage and substantial power to local Headmen and had built up two generations of loyal police, who had been the core of the 1927 punitive expedition. The power of the Headmen was often locally pitted against the power of SSEM leaders. It was the latter—men like Arnon Atoomea of Malu'u and Jastas Jimi Ganifiri in east Kwara'ae—who joined with the pagans in supporting Maasina Rule. The white missionaries, even the SSEM patriarch Norman Deck at Ngongosila, were driven from their churches by local catechists bitter at the way education (other than the Bible taught in Pijin) had been withheld from them, and at the paternalist condescension and racism of the missionaries who treated them as children.

In this climate, the Headmen had every interest in discrediting the movement. Fifi'i's account (1989:66–68) recounts how Nori and Aliki Nono'oohimae took their message to the Lau people of the northwestern lagoons:

> They had a meeting there with Tome Wate and Timi Kakalu'ae, the Lau Headmen, who were close to the government.[3] Those two Headmen deceived Nori. Nori explained his plans and his policies to them. They listened to what he had to say. Then they went back and reported what he had told them to the government. They did their best, in making their report, to discredit Nori and Maasina Rule. They could see it threatened their power. They turned everything Nori had said around so as to discredit him. They didn't tell the government what he had really told them.[4]
>
> The government wrote it all down. All the deceptions and distortions in the reports they were given were taken as truth and written down. We heard what was being said about us by the government. But we weren't deterred. We went ahead. . . .
>
> All the Malaita people joined together in Maasina Rule.[5] It was only the few places where there were strong Headmen who had been well rewarded for

3. See Keesing n.d.6.

4. See Laracy 1983 for extracts from the trial testimony of Kakalu'ae and other government witnesses.

5. Government reports in 1947–48 estimated that 96% of the Malaita population were involved in Maasina Rule.

their government service, and where the communities had been rewarded as well, that remained loyal to the government. There was Timi Kakalu'ae at Adagege, and Tome Wate at Sulufou. There was Siho at Small Malaita.

Those Headmen lied about us. They sent false reports to the District Commissioner in 'Aoke, and to the police. They said we wanted to throw the British out and form our own government. But we never said that we wanted to throw the British out, and govern ourselves. What we wanted was the power to represent our side.

The British were outraged, and denounced what we were doing. They sent out their version of it all. "You don't understand, you aren't educated. You native people are being treated really well. People working on plantations are being paid well, are sleeping on good beds; the government is taking good care of them, and they're very happy. They're treated just like white people." The government was lying, trying to discredit us. They started to threaten to arrest us. . . .

We called a meeting in 'Aoke. We wanted to talk openly to the government, to make clear what we were really saying and really demanding. What we decided to tell them was this. "You, the government, have to give us power, so that we can stand as equals. We want all of us to be able to work together. Our side has been treated badly. But this is our homeland, the Solomon Islands. It's our homeland. You are the ones who just came and invaded this place. You imposed your laws on us. You've crushed us down."

About five hundred of us went to 'Aoke, to take these demands to the District Commissioner. The District Commissioner then was Major Sandars. People from all over Malaita were with us. But people who wanted to discredit us came too. We got there, and Nori went to Major Sandars. He said, "Major Sandars, I want you to meet with us on the playing field tomorrow. We want to put some points to you."

He said, "All right." So the next day, everyone gathered there on the playing field. Nori got up and spoke: "We have come today to talk to you as Maasina—as brothers. We come as a single family. We all stand together as brothers. Up to now, we have all been divided. We were one another's enemies. But now we are here as brothers, as if we were all children of the same father and the same mother. Our minds speak as one.

"You, the government, have done many good things. You have stopped us from killing one another. You've put a stop to bad things we used to do. But our minds are not satisfied. We are treated as if we were dirt. We are treated as if we were maggots. We aren't give a decent status. We don't stand as your equals, you the white men—you the government. We want to stand as your equals. We want an equal say over what is going to happen in our country. We want, if there is trouble concerning our side, to be able to meet with you about it and straighten it out. The way things are now, if something wrong happens, you meet and decide what to do about it. You know what's happening and you make all the decisions. We don't know what's happening. You are the people with the police, the guns, the prison. So if something wrong happens, we're afraid to stand up for our side. We want to have a say in what happens."

Major Sandars replied: "Why aren't you satisfied? The government is looking after you. Killing has been stopped. Blood money is no longer put up for people to be killed. Why do you want to stand by yourselves?"

Nori responded. "It's true that the killing is finished. But we saw during the war that other black people aren't treated like dirt, the way we are. Why are they educated, while we aren't? Why do they get paid good wages, while we get only a pittance? Why are they able to sit in chairs, and mix with white people in their houses, and we're not allowed to? Why are they treated as the equals of white people? If a black man is an officer, whites have to salute him. They have to respect him. Why is it that you whites treat us like dirt?"

Major Sandars was prepared to recognize not the general injustices of colonial rule and racism, but the demands for higher plantation wages: he offered to help them bargain for increased plantation wages. Fifi'i (1989:69–70) recalls what happened when the leaders discussed his response.

Some of us spoke strongly. "We aren't just talking about money. He acted as if all we wanted was higher wages, as plantation workers. The wages are only part of it. That will come, if we have a position of power we can speak from. What we're talking about is having representatives who have power recognized by the government to speak for our side, and to talk from the standpoint of our customs. We want power for our Chiefs. We want our representatives to speak for our land. If anything is wrong, we want our representatives to be able to express our point of view. That's what's important to us. It's not just money we want. That will come. But it will come in good time, if our side is strong. We have to gain political recognition and power first." It was as though Major Sandars was just trying to bribe us into giving up our political demands by promising us more money. That wasn't what we wanted.

So Nori and some of us met with Major Sandars again that afternoon. "That's not what the people want. They want their Chiefs to be given power, to speak for their custom and for the interests of their people. Because you, the government, don't know about our customs. You come and hold courts and judge cases. But you don't know our rules for settling disputes, and you don't know the laws of our custom. So you go against our custom in your decisions, and we get angry about it." . . .

A second meeting was scheduled for 'Aoke. News went out to Makira and Ugi and Ulawa. Lots of them came to 'Aoke from those other islands on the day we had arranged. There were about a thousand people there in 'Aoke for the meeting. The station was overflowing with people. We gave a big feast when we gathered there. People brought lots of pigs and taro.

The day after we all assembled, Nori went to Major Sandars. He gave Major Sandars our answer: that we didn't just want higher wages; we wanted more freedom and more dignity. Nori said, "It doesn't matter what you do to us. We are going to keep fighting for the things we are demanding. We aren't going to be afraid. I know that you represent the government. If you want to put us in prison, go ahead! If you want to do bad things to us, go ahead! But we who have gathered here today have come prepared to be arrested, prepared to be tied up. We aren't afraid."

We didn't want to throw the government out. We were talking about our custom. We were talking about straightening out our customs, and writing them down. We wanted to follow our customs about compensation, and our custom laws about women. When someone did something wrong, they were to pay *totonga*; when someone did something tabu, they were to pay *siunga*,[6] to purify it. Then that would be the end of it. We didn't want that kind of a case to end up in government courts and be settled according to British laws. Their laws weren't fit for us and our customary way of living. Those weren't the kind of cases where someone was killed, or someone's property was stolen or destroyed. Those were the kinds of offences that were important to us, cases the government's laws didn't deal with properly.

We talked about it. "If they want to kill us, let them go ahead and do it. We can't be afraid. This is our land. This is our island. We have to hold fast to our customs and to our demands. We saw the other black people who came here during the war. They were well provided for. They were well educated. They wore good clothes. They slept in good beds. They had good quarters and good offices. But what about us? We just have to sit on the bare ground. If we talk to a European, we have to stand outside the house and just talk through the door. We aren't allowed to come in. Those other black people are well treated; but we're treated like rubbish."

It was after this meeting that a Kwara'ae man named Kefu[7] began to spread a message that the Americans were going to come and force the British out, as they had expelled the Japanese. On Malaita, where supernatural interventions are assumed to be everyday occurrences, what ap-

6. Here Fifi'i is giving the Kwaio terms. Similar categories of compensation are recognized in all the other Malaita languages.
7. Or "Kifo."

peared to the Western eye as fantastic rumors—often nowadays
incorporating Biblical elements—spread like forest fires (when I returned from a break in fieldwork in late 1963, I was greeted with some
surprise: many had heard that my ship had sunk and I had been swallowed
by a whale). Fifi'i (1989:71–72) recalls that

we didn't know what to make of what Kefu had told us. He was just lying to us,
but we couldn't be sure whether to believe him or not. We thought he was one
of us. Some people thought the Americans were really going to come, and
waited for them. Kefu called another meeting at Naafinua, and again he told us
that the Americans were going to come. "The Americans are going to come. I
know all about it." Well, we'd seen some pretty amazing things during the war,
so it wasn't impossible. But I don't know where he got that idea. I don't know
if he believed it himself, or whether he was just trying to lead our work astray.

He sent letters around to our passages, telling us to go and wait in the dark
for the Americans to come. "The Americans will come ashore at night. Go
and wait for them." The message we got was that a submarine was going to put
people ashore at Farisi. If they arrived, we were supposed to blow a conch shell
to signal their arrival. People waited at Farisi that night, but of course nothing
happened. . . .

The government supporters . . . wanted the followers of Maasina Rule to
wait for those promised miracles, so that when nothing happened, they would
abandon their leaders and give up the movement.

Kefu was the one . . . who spread those ideas around. . . . But his teachings
didn't follow the things we'd been advocating, and the things we'd been working for. He wanted to take it all in a different direction. What we had been
fighting for was a government that respected us black people, and served and
protected our interests. We wanted to have leaders for our side, and meetings
where we could negotiate with the government. We wanted a proper return for
our work, and a proper return for our taxes. We wanted education. We wanted
our customs respected.

12 Repression

Although events in India and at home were forcing the British to assess
the pre-war style of colonial rule and the empire it sustained, news of all
that had hardly reached the Solomons. With the copra industry shat-

tered by the war and many plantations in ruins, with a labor force refusing to work, and after a massive loss of face vis-à-vis the Americans, the government faced the urgent task of restoring colonial rule, white supremacy, the British presence, and the economy. Maasina Rule was an affront and an obstacle on all counts. After initial sympathy for some aspects of the movement on the part of Sandars, in 1947, the administration sent in new, tough District Commissioner and District Officers with the mandate of breaking "Marching Rule."

They were amply supplied with testimony from the Headmen and other loyalists supporting a view that the "Marching Rule" Chiefs were a handful of local tyrants extorting money and labor from unwilling followers using squads of thugs, and advocating violent rebellion. If the "Chiefs" could be pulled from their midst, a grateful populace would return to the fold, loyal to their distant King and ready to work once more on the plantations. A plan to arrest the leaders, using loyal police from the Western Solomons, was formulated—quaintly codenamed "Operation De-Louse"—and set into motion in June 1947.

Kwaio Head Chief "Jonathan Fifi" was one of the targets; and the strike to arrest him at Sinalagu almost resulted in a repeat of the 1927 massacre at Gwee'abe, a few hundred yards down the harbor. Fifi'i (1989:78–80) 81) recalls:

Word started to go around: "They're going to arrest you. The government is saying it's going to arrest you." But we leaders, and our people who followed us in Maasina Rule, weren't afraid. "Even though they arrest us, even if they kill us, the work we are doing has to go ahead. We can't be afraid." . . .

People said that Mr. Cameron and the police Sergeant Dauburi from Choiseul and a police detachment were coming to arrest me. Everyone heard about it. The other Chiefs and I talked about what to do. I told them, "Even if they arrest me, don't give up. Don't be discouraged. If they arrest us, the people you have chosen as your leaders, don't be angry—no matter what happens to us."

Some of the men from the bush said to me, "When the police come, we'll have a test of strength with them. We'll try to take them. If we can overcome them, we won't kill them. We'll just let them go." That was before the police came.

But I didn't believe these warriors. Because if there is a test of strength and one warrior overcomes another, the one who has lost the test is likely to taunt him: "Go ahead and kill me!" If that happens, then there will be killing. I said to them, "You chiefs, don't lie to me. I'm a Kwaio man. I know all about our ways. I know that if you overcome these police, they will be too proud just to let themselves be captured. They'll taunt you and you'll end up killing them. You who are saying you're going to have a test of strength with the police—I can't allow you to do it. I can't let you do it."

Other people said, "When they come, if you renounce Maasina Rule in front of them, if you make a curse against Maasina Rule, they won't arrest you. But if you stand steadfast, if you stand up for Maasina Rule, they'll arrest you." I replied, "I'm not going to give up what I believe in, just to save myself. I'll stand up to them, and if they arrest me, let them arrest me. I'm not afraid, no matter what happens.

"If I turn my back on Maasina Rule, you people will say that when things were going well, I was proud and I talked strongly. But you'll say that when the chips were down, I just turned my back in fear. Timi Kakalu'ae and Tome Wate would hear and think I was a coward. But I'm a Kwaio man. When I decide to do something, I do it. I don't give up because I'm afraid."

We heard that they were coming in two days to arrest me. The day before they were to come, everyone from the whole Kwaio District, even from the mountains above Anoano, came down to the coast at Sinalagu—men, women and children. . . . Everyone gathered at Gelebasi, where the police were supposed to come.

The government ship arrived, with the "army" on board—the police from Choiseul. A man named Dauburi was with them. He was their Sergeant Major. The white man who was in charge of them was named Cameron. He was the Captain of police. They arrived in late afternoon, on the *Nancy,* and just anchored there. They slept on the ship that night.

That night, I told the people "Don't just sit there. Play your bamboo panpipes. Hit your leaf packets.[1] I don't want you to be angry or sad tomorrow. I want you to be in high spirits when tomorrow comes. If we just sit here in silence, the people on the ship will think we're afraid."

At dawn, the police sent word that they were coming ashore. Alefo, a man from the bush who had been in the massacre in that same spot at Gwee'abe twenty years before,[2] came to me and said, "We'll lie to them. When they ask for you, we'll say, "Who is Fifi'i? We don't know anyone by that name. Where is he from? Show him to us." Then we'll see how they react. Then we'll have a test of strength. We'll set on those police, wrestle them to the ground. If you allow us to, we'll take their rifles. But we won't kill them."

1. When a Kwaio panpipe orchestra plays at a feast, women and children slap packets of leaves and sway back and forth in time to the music.
2. The Bell massacre in 1927. Alefo was the younger brother of Maenaafo'oa, one of the three principal leaders of the 1927 massacre. Alefo, from 'Ailai (=Ngudu) was himself imprisoned in Tulagi for fourteen years for killing a policeman in the massacre.

I said, "Even though that's what you say, I don't believe you. I don't want
the 1927 massacre and the terrible things that happened afterwards to happen
all over again. I don't believe you. If they ask for me, I'll just identify myself. I
don't want any killing today. I don't want any trouble. Even though you say
you won't kill anyone, I don't believe you. There's only me who is in trouble: I
can't put all of you in danger, in case something really terrible happens."

Our warriors had three hundred rifles or so, rifles they'd got during the
war—the kind of rifle we called "campaign," with lots of ammunition. They
didn't bring the rifles into the clearing. There were different groups with their
rifles, and they stayed in the bush, hidden. "If the police from Choiseul want to
make trouble for us, then we'll be ready for them. If they want to shoot our
leader, we'll get them in revenge. If Dauburi wants to show us how tough his
army is, we'll show them how tough ours is. We'll show them the strength of
Kwaio warriors. We won't kill anyone, though. We'll just throw them down
and tie them up." But I didn't want that to happen: they could just as well have
been lying to me—and when they said they were going to tie the police up,
they might have killed them instead.

In 1986, almost forty years later, at exactly the same place, Kwaio warriors armed with rifles lay in hiding waiting for another confrontation
with the police; in the end, mass bloodshed was averted by a hair. Among
the warriors were some who had been there in 1947. These continuities
in Kwaio resistance are dramatic and compelling. We here find Alefo
ready to fight the government again. Kwai'ime and other veterans of the
Gwee'abe massacre were there as well. Warriors like Basiitau, whose fathers and uncles had attacked the government force in 1927, were lying
in wait to attack the government force in 1947; and were waiting to attack again in the late 1980s, forty years later.

Fifi'i (1989:80–81) continues:

The police came ashore. . . . Moses and 'Abana stayed in the dinghy, out
in the ocean, with a machine gun. All of us—men, women and children—
were just sitting down in the clearing above the beach. Mr. Cameron and
Dauburi marched up to where we were. The police came up behind them.
There were 16 of them, those Choiseulese—people from Lauru. We got up,
and they came marching up with fixed bayonets. They got there and stood in
formation. All the Kwaio men were waiting for them. One lot of Kwaio men
was focused on each of them.

I said to the men around me, "I can't stay hidden. Don't try to hide me. Let
them take me. We can't keep control of what you might do. There might be
something like the Gwee'abe massacre all over again, and that would be the
ruin of us. The police are prepared for trouble."

Mr. Cameron spoke: "Marching Rule is a bad thing." They never got the
name of our movement right. "You are just deceived by it. The government is
good. The Americans came; they were no good, and they lied to you. So you
just have to give it up today, and not do it any more. You should let the Protectorate government just look after you and take care of you. If you don't give up
Marching Rule, the government will arrest you. If you don't give it up, the
government will strike you down, and you'll be left with nothing.

The Kwaio challenged him: "Where are you from? We don't know you!" All
the people gathered there at Gelebasi stood up and faced him. Then he asked
"Where is Fifi?" In forty years, the British have never got my name right, either. "Which one of you is Jonathan?" Our people said, "Who is that you're
asking about? Where's he from?"

"Your Marching Rule leader."

"We don't know anyone by that name."

Mr. Cameron said, "Hurry up and point him out to us!"

"We won't show anyone to you." They shouted back and forth.

I put up my hand. "Here I am." I stood up and came forward. I went to
Cameron. I knew that he was a bad man. I also knew that all those warriors
were there in the bush, concealed, with their rifles. "Slap him in the mouth!"
one of them called out. I went and stood with Dauburi and Mr. Cameron.

At that moment, several hundred warriors gave a war scream together.
The police were so frightened they were shaking in their boots. One of them
dropped his rifle. Moses . . . and 'Abana . . . stood in the boat with their machine gun. They picked up the magazine ready to load it. They tried to fit it
onto the machine gun. But they were so frightened they dropped it into the
sea. 'Abana jumped in after it and dived to find it, but came up empty-handed.

But I went with Cameron and Dauburi and the police down to the dinghy.
People called out to me, "If that's the way you want it, then you can go." I replied, "Even though I'm going, and even if I'm imprisoned for a long time, I'll
come back to you. Even if I'm an old man when they let me out, you have to
let it be and remain peaceful."

Fifi'i goes on (1989:81–82) to recount how the ship continued around
the island, arresting the Maasina Rule Chiefs. At the loyalist stronghold
of Sulufou, he was taunted:

"You are all crazy. We're standing with the government. We're not going to
mess things up for ourselves. You people are crazy!" I called out in reply, "It's
all right if we're crazy. That's up to us. You want to stay loyal to the government that feeds you, the government that's kind to you, the government that
gives you money, that's up to you. Go ahead! We're the crazy ones."

In the months that followed, Fifi'i and his fellow Chiefs were subjected to physical violence and threat, while the government cast about for an offense for which they could be tried. In their frustration, the British turned to intimidation:

They told us that if we all signed statements that we had been wrong and had lied, and if we went back to Malaita and told the people that they were being foolish, then they'd release us. . . . But we didn't believe them, and we weren't prepared to betray our cause.

Then a man from Fiji came . . . to frighten us, by testing the gallows they had built behind the place where we were locked up. Our warders said, "Oh, he's come to test the gallows. If you are tried and lose, they're going to hang you." We said, "That's up to them. Whatever happens to us happens to us. If they kill us, they kill us." . . .

"You Chiefs from Malaita, they are going to take you to a far-away island, and keep you there in exile. Just the nine of you are going to be deposited there." We said, "Whatever you do to us, you the government, you go ahead and do it. We didn't do what we did for your country, for England. We did it for our island, and for our land. We were born in our homeland, we grew up in our homeland. Our ancestors founded our homeland. But you've come, and you threaten to kill us. You threaten to send us away from our own country. But we haven't been doing anything wrong." Eventually they came to make formal charges against us (Fifi'i 1989:83–84).

In the end, they were charged with violating the British Sedition Act of 1798. Fifi'i comments wryly (1989:85) that

they charged us with holding seditious meetings. That was the kind of law that was used by the Romans when the Jewish priests turned Jesus in. We were imprisoned for holding secret meetings: that's what Jesus was convicted for. But we didn't hold secret meetings. How can meetings be secret when people come from all over the island to attend them? We were on our own island, trying to follow our own customs. We were speaking about our own land. The people of our homeland had chosen us to represent them. We were meeting to talk about our customs, about our land, about finding ways that were right for our people. For that, we were charged with holding secret meetings, under a law that was enacted far away in England in 1798—long before the British had invaded our country.

The nine Chiefs were sentenced to six years hard labor—even denied the legal means to lodge an appeal. Yet the British, who had expected the grateful Malaitans—once de-loused—to become loyalists again, faced a new array of Chiefs and a defiant population. 'Elota (Keesing 1978b:97) recalls that

even though they had been arrested and imprisoned, our work remained strong and we remained steadfast. We made big farms together. Our villages were strong. We worked hard for *kastomu* ["custom"]—that was what we called our work. We worked on straightening out and writing down the things that were taboo, and the history of the land, and the shrines. The old people heard what we were doing and were glad. So our work went ahead even though Fifi'i and the other chiefs were arrested, tried, convicted, and imprisoned.

The solidarity achieved during Maasina Rule, uniting Christians and pagans, Kwaio and 'Are'are, kin groups and old enemies, was remarkable. In some ways, it entailed the realization of a potential order foreshadowed in pacification: a Malaita project to achieve politically and socially what had been impossible in the days of blood feuding.

The old divisive pressures, the old enmities and the male pride that fuelled them, the old temptations to steal and seduce, remained; they were kept below the surface much of the time by rhetoric and collective pressure, but they recurrently exploded into view. 'Elota (ibid., 98ff.) recalled that

we were all suposed to join together, to live together in peace, to work as one people. But people didn't always have good sense. I had to work hard trying to keep the peace. . . .

We had problems living in big villages. There were sexual affairs that caused trouble. And some people still stole pigs. Those were the things that provoked the kinds of feuds we had always had. We who were leading had to try to keep the peace.

'Elota went on to recount confrontations, feuds narrowly averted. He remembered (ibid., 100) that "there were troubles in those days we couldn't prevent. Troubles over stolen pigs, troubles over seduced girls."

Maasina Rule was in many ways a men's project, one heavily dependent on women's labor. It is worth pausing to look at the perspectives of Kwaio women toward pacification, and toward the unity of Christian and pagan communities forged during Maasina Rule. We have seen (chap. 2) that Kwaio women had a deep ambivalence toward blood feuding and male aggression. On the one hand, the threat of execution could be portrayed ideologically as a force for virtuous living: chastity, honesty, responsible observance of pollution taboos, and hard work are idealized as moral virtues. Indeed, a woman or girl who ignored pollution taboos or

failed to report an involuntary transgression put lives collectively in danger of ancestral punishment—illness, death, or grave misfortune. The
irresponsible risked death at the hands of their own kin, directly or through
being given up to enemies as a vengeance victim. As Oloi'a put it,

> I saw the men who had been killers. We little children were afraid of them,
> we whimpered and ran away. We saw them and shook with fright. But nowa-
> days young people aren't afraid of anything at all. People of our parents' gen-
> eration saw people who killed. They saw killing. They were afraid, that's why
> they steered clear of bad ways. In my generation, we were afraid too, because
> we believed the grownups when they warned us what would happen.
>
> In the old days they'd kill a woman who urinated in the house, or men-
> struated—kill her for their purification, to purify that place. The women in the
> old days were afraid of that! So women didn't go around menstruating. They
> didn't hide their pollution violations, didn't go around defiling places. . . .
>
> But the young people of our children's generation don't know about what
> happened in those days, so they're not afraid of the consequences. They aren't
> afraid of being killed. They aren't afraid of any of those things from the old
> days—they are just thinking about how things are now. And nowadays, what-
> ever someone does, however badly someone messes things up, nobody thinks
> of killing them. They only think of [settling the matter with] talk.

Fa'afataa put it more briefly, but with metaphoric eloquence:

> People nowadays don't realize what it was to live amid people who lived
> with threats and anger, who killed and seduced and fought. The taro had sting-
> ing crystals then, but now it is all soft and sweet: soft with foreign ways. The
> customs used to stand straight up, but now they've been dug out and set askew.
> What is there to be afraid of, to keep you from taking what you like and doing
> what you like? You slip and slide about, doing anything you please.

Maasina Rule put women in a new situation. It was the men who met,
talked endlessly, "straightening out the custom." Yet it was the women
whose labor had to feed and sustain the expanded communities, the endless meetings; it was women who had to do the daily work in the "communal" gardens while continuing to grow taro and yams and sweet potatoes
in family swiddens. It was women who had to feed the penned pigs, where
in scattered homesteads the pigs had foraged loose, penned in houses
only at night.

And although girls were constantly enjoined by mothers and older sisters to follow pollution taboos punctiliously, and these virtues were a
constant theme of men's—and women's own—talk about *kastomu*, the

strict separations of male and female realms were threatened by Maasina Rule's appeals to unity.

Several of the women from whom Shelley Schreiner and I recorded their perspectives on *kastomu*, virtue, and recent Kwaio history emphasized the shift in rules regarding pagan-Christian interaction and how they had deteriorated, especially during and since the time of Maasina Rule. Oloi'a summed up the changes and used them to explain the present:

My mother told me how, in the olden days, if you got something at a mission village, you couldn't put it in your bag. You'd have to tie it onto a stick and let it hang down. But not now. . . . Now . . . people there say, "Well the mission villages are like those foreign places" [i.e., the places abroad the men go to where people don't follow Malaita customs and where they are exposed— harmlessly—to pollution]. But that's not true. Those foreign places are different. . . . Foreign is foreign. What white people do is their business. When [men] go abroad, maybe they do mix up with foreigners, with women who are menstruating or giving birth. Maybe so—who knows? But in the mission villages, when a woman is menstruating, we can *see* it. They are the same people as we are.

Why don't men nowadays say the same things about the mission as they did when it first came? In the days of the old people, even a woman couldn't light her pipe from a coal in the mission villages. The food cooked [there] couldn't be eaten by any male, not even a young boy. They classed the mission villages as menstrual areas. Only a baby boy we still held in our arms, one who was still nursing, could eat food from there [such a male infant, in traditionalist communities, is taken to the menstrual hut by his mother].

In my parents' day—I remember this, because I went with them—if we went down to a mission village . . . all of us womenfolk would stay just at the mouth of the clearing. The men stayed at the mouth of the clearing. We put all our sacks there. If a woman was to visit with some woman or man in the mission village who was her close relative, she'd wait till they told her to come. Then she'd leave her pipe behind, she'd leave her bag behind. She couldn't even bring a coal from the mission village to kindle her pipe. She had to go there empty-handed. In those days when I was young, they cut paths that circled around those mission villages. I saw that with my own eyes. When we women went down to the mission, we didn't have skirts we put on. A girl who wasn't married yet had to go there naked. One who had a pubic apron [i.e., a married woman] would have only that on.

But that's not the way people follow the taboos nowadays. Christianity has caused our living to go bad. Now, even a [customary] priest will go to the mission village and ask for a coal [to kindle his pipe]. People say that's the rule that governs us now.

When Maasina Rule came, the men said, "We have to work close to the coast now, mixing up with the mission people. And those mission people have to mix up with us non-Christians ['wicked people']." And so bags were taken back and forth, people asked for tobacco back and forth, and for fire. Even men ate things from the bags of the mission people. And we women started to kindle our pipes from the coals of the mission people. "Oh, the men are taking their bags into the [mission] clearing." They were taking them into the clearing, and *they* were the ones who ate consecrated pigs. "When we go down to the mission, let's take our bags into the clearing. Let's leave our bags outside the church and peep inside. Let's kindle our pipes with their coals." The important men saw us do it and they said, "Oh, that's all right." That was the beginning of things turning in a different way.

The crossing of boundaries—the flaunting of old rules about sacredness and ancestors—is used to explain the dwindling power of the Kwaio traditionalists, in terms both of the withdrawing of ancestral support and of the weakening of the ancestors and their powers—powers that were sustained by the sacrifices of the living.

Men take bags they have had in mission villages into their shrines. They wear the clothes they've worn down there in the mission villages when they go into the [ancestral] shrines—even important men, men who eat consecrated pigs. But shrines are sacred. . . . In the old days a man would sacrifice there for success in fighting, to be able to kill. Nowadays . . . the ancestors are angry because we don't follow their rules properly.[3]

As we will see, this is a major continuing theme in contemporary interpretations of modern Kwaio history.

3. For these and other accounts of Christian life and recent history as characterized by Kwaio women, see Keesing 1989c.

13 *Kastomu*, Law, and Tax

The collective enterprises, the big meetings, the expanded communities, all gradually succumbed to internal pressures and contradictions as well as to external pressures from a repressive administration. By the time the nine Maasina Rule Chiefs were pardoned in 1953 (by intervention of a new High Commissioner sent from London to mend fences—he had helped rebuild bloody, shattered fences in Kenya), much of the idealism and political energy of Maasina Rule had been dissipated. Tiny Kwaio settlements spread across the bush again.

But the political goals of Maasina Rule, as conceived in the Kwaio mountains, remained clearly in view. The Kwaio pagans resisted the penetration of evangelistic Christianity into the mountains, resisted as best they could the imposition of alien laws and the exaction of the head tax.

A central theme for the past forty-five years has remained the one 'Elota hearkened back to in recalling Maasina Rule: "writing down" and "straightening out" *kastomu*. In the late 1950s, concern with *kastomu* began to catalyze again the political energies of Maasina Rule. Jonathan Fifi'i recalls (1989:104–5) how he was summoned back from 'Aoke, where he had been working in the Department of Agriculture, to help the pagans in their project of codifying *kastomu*.

They wanted me to help them work on custom. "Our customs here aren't straight," they were saying. "Things are getting messed up. The judgments that are supposed to be made according to custom aren't following our old ways. Some of our customs are being turned in the wrong way, and some of them are being lost. Come with us and help us work to straighten out the customs. We want you to help us write our generations, too—our genealogies."

I told the people in Agriculture that I wanted to quit. "My people have asked me to come back and work with them. So I want to quit."

I came back, and I started working with the leaders from the bush. "We want you to write the customs. We want you to write down everything about the land. We want you to write down our generations." I told them that I really didn't know how to do it properly. "Well, do the best you can." They were afraid that their old customs were going to be lost. They were afraid that rights over the land would be lost track of. "We're worried about our old ways being lost." So in the last five months of 1961 and through 1962, I worked with them, writing down customs and generations and things about the land as best I could.

Our people were trying to write down their customs partly because of the work of the 'Are'are chief Waiparo of Takataka.[1] . . . Waiparo had said to his people, "All our customs are going to break down. It's not the same for us as it is for Europeans. They write things down in books. We see in their Bible how everything is recorded: the generations, the passing of the years. But we pass our custom down from generation to generation, and unless we preserve it, it will break down and eventually disappear as the elders die. We have to raise it up and make it strong, and we have to write it down so it won't be lost."

People at Sinalagu heard about his [Waiparo's] work. "When we worked on Maasina Rule, *kastomu* was a part of it. But now, Waiparo is working on *kastomu*, but we're not doing anything about it. We want to do it for ourselves." People from 'Oloburi—Geniriria and Nunumae—took up his idea. So did Maesubaa from Uru. In our place, 'Elota started talking about this work of writing the custom down. They said, "What he says about raising up the custom, what he warns us against—customs being messed up or forgotten—is true."

Waiparo had picked up the Small Malaita title of Araha 'Ou'ou as the chief who was supposed to be in charge of customs. That idea had been around in the time of Maasina Rule: having a chief who would speak for the side of custom, and help settle disputes according to our traditional customs. . . .

Some of Waiparo's people were trying to get Kwaio people to join in their work, and pay lots of shell money to have their generations recorded at Takataka. But the leaders in our area were trying to write down their *own* customs, with me as their scribe. That was why they had asked me to come back.

The project of "writing down" and "straightening out" *kastomu*, which has been so central in Kwaio ideologies of resistance, requires clarification in several directions. First, what do Kwaio mean by *kastomu*? The label obviously comes from English "custom," but that does not tell us local meanings. *Kastomu* corresponds roughly to the Kwaio terms *tagi* or *fui'ola* (lit., "bunch of things"), in referring to the realm of customs, knowledge, rules, and taboos related to ancestors (and hence, the land and knowledge of the past as well as "religious" customs). But *kastomu*, and the project of writing it down, have an emotional salience and a political force that go far beyond any ideas Kwaio may have had about their way of life prior to European invasion. It is this added force that demands explication; and this will be a theme for the rest of the book. We can well have a first look at these questions now.

First of all, there is the apparent contradiction between talking about customs and enacting them in one's everyday life. The Malaitans united in anticolonial struggle in the 1940s have gone along very different paths

1. See Coppet and Zemp 1978.

in the intervening decades. As I have observed (Keesing 1982b), some of
the Malaitans who nowadays make rhetorical pronouncements about
"custom" and fill endless exercise books with "generations" (genealogies)
and lists of taboos have long been Christian; and many are embarked on
projects of cash-cropping, cattle-raising, or petty entrepreneurship.
Why, if you have abandoned your ancestral religion in favor of a white
God and Jesus, left the land where your ancestors lived, abandoned the
rules and ways and values enjoined by your forebears, should you talk endlessly and rhetorically about the "custom" you have mainly given up?
And equally puzzling, why—if you are still sacrificing to your ancestors,
living on the lands they cleared centuries ago, following their rules—do
you need to "straighten out" or write down the customs you are following
anyway? Indeed, as I have pointed out (Keesing 1968a), in the contexts
where Kwaio invoke *kastomu* most rhetorically, they defer to the authority of "chiefs" that do not act as such anywhere but in a *bungu 'ifi* ["meeting area"] on a Tuesday afternoon.

A partial answer, at least for the Kwaio, lies in the disintegration and
disappearance of customary practice and knowledge in other parts of the
Solomons, which the Kwaio pagans view as a concomitant of the alienation of land and the loss of local autonomy. We will see this as a recurrent
them of Kwaio rhetoric: the people of the Russell Islands, center of the
Lever plantations where they have worked for decades, have lost their
customs and lost their lands. So have people in the Western Solomons,
and on Guadalcanal; and even their own cultural cousins inland from the
western coast of Kwaio country, where plantation lands were alienated
decades ago. For the Kwaio, writing down genealogies and histories of
lands and shrines provides the foundation for their struggle to hold their
homeland against invasion by plantation (and now logging) interests.

Writing *kastomu*, in the form of lists of shrines, lands, and ancestral
genealogies, and in the form of ancestrally enjoined taboos, also provides
a defense against invasion by the Christian evangelists on the Kwaio
coast. This, too, has been a continuing theme in the political rhetoric of
the pagans; we will see it expressed in 1990, as it was in the 1960s.

Finally, writing down *kastomu* is seen as a mode of struggle for customary autonomy, for the legitimacy of customary law (in opposition to the
alien laws of the colonial state, and now the postcolonial state). *Kastomu*
is sometimes conceptualized as *loa*, "law." A central element in Kwaio
political struggle for 45 years has been a sustained effort to codify customary law in a form parallel and counter to the British-derived legal statutes
that have been an instrument of their subjugation. For half a century,

Kwaio have been getting imprisoned, and until recent times, hanged, for homicides deemed legitimate in customary law—sentenced by magistrates citing the written statutes of the white man's law. For half a century, offenses that are heinous in customary law—adultery has been the main sore point—have been dealt with lightly, by magistrates citing the same lawbooks. Where fines or imprisonment have been meted out by colonial (and now postcolonial) magistrates, the aggrieved parties get no compensation or satisfaction, as they would in customary law: it is the state that exacts redress. Two generations of Kwaio ideologues have imagined that if they could confront the government with *their* laws in a similarly codified format, they could demand their recognition and legitimation.

During Maasina Rule, a major demand had been for courts run by the Malaitans themselves, according to customary law. When the Protectorate Government attempted a reconciliation by freeing the Chiefs and forming a Malaita Council (initially, with virtually no powers), a system of "Native Courts" in which local elders sat as experts on custom was instituted. In the Kwaio situation, with Christians in the coastal villages praying against the ancestors and violating their rules and defiling their sacred places as a matter of political confrontation with the pagans, and with some Christians refusing bridewealth and compensation for sexual offenses as a matter of scriptural principle (and thus denying the rights of their own kin), there was no easy way to resolve disputes that cut across Christian and pagan communities (Keesing 1967b, 1989c). The pagans mainly rejected the Native Court, controlled as it was by coastal Christians and subject as it was to government review; they settled their own disputes and pressed for a legal system they controlled themselves.

To a nonliterate people, writing is a special magic, a special medium of power. The Christians, too, have their own codified sacred charter, their own Biblical genealogies in the form of begats and their Ten Commandments; so that in militant defense of the ancestral ways against Christian invasion, writing becomes a key weapon, and one ancestrally empowered, as the Christians believe theirs to be divinely empowered.

Just as the codification of *kastomu* has become an historical leitmotiv of Kwaio resistance, so has defiance against the exaction of tribute in the form of a head tax. There can be few taxpayers who have expressed their grievances more dramatically than the Kwaio warriors who assassinated Bell and wiped out his tax collection party. The resistance has continued ever since: refusal to pay the head tax has been a more direct means of resisting domination than the writing of *kastomu*.

The Headmen and their deputies appointed during Maasina Rule, notably David ("Captain") Riddley at Sinalagu, had been staunchly loyalist, and mainly evangelical Christians. But they had limited means to deal with mass resistance by taxpayers who saw as clearly as their fathers had that the head tax was an instrument of subjugation and a device to force them into plantation work at low wages. The postwar administration lacked Bell's resolve and energy, and the constabulary no longer could or would impose domination by force. A District Commissioner wrote in his 1959 patrol report that "the [Kwaio] bushmen know quite well that we have not the resources to bring them all to court. Consequently, while their bloody-minded attitude persists there will always be a canker of discontent [in other areas]—if they don't pay, why should we?"

The historical ironies here are striking. When Bell had first been asked his opinion about the introduction of a head tax on Malaita, he had warned against the difficulties and hardships a tax would create, and pointed out the problems collecting it would pose. "There was virtually no economic development on the island, and few Malaitans would be able to raise even a nominal sum of money each year. The bush people could easily disperse and regroup to frustrate any attempt to tax them; and it would be unfair to tax only the coastal people" (Keesing and Corris 1980:75).

In 1960, the District Officer, South Malaita, wrote in his patrol report: "Sinerango [Sinalagu]: A large assembly, and detailed reasons for paying tax given by me in a two hour meeting. To sum up: all feel that there is little in return for tax paid." Again, historical ironies loom. The reluctant taxpayers were asking a question Basiana and his comrades had been asking thirty-five years earlier. When the tax had first been collected at Uru, Sinalagu, and 'Oloburi, the Kwaio wanted to know what they were going to get in exchange: to Melanesians, there is no such thing as a strictly one-way transaction. Recall the Kwaio grumbling about the tax in 1924 reported by Pastor J. D. Anderson, the first SDA missionary stationed on the Kwaio coast: "What is this government? It's just stealing our money. We're not going to give any more money just for nothing."

When, in 1925, the Resident Commissioner arrived on tour at Sinalagu—while Bell was on leave—he had been confronted with hostile questions about what was to be given in reciprocation for the tax. Captain Kane spoke Pijin badly, and when Bell returned, he found that "the natives" had erroneously been given the impression that they could expect to receive medical treatment. Bell added that "they also understood him to say that they would get all their money back, which was probably an interpretation of something said to the effect that all money obtained from the tax would be spent on them" (Keesing and Corris 1980:104).

The Kwaio of 1960 were still asking the same questions; and though the same vapid answers were being given, whatever money was collected was being spent elsewhere. The Kwaio of the interior were in 1960 no closer to receiving medical care, education, or any other benefits from the government than their parents had been in 1925; and their own children, in 1990, were to see things little changed.

In 1961 and 1962 Jonathan Fifi'i worked with the senior leaders of the interior, writing down as best he could lists of lands and shrines and taboos of Kwaio descent groups, and recording genealogies using the Bible as a guide. *Bungu 'ifi* meeting areas were cleared and houses built, as a cluster of senior leaders from the interior—notably 'Alabai, Bui'a, 'Elota, Fuamae, Osika, Riufaa, and Tagi'au—sought to establish the legitimacy of *Kwaio* custom vis-à-vis the 'Are'are hegemony emanating from Waiparo's movement to the southeast.

14 *Kisini* and *Kastomu*

In Kwaio country, Waiparo's agents from the southeastern fringe of Kwaio country had been collecting shell valuables from pagan descent groups and taking them off to Takataka. These emissaries and their Kwaio supporters were locked in struggle with the rival movement in which Fifi'i was working. 'Elota's account (Keesing 1978b:112–13) recreates the background of contestation:

The 'Are'are people came to collect our money—our red shell, our good valuables. . . . They worked to straighten out everything from the custom—everything from their ancestors. . . .

We Waariu people did that too, we worked on it. But we didn't give them any money. We . . . made a meeting village to follow that work. It went on for a long time. We had chiefs for that. I was chief for the women's work group; Geleniu was chief for the men's work group. The people in the ['Are'are] movement kept to themselves; even their in-laws were excluded. Even brothers who lived in different places were excluded. . . . "You can't hear

about Committee's work [the 'Are'are movement]. You belong to 'Authority'"
[the Kwaio counter-movement, associated with Fifi'i].

'Alabai, a leader in the Kwaio counter-movement, told his son-in-law, in
the rival movement, he wanted to attend their meeting. 'Elota recalls:

I'atalau wouldn't let him come to the meeting. "You can't come here—you
belong to 'Authority.' Nobody from 'Authority' can hear the work of the Committee. If you hear anything about us the government can put us in jail for
seven years." But 'Alabai came anyway. . . .

'Alabai heard . . . that the 'Are'are people were gaining strength. [Former
Headman] 'Adi from Uru heard that too, and his people sent money down for
it. Only we at Waariu didn't give any. We only gave some money for thatch.
Then 'Alabai and Fuamae had a meeting. They sent word down to Waiparo.
"What are you doing down in 'Are'are to straighten out the Custom? The roots
of the Custom, the base of the tree, are here in Kwaio. We have the proper and
true customs. You come here and find the real foundation of Custom here in
Kwaio." 'Alabai and Fuamae started doing that work. They started tracing after
our genealogies and writing them down.

In early 1962, the District Officer discussed with the 'Are'are leaders
in Takataka a request received from an American who had proposed to
come and write down their customs. The pro-American ideology of
Maasina Rule was still strong on Malaita, and the prospect of an outsider's coming to lead the project of codification and legitimation of *kastomu* seemed Heaven-, or ancestrally, sent—particularly when Waiparo
himself had just died. 'Elota's account recalls the shock waves in the
Kwaio interior when news came of an American coming to Takataka.

Old Lafudari ['Elota's uncle] heard about our problems and he said, "An
American will come here to Sinalagu, you must sacrifice a pig to ancestor
Gilogilo. The people in other places aren't sacrificing for that—we must do it
here at Sinalagu. You must raise a pig for Gilogilo, so the priest can sacrifice. If
there is nobody to sacrifice it, you people must enlist someone to do it."

We talked about it. 'Alabai contributed a string of [shell] money and a piglet; the rest of us contributed three strings more. We put together a *fa'afa'a
nima bata* [a substantial valuable]. "We must raise a pig for all of the people
here in Kwaio. But there is one problem—there is nobody to sacrifice that pig
to Gilogilo. Nobody took over that priesthood when [former Headman] Sirifa
died."

"If we sacrifice that pig, the American man will not go to 'Are'are; he will
come here to Sinalagu." . . . 'Alabai had got quite sick when these prepara-

tions were being made. And then after three months he had died. But before he died he told us that we must go ahead and sacrifice to Gilogilo so that the American would come here to us.

. . . We told [Fifi'i] that he must go to find old 'Aika in the Western District and bring him back to sacrifice that pig. Fifi'i found him and persuaded him to come back. He must come back and sacrifice the pig for all of us. Though 'Alabai had died, we did what he told us. . . . We told ['Aika], "Maasina Rule has gone astray. . . . Fifi'i's side, 'Authority', and the 'Are'are side 'Committee', have been separate. The 'Are'are people have been doing 'Committee' in preparation for an American who is to come. But 'Alabai said that if someone replaces Sirifa as priest and sacrifices to Gilogilo, the American will come here to Sinalagu instead. You have to take over the shrine and priesthood."

'Aika agreed. We brought the pig and tethered it, along with a piglet. We all took the pigs to Foumalo shrine. In the shrine he said, "Our place here, Sinalagu—the 'Are'are people have all insulted and deprecated us. Even the bush people from Sinalagu have said that the American would come to 'Are'are. Only Fuamae is left, and his people—'Alabai died. But you, Gilogilo, the pig they raised, you are to bring the American here to Sinalagu." The ancestor answered through 'Aika there at Foumalo shrine, "This pig you raised is good. You are waiting for the American here at Sinalagu. He will come here in six days—you will see his face." We heard him. He sacrificed the pig, and we ate it. We waited the six days, counting.

In Sydney, in late 1962, I had been making final preparations for my voyage to the Solomons with my wife Zina on MV *Sinkiang.* I was on my way to Malaita, to do fieldwork with the 'Are'are, from a base in Takataka. Permission—rather reluctant, as I later found out, in view of continuing anticolonial and pro-American sentiment in culturally conservative areas of Malaita—had come from the administration, expressing the support of the community where I proposed to work. I had narrowed my search for a fieldwork site through reading all the published scraps of historical and more recent evidence I could find, and on the advice of a former Malaita District Commissioner who had since moved on to the New Hebrides.

On the night before we were to sail, there was a knock on the door of our King's Cross flat: the young man introduced himself as Daniel deCoppet, a French anthropology student, who had just arrived in Sydney.

His story rocked me back on my heels. Student of the famed French anthropologist Claude Lévi-Strauss, and advised by Melanesian specialist Jean Guiart, he had decided to work in the Solomons, and had narrowed his search for a fieldwork site to the most culturally conservative island, Malaita. Poring over the scant published materials, he had chosen the eastern coast of 'Are'are as a fieldwork site. Amazingly, he too was bound for Takataka, but I was several months ahead of him.

I was in a position to claim Takataka as my own field base, leaving deCoppet to find an alternative site. But given the large blanks on the anthropological map of Malaita, it seemed more reasonable for me to find an alternative venue if I could, leaving Takataka to him. The former District Commissioner had written from the New Hebrides of "shifting cultivators" living in the "Koio" interior, but virtually nothing had been written about them: only a tantalizingly brief reference in a 1957 survey of customary land tenure in the Solomons (Allan 1957) to the large number and small scale of Kwaio "clans" in contrast to those of northern Malaita, and the importance of the "female principle" in an otherwise patrilineal landscape.

When I arrived in Honiara I sought more information on these "shifting cultivators" of the central mountains. I soon found a young administrative officer, A. V. Hughes, who had patrolled in Kwaio bush as District Officer. He laid out a picture of striking cultural conservatism among the pagans of the interior, and of a social structure still relatively "intact"—just what I wanted to hear, since my research project as then conceived was to study kinship, descent, and residence from a cognitive point of view, and their relationship to cultivation strategies. The "female principle," too, was intriguing, since what I was looking for was a cognatic descent system.

A few days later, I was in the tiny District headquarters of "Auki." A chance came to travel by ship down the western coast to the Kwaio village of Anoano. When I asked the local administrative clerk about the people of the steep rain-forested mountains that rose above the coast, he was contemptuous: "They're like animals. They live in little houses with earth floors, like pigs." Anthropological romantic, I was enchanted.

Two days later, I was struggling through those mountains—almost uninhabited now—on my way to Sinalagu by way of the interior. Arriving by sea on a government ship, I thought, would prejudice my acceptance by people I knew by then to be staunchly resisting colonial domination.

Eventually, after a night in the high mountains at a Kwaio pagan marriage feast when all had been too frighteningly wild and unintelligible for romanticism (see Keesing 1991) I found myself on the eastern coast. I reached Sinalagu exhausted, and was taken to meet Fifi'i. It was the day that had been prophesied, the sixth day since 'Aika had sacrificed to *adalo*

Gilogilo at Foumalo. 'Elota (Keesing 1978b:114) remembered that "we waited for the six days, counting. On the sixth day, you, Kisini, you arrived at Malo'u, here at Sinalagu. You, Kisini, you came on the sixth day. And you told us that our search for the Custom, our effort to straighten it out, was true." Fifi'i recalled that I told him,

> "I'd like to go up the hill and talk to the bush people. My work is to write down other people's customs. I've come from America to study Malaita customs." I'd never heard of anthropology then. But he told me he wanted to study our Kwaio customs, learn about our land, write down our genealogies. . . .
>
> That day I went up to Uka'oi and I told people that the white man they had heard about had arrived. I said that he wanted to work with us, and write down our customs. . . . The next day we went up the hill, where the men from the bush had gathered, and he talked to them. I interpreted for him. He told us, "I want to come and write down your customs. I am an anthropologist. We don't come to a place like this to teach you. We come to have you teach us. I want you to teach me your language and your customs and your way of living. I will write it all down."

I had no way of knowing, then, that I had come in fulfilment of prayer and prophecy, that I was caught up in their historical project.

Since 1962, then, I have been part of their story. My place in it would be easy (and tempting) to exaggerate; and what is important is not what I thought I was doing, but what they thought I was—or should be—doing. There has always been a wide, and perhaps unbridgeable, gulf between my project and their project, my goals and theirs, my aspirations and theirs (and "they" do not, of course, speak with one voice). Fifi'i's telling of the first fieldwork we did together is no more "objective" than mine, but it will serve to place my work in its context:

> We had a meeting after he had gone back. People said, "Let's trust that man. If he turns out to be a good man, he will work with us and help us write down our customs. If he's lying to us, we'll find out."
>
> Fuamae, 'Aika, Osika, Tagii'au, Tau'ifelo, 'Elota, and Talaunga'i discussed it with me. "What are we going to arrange? We're bush people; we still follow our customs."[1] We discussed it. He didn't want to be too far from the coast, but

---

1. There were several issues involved. One was that they knew Europeans lived on or near the coast. More importantly, they were concerned about my presence in relation to ancestral rules and restrictions, particularly since I had a wife who was going to accompany me. It was unimaginable that she might be willing to follow taboos regarding menstruation and take off her clothes when going to the latrine, as she would have to in a pagan settlement or in the mountains surrounded by ancestral shrines. A liminal, neutral point in between coastal Christians and bush pagans was the ideal categorical solution, even though pagan settlements (where I later lived) are nearby.

most of those men lived far up in the bush. "Let's clear a meeting area half way up the mountain, and build his house there." It was to be a *bungu 'ifi*, a 'conch shell village' of the kind we had started to build during Maasina Rule—a place where everyone could gather for work. . . .

The leaders from the bush called for everyone to come down and clear the area [at Ngarinaasuru], and build a house for the man who was coming to write our custom. People were happy to come and work. People brought sago thatch from around Sinalagu, and from Uru and 'Oloburi as well. They came from all over the bush to work. It was like the old days of Maasina Rule, with so many people working together—more than a hundred people at a time. People built a house for Roger and his wife. They also built houses for people to stay in when their groups came down from the bush to meet there.

For two years, Roger Keesing and I worked together. My house was down at the coast, but for those two years we went around in the bush together. I'd work with him all day, and then at six o'clock in the evening, I'd go down the hill. At dawn, I'd climb up the hill again, and start work with him. At first he had me interpret for him. I'd translate what he wanted to say to them into Kwaio. I'd translate their answers back into English. He quickly started to learn the language, even though there was no grammar or dictionary, not even a proper system for writing our Kwaio language.

Everyone would gather at Ngarinaasuru each week. Roger was working on his notes, and also on a dictionary of our language. When people gathered there, he would sit with us while we talked, all day and sometimes into the night. He would listen to us. The elders—Fuamae, Osika, Tagii'au, 'Elota— would discuss problems about custom, or how to settle a particular dispute. Even if it went on day and night, Roger would be with us, writing down what was happening, or tape recording it. He'd take notes. He wouldn't speak; he'd just sit quietly listening to what we were saying and taking notes.

He wrote and wrote. Then when just the two of us were left together, he'd say, "This word such-and-such I heard, what does it mean?" I'd explain the new words he picked up, and then he'd put them into the dictionary he was building up.

We worked on customs. We worked on recording genealogies—genera-tions—from the old people, people who are dead now, whose knowledge would have died with them if we hadn't recorded it. We walked up in the bush. He was really strong for climbing up the hills. Foreigners can't usually get on well if they go into the bush; but he was just like one of us. He'd see how we lived, and do the same way. He'd sleep in our houses, even though they're built on the ground and dark and smoky. He'd eat our food, and never acted dis-gusted by the things we ate. He'd eat whatever we were having—roasted

cyathea fern, plantain bananas, taro leaves, or whatever it was. He never recoiled from it, or smelled it to see if it was really edible. He'd just plunge in,
with the rest of us. We'd go to feasts together. Whenever there was a gathering—
a compensation claim or something like that—we'd be there together. He was
like one of us, and people really were pleased about it. Something that never
had happened before was happening.

When there was a mortuary feast and people contributed shell money, he
would give shell money along with them. He'd sell a bit of tobacco or rice at
his house sometimes, in exchange for shell money, so he could give the shell
money away to people. The son of 'Elota, a very important man, brought his
girlfriend home as his bride. 'Elota was down with us at Ngarinaasuru when the
news came; he was annoyed about it, because he wanted to use his shell money
to get remarried himself. Roger said, "Don't worry, I'll help you. I'll contribute
a string of shell money."

He had just started his work then, and he hadn't understood that contrib-
uting a small string at the opening marriage payment amounted to making a
pledge that he would make a major contribution to the brideprice when the
main feast was held. He had pledged to stand for a *kabu*. [2] People said, "Hey,
that's really something!" Only people's closest relatives help that way when
they get married. I had to help him put together the *nima'ae* [3] he presented. He
accumulated most of the white shell money himself, but he had no way to get
the red money we put on top of big valuables. He hung that up himself, and
some of his friends "stood with" him and presented smaller valuables. At other
marriages, when people would *laga*—that is, run back and forth and shout and
stamp his heel before presenting a small valuable to one of the people standing
for a *kabu*—he'd do the same thing. Roger and I would go off for three days or
sometimes five.

Usually when we'd go to a feast in the bush or travel around, his wife Zina
would stay home and take care of things in the house. But sometimes she'd
come up into the bush. That was harder for a white woman, because of all the
strict customs that apply to women in our settlements. If a woman has to go to
the latrine, she has to take all her clothes off. When people divided pork or

2. When an initial marriage payment is made (in those days, consisting of ten strings of shell
valuables), each of the strings is taken by one of the bride's relatives (who is entitled to a share of the
brideprice). The person who takes the string accumulates large amounts of taro, fish, and pork
(which together constitute a *kabu*). The person who contributed the string, and his or her relatives,
then present large valuables to the bride's relatives and receive the food—which they then
distribute—in return. The contributor of the string "stands for" (*ula fana*) the *kabu*.

3. A large five-stringed valuable (lit. "five legs"; compare the *taafulii'ae*, "ten legs," of northern
Malaita).

taro, they'd send a share down for Zina and Roger. People were really happy to have them there.

When I worked with Roger, I kept watching how he did his work. After they'd been there for eight months, Roger told me, "We're going to go to Australia and have a break." He didn't ask me to work for him while he was away. But I'd been watching the sorts of things he was interested in, and the way he wrote them down. I had learned to write down genealogies. When they went away, he'd given me a notebook. So I tried to write down what had happened. When he got back, I showed him my work: "If it's not good, it's the best I could do. If there's something that's not done right, or not clear, ask me about it and I'll explain it." Roger was very pleased to see the record I had kept while they were away. By then he was able to speak our language pretty well, and he was getting better at it all the time. So he asked me to keep writing things down myself, but to use our Kwaio language. When he was away, I had tried to write in English. He had taught me a proper way of writing our language.[4]

After they'd gone off to Australia and came back, Zina stayed only until Christmas[5] and then she went home. She went back to go to university. So Roger stayed on for another year by himself, working with me. When he was by himself, he spent even more time patrolling around in the bush—mapping gardens and visiting settlements and going to feasts and sacrifices. No white man had ever been allowed to go into the shrines and sacred places. But once Zina had left, he was allowed to go and stay with them when they sacrificed sacred pigs. He became taboo with them.

He was speaking Kwaio well enough to work by himself, so often he'd go off in one direction and I'd go off in another. He knew the bush so well, he'd often go off by himself for the day, visiting around in Waariu and other places. I was recording lots of things myself, and he was recording lots of things himself. Then we'd go over the things I had recorded, and the things he'd written down he didn't understand, or the new words he had run into. That second year, he was travelling around the bush for days at a time, and I had a busy time, too, getting records of feasts and brideprice payments. Kwaio bush people, with no way to write things down, remembered twenty or thirty years later exactly who had contributed what to their brideprice or their mortuary feasts.

When the time came for him to go back to write his doctor's thesis, at the end of 1964, he asked me to keep doing that work for him. He left books and

4. The orthography some Christian Kwaio had learned from missionaries failed to mark the crucial difference between single and doubled vowels (e.g., *faafia* 'on top of' vs. *fafia* 'bake it in a leaf oven'), and failed to mark as such the most common consonant in the language, the glottal stop (*'abu* 'blood' vs. *abu* 'sacred, taboo').

5. Of 1963.

notebooks and envelopes and pens and things for me. I'd write down all the things that happened, and send the notebooks to him. He had found a research grant to pay me for my work. When he was writing his thesis, and he found some question he'd forgotten to ask, or some piece of information or custom that wasn't clear, he'd write to ask me, and I'd write back to him in California. I suppose I filled up fifteen shorthand notebooks.

For me, "writing down the custom" meant probing the intricacies of kinship, descent groups and local groups, the complex exchanges in mortuary feasting and bridewealth. The ancestors were crucial beings in this social world, but mainly as points of reference in terms of which the living defined themselves; I explored the sociology of sacrifice and the shrines that anchor the living to the land and the culturally constructed past.

In this task, my interests and theirs partly overlapped. I spent many early months recording genealogies that went back twelve or fifteen generations. I recorded lands and shrines, the rituals of sacrifice and the complicated sequences of desacralization that followed the death of a priest; and I explored the rules defining the strict separation of men's and women's realms in terms of "pollution." My hosts were happy when I documented what fell squarely into their category of kastomu. I wanted to know, too, how people went about their daily lives. Who slept where? Who chopped the firewood? Where this could be cast rhetorically in terms of taboos or women's virtues, the Kwaio ideologues were satisfied; but often, my interest in the mundane was in their eyes a waste of time. Moreover, my genealogy-taking had to stop somewhere: I had probed the sociology of some fifty tiny settlements scattered over many miles. My Kwaio hosts concerned with documenting kastomu expected me to keep endlessly expanding my geographical sweep; having defined a reasonable sample group within five or six hours' walk, I was intent on documenting social life within it.

There were other notes of discordance where their expectations and projects and mine were at odds. For the Kwaio ideologues of kastomu, the high point of our collective work came every Tuesday, when people would gather from far and near at the meeting area they had constructed around our house at Ngarinaasuru (Keesing 1968a). The women kept the grass cut, carried firewood, cooked; the young people flirted and played and visited. The senior men, in their guise as "Chiefs," gathered in what they were calling the "Sub-District Committee" house to pontificate and adjudicate on matters of kastomu. Often, this took the form of a quasi-court, with the senior men sitting in judgment as two sides presented their grievances and their versions of events. The "Chiefs" would then decide on an appropriate resolution, usually payment (or exchange) of compensation. (The adjudications were binding only insofar as social pressure and a desire to keep the dispute out of the government's Native Court impelled the parties to accept them.) All this was grist for an ethnographer's mill, and I spent hours listening to disputes being aired and debated.

But often, instead, the "Chiefs" spent hours talking rhetorically about the project of writing down *kastomu,* or voicing their grievances against the government or the missions. For me, this was a deflection of time and energy from real ethnography.[6] In those days anthropologists operated with rather unreflective stereotypes of the "Big Man" in Melanesia, and I found it ironic that in these contexts of "Committee" meetings the Kwaio divided themselves up into *sifi* "chiefs" and *koomani fiifuru* "common people." I wrote an early paper (Keesing 1968a) on the strange phenomenon of a society that had chiefs only on Tuesdays.

The anticolonial rhetoric of the *sifi* in the early 1960s, as I have gone back to reexamine it, shows clear continuities with earlier phases of their political struggle and the phases that were to follow; and it shows the same keen sense of history, expressed in terms of the processes that had transformed other parts of the Solomons. An example from my tapes (see Keesing 1978a:54–55) will serve to illustrate:

The land is yours, these are your customs. If anyone comes and tries to get the land from you, go ahead and talk but don't agree to anything. The white man will lie to you and you will die because of it, and your children after you. The Headmen and the white men know about the foreign ways, how to talk people out of their own things. We've all seen what happened in the Western Solomons, in Guadalcanal. I've seen the plantations. Lever's just took people's lands, and now the people have to stay outside the boundaries of the land their forefathers lived on, and just look in. Lever's takes all the copra and makes the profits—but it comes from native peoples' land. Malaita people go and cut copra there, but the people who really owned the land don't get anything. All the things white people developed in the Solomons they did for themselves, not for us. When they take land, they say to us, "Here is your money." They lie to us: they only give us the ashes of the money. The money really goes to build up everything for the foreign people who make their business here in our islands. If we are wise we'll stand against their business ventures. We told the

6. Only in writing this book have I been led to go back and listen to some of my early tapes.

Kwara'ae people what would happen at 'Aoke, told them they shouldn't give
over their land. But they said "I have to get money now, in my lifetime." And
now you see them moved far from their proper places and things are very bad
for them. Those people always say we 'Welakau' [Kwaio] people are backward.
But I say we are the wise ones, holding onto our land, holding on to our
customs.

The sense of alienation from the political processes the British introduced paternalistically (and in response to the demands of the Maasina
Rule leaders) as the first steps toward eventual self-government also
comes out clearly. Bui'a, a Sinalagu pagan who was the "delegate" to a
quite powerless Malaita Council, observed that "we members watch what
happens [in the Council meetings]. The things we speak for on behalf of
our people turn out to be impossible. The government just treats us like
children—they listen to what we say, then do what they want."

The British administration in 'Aoke had a limited understanding of
what was happening among the pagans of the interior. Every two or three
months, the District Officer would come around on a ship, and visit the
three east Kwaio "passages." In an hour or two at each place, he would be
briefed on the local situation by the Headman and Clerk, and would go
over the records of cases resolved in the local court. His vision of local
politics was the one presented by the Headman—which prominently included a Headman diligently visiting the bush settlements regularly and
maintaining law and order. In fact, the Headman was only seen in the
bush during a perfunctory tax collection (at which the pagans would put
forward a few token taxpayers) or in the event of a murder, attempted
murder, or similar drastic breach of the law. Several wanted murderers
lived unhampered in the bush. [7]

There were no serious educational or medical facilities extended to the
Kwaio of the east coast. When the administration did make some effort
in that direction, they bumbled into cultural obstacles. In 1964 a small
clinic was built at Gelebasi, the old market area on the coast at Sinalagu
where the Maasina Rule *bungu 'ifi* had been built, and where Fifi'i had
been arrested. The government sent materials for a maternity building,
and when the ship delivered them to 'Ilemi the District Officer ordered
them stored in the small court building. Following Kwaio rules regarding

---

7. In 1990, a quarter of a century later, when I was in the Kwaio interior, a young murderer was
hiding in the bush; he had held up a white plantation manager, stolen the payroll, and then killed
him. The police were too frightened and intimidated by Kwaio demands for political and legal autonomy to come and look for him. See p. 182.

pollution, which require that a childbirth hut be hidden in the forest away from the eyes of men, the pagans then refused to enter the courthouse—an impasse that was resolved only by shipping the materials back to 'Aoke to be used for another purpose, and abandoning the plan for a maternity clinic—(see Keesing 1967b).

15 A Growing Christian Presence

In 1965, just after my return to the U.S., a new Christian presence began to be felt. In the 1930s, the Seventh Day Adventists had explored and drawn tentative plans for a hospital site in Uru Harbor, across the water from where Pastor and Mrs. Anderson had lived in the 1920s. The southern half of the eastern coastline of Malaita—more than a day's travel from 'Aoke by sea, in either direction—had been left virtually without governmental attention or facilities. The SDA medical facility at Kwailobesi, near the northern tip of the island, was too far away to provide effective services. With growing capital investment in Melanesian mission work, the Adventists decided to push ahead with the early plan, and began negotiating for the land.

In the end, a single owner, a man named Ma'unisafi, was accorded the right to lease the land above Taunau'a to the Adventists. He was paid a large sum, and kept it himself. In Kwaio eyes, this was a massive inequity: there were several land tracts involved, and several dozen people had strong and direct, collective rights to them; and scores more had secondary and more tenuous rights. Jonathan Fifi'i (1989:112–13) recalls the conflict and its spurious resolution, in terms of custom.

The court didn't consider the rights of all the others who were related to the land. Custom wasn't taken into account. The land was awarded to Ma'unisafi, at the expense of Falaifu and all the other people who had rights to it. The Government had promoted Ma'unisafi as if he were the only one who owned the land—so he was the only one who was going to get paid for the sale. But that went against our custom. All the other people related to it were to get nothing. That's not the way our customs define rights to land. Land isn't something you grow yourself, like a plant. It's not something you feed. Land is something an ancestor cleared, generations back. He married and had descendants. Generations later, the descendants of the man who cleared the land all own it. They live on it together, and they own it together. So it's not something only one man owns. That decision went against our custom.

Moreover, the land acquired for the hospital extended up the hill close to several shrines, some of which were still used by the pagans for sacrifice. Disputes raged, and hostility simmered among the aggrieved landowners and militant pagans fearing the consequences of further invasion and desecration of sacred places. (The hospital was to be built just across the water from 'Ailamalama, where Fred Daniels had been assassinated in 1911, and just down the hill from Farisi, the settlement destroyed by the punitive expedition: the old grievances became entangled with the new ones.) Fifi'i (1989:113) describes the sad culmination of these grievances.

They finished building the hospital in 1965, and a man named Dunn came. He worked there for only a few months—maybe it was five months, or six. That anger about the land, against Ma'unisafi, was still intense. People said, "Ma'unisafi didn't plant the land, or feed it.[1] It's not just his. It belongs to the rest of us too!"

With all this anger around, someone got the idea of killing Mr. Dunn. That was in December, 1965. Whoever it was came in the night. Mr. Dunn was called to treat someone who was sick. He sent for the dresser and talked to him. Then the dresser left and Mr. Dunn turned to go into his house. His assailant was hiding, and threw a reinforcing rod spear through his back. The wire rod pierced through the lumbar area of his back.

They took him, gravely wounded, to Honiara—with the spear still through his back and out the front. The doctor examined him and thought he might live. But according to our custom, if a warrior prays to his ancestor for the power to kill someone, and then spears him or shoots him with a bow and arrow, even though the spear or arrow inflicts only a minor wound, no one will be able to save the victim. He'll die. Because the ancestor the warrior prays to is really powerful. It's the ancestor that kills him. The doctor thought Dunn would live, but he died.

The police arrested a senior man named 'Ada'ii, a landowner who had been heard to proclaim that someone should go down and kill Brother

1. In Kwaio custom, you get clear title over a productive resource if you plant it or feed it (and in the latter case, only if you have acquired title to it in the first place).

Dunn, and a young man named Susu Fa'ari. They were tried, 'Ada'ii for inciting the murder and Susu for committing it; but both were acquitted because of insufficient evidence. Jonathan Fifi'i, who served as court assessor, was convinced of Susu Fa'ari's innocence (and, having discussed those events with Susu in 1990, so am I). When Fifi'i died, he still carried private suspicions that the murderer was a pagan priest, a friend and colleague of his and mine, who had later become a Christian; if so, it was a killing enjoined by his ancestors, and by Western standards, without motive.

In the face of this tragedy, establishment of the hospital went ahead. The hospital opened in mid-1966. (I was there as tour guide and interpreter for a Harvard-based biomedical expedition [see Friedlaender et al. 1987], a visit that allowed me to ask the questions I had forgotten to pose, update my sociological census, and make final preparations for Jonathan Fifi'i to accompany me to the U.S. for a year of collaborative work.)

Establishment of the Atoifi Adventist Hospital marked a major shift in power relationships and regional political economy in Kwaio country. The hospital was initially well funded, equipped, and staffed, with a complement of white doctors and nurses, including the best qualified doctor in the Solomons, a Fellow of the Royal College of Surgeons. In the next several years, as an internal air service was established in the Solomons, the regular SDA shipping service was dramatically augmented by construction of a small airfield near the hospital, and the commencement of regular air service. Kwaio country was, after decades of less-than-benign neglect, connected quite directly to the outside world and the technology of the latter twentieth century.

The presence of the Atoifi Adventist Hospital will be a theme in the chapters that follow: pagan resistance has for the last quarter of a century been formulated in response and opposition to this dramatic and powerful alien presence, as well as to the institutions of what has become the postcolonial state.

The pagan response to the medical services provided by the hospital will emerge progressively. Some important themes were established in the first years of the hospital's operation. One was that by the circumstances of the hospital's construction, the entire area is defined by the pagans as more radically polluted and polluting than the Christian villages. The Adventists on Malaita have steadfastly refused to take the religious beliefs of the pagans seriously enough to accommodate to them. When the hospital was designed, the maternity ward was attached to the rest of the building by a continuous roof—thereby rendering the entire hospital complex polluted by childbirth. (The Adventists have recently made matters even worse by building a second storey of administrative offices above the out-patient ward: the presence of women above the ward causes drastic pollution.) In Enga country in Papua New Guinea, the Adventists have gone to some lengths to design the hospital to meet local pollution rules; on Malaita they have gone to some lengths to disregard them.

For pagan women, this poses no problems; and boys and young men treat the matter fairly lightly. But no ritually adult pagan man will venture beyond the margins of the hospital complex; a man who, with his life in mortal danger, gives in to hospitalization must undergo drastic rites of purificatory sacrifice if he returns to the bush.

The early operation of the hospital caused other lingering hostilities. Kwaio pagans claim that the bloody dressings of the maternity ward and the afterbirth are burned, and the smoke allowed to blow across the shrines up the hill, massively polluting them. (European hospital staff have claimed that for years they have been buried; I have been unable to ascertain whether either procedure is consistently followed. I believe both methods are used.)

These conflicts and cultural disjunctures notwithstanding, the regional political economy has through the last twenty years been substantially altered by the presence of the hospital. The Adventists have partly supplanted the SSEM (now South Sea Evangelical Church) as the dominant mission in the area, particularly in terms of educational facilities and economic development. The pagans as well as the Christians (allowing for their differential access to the cash economy) use the air service and other facilities provided by the Adventists (including postal and banking facilities and a small store). A weekly market at Taunau'a, below the hospital, has become the major regional redistribution point for fish, fruits, and vegetables, to which many pagan women (and some men) go to trade. And gradually, through the years, the hospital and market have seen an escalating demand for modesty, in the form of dresses covering breasts, rather than the earlier skirts. Even in the mountains, where girls were nude and women wore tiny pubic aprons of blue cloth, many now wear grimy dresses.

Where in the 1960s, the Kwaio in the Christian villages down the hill had little more access than did their cousins in the mountains to Western education, cash economy, and the outside world, all that has shifted markedly. Many Christians have now become well educated, a good many of them overseas. The nephew of Headman David Riddley has been an AAP International newsman in Brisbane, a man from 'Oloburi is a well qualified doctor, another is a pilot. Other Kwaio men (and a few women) have risen to some prominence in the worlds of politics, business, and public administration. Where in the 1960s, opting for one world or the other made little difference in terms of materials rewards and paths of life, in the 1980s the gulf between worlds, and paths, has widened dramatically.

But in the face of all this, and despite a trickle of pagans shifting to a Christian life on the coast (a trickle rather greater than a counter-trickle back to the ways of the ancestors), the traditionalists in the bush have for the last twenty years remained diehard and defiant.

In many ways, despite the growing Christian power and the slowly thinning pagan numbers, the two communities have remained locked in a situation that had prevailed since Maasina Rule. One important consequence of the closer interconnection of Christian and pagan communities brought about by Maasina Rule is that the pagans are in many cases very familiar with Christian teachings. On the one hand, the pagans know exactly what the Christian alternative is, both in doctrinal terms and in terms of the round of daily life in Christian villages. On the other, in a curious way, both Christians and pagans require the theology of the other "side." The pagans must "believe in" the existence and the power of the Christian God in order to account for the way Christians flout the most binding and awesomely dangerous rules of the ancestors— the rules about menstruation and childbirth—with impunity. But God can be edited out as best possible. As Fei'a expressed it when I asked why the Christians could survive, "Down there? Because their *adalo* aren't with them. Their *adalo* have gone away and left them. Because they polluted them. They abandoned them. That's why people survive there. That's why they live all right there, without getting sick."

The Christians in turn "believe in" the powers of the ancestors (although in some contexts, at least, they regard them as manifestations of Satan). It is their opposition to the *adalo* that gives the Christian villages their coherence and their ideological rationale; they pray against the ancestors, they conduct exorcisms and prayer meetings to rid refugees from the mountains from the evils that threaten their lives or those of their children. Moreover, most of those of the parental generation, at least, themselves came down as refugees seeking sanctuary from punitive ancestors; it is the power of the ancestors—as it is still manifest in the mountains—that justifies and rationalizes their move to the coast.

In the women's accounts of the mission villages, we have glimpsed a symbolic construction that can usefully be spelled out. The regional geography whereby the Christian villages mainly cluster at the foot of the mountain wall or along the coastal margins and lower slopes and most of the pagan settlements are scattered through the interior above the mountain rim represents a curious macrocosm of the symbolic geography of the pagan settlements. A pagan settlement has as its center the middle part of the clearing where one or more dwelling houses are built. On the upper side of the clearing stands a men's house, with a sacred area around and above it; and on the lower side of the clearing is the *kaakaba*, the menstrual area, with a *bisi* or menstrual hut. The upper side, sacred and open only to males, and the lower side, "polluted" and open only to women,[2] are symbolic mirror-images (the mirror-imaging extends to the shrine above and the childbirth hut below). To the pagan ideologues, the Christian villages and the surrounding area are equated with the menstrual area, and the interior is equated with men's houses, ancestors and the sacred (see Keesing 1989c).

The familiarity of pagans with Christian theology will be examined in chapter 16. However, a preliminary example from my 1963 tapes will serve to illustrate both this familiarity and the confrontational politics in which it is deployed. A Kwaio man locked in conflict with a Christian kinsman over who had what rights over compensation for a sexual offense turned the ideological tables:

You mission people have a Book. We pagans don't have a book. Your Book says "Though shalt not kill." If I want to kill, I go ahead and kill. Your Book says "Though shalt not commit adultery." If I want to commit adultery, I do. And here you are demanding that you should receive the biggest share of these ten valuables as compensation. Your Book says, "Thou shalt not covet." So why do you covet these valuables?

Because women can go into the mission villages with few restrictions, and because a number of the pagan women have spent periods as Christians before returning to the mountains, many give critical commentaries on the laxity of life without the virtues and structures of pagan communities. The pagan woman Fei'a commented that

women down there in the mission don't live properly. The things we 'heathen' people taboo—they just walk over the top of them. They just eat any way they like, not the way we 'heathen' do. For us, men's things are separate, women's

2. And infant boys. As I argue in Keesing 1982a, some distortion is introduced in characterizing menstrual seclusion in terms of pollution.

things are separate. Men eat their food separately. I don't want the Christian ways. "It's wrong," I tell them [her children]. The things associated with menstruation just get taken into the house. I'm disgusted with it. So I'm just going to stay here on my ancestral land. If we don't live by the ways passed down to us—if we eat any which way, take anything anywhere—it's just not right. The old people observed the separation of men's things, . . . men's bark sitting mats, . . . men's water. Our water, our sitting mats, were women's things. "We throw things away in the proper places [I tell the mission people]. When we menstruate we stay in the menstrual hut, away from the house. You mission people menstruate and you just stay in the house. I'm disgusted with it—and I'm going to stay in the bush."

Boori'au, a highly respected senior woman almost all of whose relatives (from the coastal slope) had become Christian, echoed Fei'a's view of Christian life:

They give up all the taboos. They just menstruate in the house. They urinate in the clearing. They just break any of the ancestral rules about not eating food. They can eat anything they like. They have no taboos. They run away from the *adalo*. They run away from the taboos. They take up the Christian rules. Even a man who has been a priest . . . will give up all his restrictions if he becomes Christian. He eats with women. He eats with menstruating women, or women who have just given birth. He stays with them.

The Christians and the pagans remain locked in ideological and political struggle, sharing a common cultural heritage yet taking strikingly different stances toward it.

16 Lull Before the Storms

I had spent much of a year in Kwaio country in 1969–70, with our three young children. Committee activities had continued, although the energies directed toward *kastomu* seemed to have abated. This lull in political activity, with *bungu 'ifi* built in the bush and then falling into disuse, continued into the late 1970s.

Perhaps there was a measure of sheer inertia in this, as the investments of time and energy and women's labor in Committee meetings were balanced against the diffuse results. But it was also a time of political change within the Protectorate, as the British moved progressively toward self-government and eventual independence. The Kwaio pagans for the first time were vigorously represented at a national level, as their former Maasina Rule Chief Jonathan Fifi'i became an active parliamentarian and an effective spokesman for the interests of conservative rural communities, and his constituents in particular. It seemed that as resources and political power were progressively passed into the hands of a Solomons government, the Kwaio would at last start to get what they wanted.

But what was that? Seeing people in other parts of Malaita gain access to and relative prosperity in the cash economy, many people in the bush looked forward to gaining some of this prosperity and becoming less dependent on plantation labor at low wages. Since the mid-sixties, the plantation labor itself had become more precarious. Lever's had owned its own recruiting ships, and plantation workers had been assured of free transportation to and from the Russell Islands, and of returning with a full box of trade goods; but all this had changed. Kwaio looking for plantation work now had to find (and pay for) their own passage and, in many cases, to find their own housing and provide their own rations; many returned empty handed after two or three years of work.

A road was constructed across the island to the north of Kwaio country, and Fifi'i pushed vigorously for its extension down to Uru—which would have given potential access to road transportation for cash crops. With this possibility opening up, and with an airfield at Atoifi, the sense of isolation from the outside world was beginning to evaporate. But at the same time, and with the growing strength and prosperity of the Christians on the coast, the Kwaio sensed that the viability of their ancestral way of life was in danger. The Kwaio wanted the best of both worlds: they wanted access to cash and a limited prosperity without losing their customs, their land, and their ancestors. This two-sidedness, a contradiction-laden aspiration both to preserve traditional life and to attain the benefits of economic development, has marked Kwaio political rhetoric and struggle since the mid-1970s.

Another factor of change was the passing from the scene of a number of the leading figures in Maasina Rule and the Committee activity of the 1960s. 'Elota died in 1973; Alefo, Fuamae, Osika, and Talaunga'i had joined their ancestors; and this created something of a political vacuum, with only a few of the strongest leaders in anticolonial struggle—Bui'a, Ma'aanamae, Riufaa, Tagi'au[1]—still active.

Two men who stepped into the breach were fiery characters who were

---

1. And their counterparts in the bush above Uru and 'Oloburi.

to play important parts in the confrontations of the 1980s. One, Folofo'u, was a man of limited prominence in feasting and ritual activities, but a spellbinding orator with a charismatic presence. His bad temper and proclivities to fling ancestral curses had by the early 1970s contributed to the breakdown of kastomu activities (since several prominent leaders, notably Tagi'au, refused to come to Ngarinaasuru). Folofo'u lived next to Ngarinaasuru, and so was able to exercise a direct and continuous influence on a place that otherwise was only sporadically occupied. Folofo'u's anger about colonial domination had crystallized when he was a young man, after the 1927 massacre; he had worked as a cook for a District Officer named King (actually a German who had changed his name from Koenig) whose racism and scorn for the "natives" was typical of the period. Folofo'u's understanding of the political processes that were carrying the Solomons toward independence was limited and simplistic.

A second leader who was coming to the fore was Laefiwane, the younger son of Basiana (Bell's assassin). (Recall that his older brother Anifelo had been raised as a police bugler in Tulagi, after the two boys had been forced to watch their father die on the scaffold; and then he had been taken to the SSEM headquarters at Onepusu and trained as an evangelist. Anifelo's anger had led him to be a Maasina Rule leader.) Laefiwane was a tiny, wiry firebrand of a man, still a pagan though he had spent years on plantations, whose psychological stability was precarious, and who found in a growing extremism of Kwaio politics at the end of the 1970s an outlet and focus for long accumulated rage.

As the District administration in 'Aoke began to slacken its reins in anticipation of independence, during a further year I spent in Kwaio country in 1977, conflict began to escalate. One point of conflict—yet again—was the tax. The Kwaio were refusing to pay; the British Clerk[2] to what was to become the provincial council had mooted a plan to convert the head tax (euphemistically recast as a "basic rate") into a sales tax, but meanwhile was trying to enforce the laws as they stood—even though the annual tax obligation exceeded the annual income of most of the pagans. The Clerk also discussed the imposition on the pagans of such long-disregarded by-laws as annual dog licenses and the prohibition of pigs in dwelling houses (the dog licenses were viewed as yet another ridiculous harassment; the pig prohibition as an outrage, since for the Kwaio pig-theft is a culturally valued and ancestrally enjoined art and the pigs are kept in houses for surveillance).

---

2. Dudley Cook.

Another point of conflict—again—was the imposition of Protectorate law. Matters came to a head over two attempted killings. In one, a
man attacked a visitor he suspected of having a sexual affair with his wife,
hacking him in the head with a machete; only luck and the proximity of
the Atoifi Hospital saved the victim. In another, a girl was seduced and
left pregnant by a lover; in grief and shame, the girl hanged herself. The
girl's mother then attacked and almost killed the sister of her daughter's
seducer. In each case, the Kwaio "chiefs" demanded that the attempted
killings be resolved by exchanges of compensation, with valuables paid
for the sexual offenses on one side, and for the physical injury, on the
other. The government demanded that the attackers be turned over to be
tried and imprisoned for attempted murder. Meetings at Ngarinaasuru
sought to effect compromises, with the District Magistrate from 'Aoke[3]
negotiating with the "chiefs" to achieve both the exchange of compensation and trial according to Protectorate law. But in each case, after initially agreeing, Folofo'u overturned the proffered compromises with fiery
rhetoric and ancestral injunctions and curses.

By 1977, Folofo'u and Laefiwane had intensified and radicalized their
political demands as talk of impending independence spread around the
Solomons. Folofo'u talked of how independence would mean that the
Kwaio would at last be free of Protectorate law, and could follow their
customary laws. He and Laefiwane discussed the possibility of seeking assistance, political and economic, from the Americans: being independent, they could conduct their own foreign policy. Laefiwane was
particularly attracted by the idea of "Republic Government" (one issue in
Solomons constitutional negotiations, in which Fifi'i had been prominent, was whether the new country was to retain the Queen as sovereign). Again, understanding of what that might mean was blurred and
mystical.

Kwaio Christians were also important in the political negotiations
with Malaita Council. In November 1977, a Christian leader named
Mahlon wrote to me:

> On 8th November 1977 we met Council Presidence, Clerk to Malaita
> Council, and Planning Officer for the Malaita Council. We talk[ed] about cul-
> tural education, pigs, dogs, marketing, medical for bush people and others
> more. This is our problem.
>
> Then we ask them a question, where is our Tax? Since Government Rule
> over this island about 50 years now, and our own people pay tax, also we are
> today we still paying tax, but no result, why?

3. Francis Daley, who later became Solomons Chief Justice.

Angry that governmental priorities supported development in the north and south of Malaita, and none in the middle, Mahlon concluded that "therefore we don't want Government or Council to rule us. We want to live as a isles. If we didn't see any help from Council."

In this climate of confrontation and mounting frustration, the Malaita Council was talking of some power and resources being devolved on "Area Committees." This suggested a local strategy with regard to the tax. A young and politically ambitious Kwaio Christian, Lee Siilamo, wrote to me in early 1978 about these developments: "There was [a] meeting conducted by Council Member Alick Konai in regards to the reduction of the council tax rate from $6 to $2 per head and this money will be kept by the Area Committee and not to send it to the Malaita Council."

In this climate, too, Konai and other Christians had decided that it was appropriate for the Kwaio Area Committee to have a Kwaio label, not a government one, to make clear that its responsibilities were to the people, not the Council. They named it "Kwaio Fadanga" (fada is 'meet, discuss collectively'; -nga is a nominalizing suffix; thus Kwaio Fadanga can be translated as something like "Kwaio Council"). In early 1978, Konai wrote to me: "We are paying two dollars in tax now. And we're keeping it from the Council as well. . . . Independence for us in Kwaio is to be in July [1978]. We of Fadanga changed the tax Council imposed on us of $7.00. I'm asking you, what are we to do with our independence? I want you to advise us, what are we to do with our independence?" I obviously could give no advice: foreigners are understandably not permitted to engage in political activities in the Solomons, and I have repeatedly emphasized publicly and privately in Kwaio country that I can write down customs but not advise on questions of politics or business.

Soon after, Mahlon wrote to me again: "The Area Committee tell people not to pay their tax for $6.00 but $2.00 just for only Kwaio. WE AREN'T AFRAID. WE ARE CLOSE TO INDEPENDENCE AND WE WON'T GIVE THE TAX TO AUKI."

I returned briefly to the Solomons in July 1978, representing The Australian National University at the independence celebrations. The committee planning the celebrations had left traditional leaders out entirely, and only grudgingly provided limited funding for feasts in village areas. In anger and resentment, Jonathan Fifi'i boycotted the independence ceremonies entirely. Ironically, the British Governor who turned the country over to Sir Peter Kenilorea, its first Prime Minister, was Sir Colin Allan, who had been District Commissioner of Malaita in 1947–48, overseeing the repression of Maasina Rule. The new Prime Minister, an 'Are'are man educated in New Zealand as an SSEC evangelist, was locked in local political struggle with 'Are'are traditionalists, and pointedly made no mention of Maasina Rule. It was a special irony that, as I sat with the other official guests in the VIP area at the independence ceremonies at the sports stadium, the old Maasina Rule Chief Aliki Nono'oohimae came in, with great dignity—uninvited. Fortunately, he was escorted to the VIP area by a sensible policeman.

I was able to go to Malaita immediately after the ceremony, and spent a week at Ngarinaasuru. Folofo'u and Laefiwane were brimming over with antigovernment rhetoric and wild ideas that independence would mean that they could resume ancestral ways and customary law without outside interference. Folofo'u's rhetoric, though, has a special kind of bite because he perceives so clearly the contradictions of the colonial and postcolonial claims to sovereignty. He told me that

> I want to live on the land that has been passed down from my ancestors, down to my grandfathers. I want to live there in freedom [*firiidomu*]. You, the government—if I want to be free here, who are you to wreak destruction on me? If I'm just living peacefully on my own land. You, the government, what have *I* destroyed, that belongs to you, just living here peacefully on the land passed down to me through the generations? Who are you, the government, to strike me down for living here peacefully on the land inherited from my ancestors?
>
> What I envision is that kind of freedom that came down from ancient times. Who are you, the government of Solomon Islands, to come here and mess up my living? . . . What have I destroyed of yours, you "native government" of the Solomon Islands? Nothing! What have I transgressed, that you can come here and say I've done something wrong? When I'm following the ways that have come down to me from ancient times! . . . You, the government in Honiara—what right have you to seize control of us here in Kwaio? None. We have always been free, responsible for ourselves. But you, the government, have just come and messed us up!

Folofo'u's rhetoric turned to the issue of legal autonomy:

> My shell valuables—that's the foundation on which I stand. That's what's been passed down to us. If there was a fight, if something bad happened, it would be straightened out with valuables [as compensation], as has always been our way, for twenty or thirty generations. If there was a fight, I would settle it; if there was an illness, I would cure it—and it would be settled. Settled the way

I just fixed up the conflict over 'Akwaa'i [the woman who avenged her daughter who had hanged herself], following my custom. It's not like the law brought here from outside. We pay compensation and that's the end of it—the two sides are joined again. That's our Kwaio way. That's the freedom I'm demanding—the freedom passed down from olden times. . . .

From olden times, whatever bad things happened, we straightened them out with our own [shell] money, our own Kwaio money. Nothing is left in a mess after it has been fixed up. The hostility doesn't keep spreading like vines on a trellis.

But the law [loa] you've brought doesn't fit our living here in Kwaio. See what happened in this case. 'Akwaa'i was angry because of her daughter. Her daughter hanged herself. She ['Akwaa'i] was angry, and smashed the water containers, tore up her bag. And then, while we were all there, at midnight she hacked up the sister of the man over whom her daughter had committed suicide. Because of her daughter.

The government arrested her and took her away from us, from our Koumitii ["committee"]. They took her to 'Aoke, and then the Koumitii demanded that she be returned. The Koumitii settled it with payment of compensation—21 valuables. We joined the two sides together—with 21 valuables as blood compensation [tori'abunga, lit. "blood spilling"], from 'Akwaa'i's side. And they gave ten valuables in the other direction, to 'afumaa, compensate her for her grievance [lit., "shut eye"]. So it was all even [lefolo, Pijin "level"]. And that was the end of it.

That's the kind of freedom for the Kwaio. That's the real kind of government for Kwaio. Resolving things—quarrels, fights—with the exchange of valuables. It's shell money that settles things.

As the new country sought to create effective structures of government, and as what had become Malaita Province sought to extend its control around the island, more serious confrontation was becoming inevitable.

17 The Kwaio Cultural Centre

Solomon Islands, the 150th member nation of the United Nations, faced serious problems of internal disunity. What had become Western Province, the country's most prosperous area (along with the Guadalcanal

Plains), had threatened secession and boycotted the independence
ceremonies. Provinces were flexing their muscles over the use of newly
decentralized financial resources and powers.

In this climate, the growing militancy of Kwaio Fadanga was a minor
irritant, noticed mainly at the provincial level. A new element had been
introduced in the Kwaio political scene, albeit one that was inherently
nonpolitical: the Kwaio Cultural Centre. In 1977 I had discussed with
pagan leaders my idea of trying to establish a school in the bush where
literacy in Kwaio could be taught, with elders teaching traditional
knowledge—'ai'imae epics, ritual, genealogies. Literacy, we agreed,
would not only help them preserve traditional knowledge (and free them
from dependence on coastal Christians in writing letters to relatives in
town and on plantations), but it could also empower them as agents in
writing down customs themselves in the form they envisioned. I also saw
the possibility of a craft cooperative, where traditional craft skills of making the beautiful plaited combs, weapons, body ornaments, and other objects could, with effective marketing, provide a modest income as an
alternative to plantation labor.

The idea had been strongly supported by the elders, who resented their
dependence on Christian scribes but saw the government and mission
schools as subverting traditional knowledge and ancestral religion. They
saw, as I did, that the ancient craft skills were vanishing with a last generation of elderly experts. My plan was to seek to persuade the US Peace
Corps, through its energetic and enlightened Solomons Director Terry
Marshall, to recruit a couple who were trained in anthropology to establish the school and craft cooperative, working with and for Kwaio
traditionalists.

The Peace Corps accepted the plan, and when in the US on sabbatical
I wrote to all likely anthropology departments there to advertise the
project. Eventually, David Akin and Kate Gillogly, a young couple who
had just graduated from the University of Iowa, with majors in anthropology and a strong interest in Melanesia and anticipated graduate
work in the field, was selected. I was to spend seven weeks in Kwaio country in 1979, giving them an introduction to Kwaio language and culture
and an orientation to the area. Meanwhile, I had obtained a small grant
from the Australian High Commission to fund the initial physical establishment of a Cultural Centre at Ngarinaasuru, a thousand steep feet
above the coast.

A complex of thatch buildings, for the school and for Akin and
Gillogly, was constructed, mainly with volunteer labor. In mid-1979 I

gave the orientation and introduced them to the landscape and my Kwaio friends. Just before we left, an official—albeit inevitably preliminary—launching of the Kwaio Cultural Centre was held, with a number of representatives from Malaita Province, the Ministry of Education, Training and Cultural Affairs (METCA), and the media. Folofo'u orated about Kwaio *kastomu*, but with a measure of restraint; Laefiwane danced around stark naked for the benefit of the white visitors, and optimism prevailed.

The optimism and harmony were to be short lived. The Australian grant had been given to METCA, to which the project and the Peace Corps volunteers were supposed to be attached. But there was much resentment against the Kwaio project within the Province and among Malaitans in the government: who were the despised Kwaio, the killers of Mr. Bell and themselves still recalcitrant heathen, to imagine that *they* had a culture? METCA refused to include the bush school within their primary school system—it did not have the requisite hours of Christian Education classes, and did not have a playground of suitable size (built as it was on a ledge on a steep mountainside). So METCA progressively disowned the project and the Akins, and most of the Australian grant was never released.

Cast adrift, the nascent Centre pushed ahead. The Permanent Secretary of METCA wrote agreeing to my proposal that I be allowed to seek outside funding from nongovernmental aid agencies, and I succeeded in getting modest funds from the Freedom From Hunger Foundation in Australia and the Dutch agency NOVIB—the latter to allow construction of a semipermanent school building and office complex as well as providing duplicating facilities for the written materials in Kwaio language that were emerging.

The Akins were meanwhile achieving dramatic results. I quote from a 1986 paper I published in India (Keesing 1986b):

As the Centre got underway, the Akins faced serious difficulties as well as government doubts and hostilities. They had, first, to acquire fluency in a new language, and familiarity with a complex tribal culture; they had to survive physically in an isolated and difficult setting. There were grave sociopolitical problems as well. Despite the nominal "chiefs" . . . Kwaio society is in reality very fragmented and almost anarchic politically; the Kwaio are fiercely egalitarian, and nobody trusts anyone else with money or responsibility. The only possible teachers for the school were Christians, so a teacher had to be carefully chosen and persuaded to support, not erode, traditional customs. The doubts and fears of the community had to be overcome before young people

would be allowed to come to school. The sheer logistical difficulties of organizing a school from nothing would be considerable even in a city; in an isolated
jungle clearing, they are immense.

The Akins managed brilliantly. Within eight months they had acquired a
score of students, a committed teacher (working with them as they acquired
fluency), and strong support from the community. A craft cooperative was beginning to take shape. Young Kwaio—mainly boys, but a few girls—were
showing a striking aptitude for reading and writing their own language. . . .

. . . . My strategy . . . to use elders as teachers, to try to create continuity
with tradition and avoid widening a generation gap . . . , put effectively into
practice by the Akins, worked splendidly. Elderly craft specialists, like the
master craftsman Sulafanamae, not only taught their skills to the young and revived old crafts they had seen in their childhoods or copied from heirlooms;
priests and other experts also served as teachers in the classroom, instructing
young people in the intricacies of custom and religion, in the deeds of the ancestors. . . . As training in literacy and arithmetic progressed, then, it could
be put to use to record customs and traditions (with the aid of cassette tapes)
and to keep track of the complex transactions of mortuary feasts and marriages.

As the Centre began to achieve visible successes both in education
and craft marketing, political jealousies in 'Aoke and Honiara intensified. Moreover, Kwaio Fadanga—both through Folofo'u and leaders
from the Christian villages—was taking an increasingly confrontationist line toward the Province. A new Provincial Premier, Stephen
Tonafalea, was particularly hostile and unsympathetic toward the
Kwaio leaders and their demands. The Akins did their best to stay out
of politics. But as Folofo'u was elevated by his Christian backers, with
reluctant assent from the pagans, into the newly created position
of "Paramount Chief," Ngarinaasuru became headquarters of Kwaio
Fadanga. His settlement virtually adjoins the meeting area, so from the
standpoint of outsiders, the Cultural Centre came to be associated with
Fadanga politics.

In 1982, a large feast was given to celebrate the opening of the new
buildings funded by the NOVIB grant. A long list of government digni-
taries including the Prime Minister and Provincial Premier was invited.
None turned up. The occasion turned into a forum for Folofo'u's anger
and defiance. Responding to the government's conspicuous absence, he
proclaimed in fiery terms the independence of east Kwaio from the Province and the country. Among the invitees who did come was the intrepid
Australian High Commissioner Trevor Sofield, who recorded the pro-

ceedings on videotape (despite his politically embarrassing position as
the talk turned to secession).

The political events that had begun to unfold, the confrontations and
conflicts that were coming into view, and the crystallization of years of
resentment are of more concern here than the Cultural Centre. But the
latter too—the breakdown of the Ngarinaasuru complex but the continuing commitment of the pagans to schooling in the face of adversity—
are part of the story that leads into the present. Some extracts from David
Akin's report to the Peace Corps before they left at the end of 1982, after
almost four years at Ngarinaasuru, will be illuminating.

The two major subjects were practical mathematics and book-keeping, and
literacy in the Kwaio language. In addition, I taught classes in geography, art,
kinship diagramming, social studies, basic science, and limited, appropriate
English for business.

Classes were held three days a week, as most students lived some distance
away and their parents did not want them absent for long continuous periods. . . .
About 40–60 students attended the Centre school at any one time. . . .

In mid-1981 a bush school was started at K, a meeting place about four
hours walk inland. Two teachers, both former students at the Cultural Centre,
were trained, and regular visits made to the school to check progress. About 30
students attend the K school.

In early 1982 a second bush school was started at B, about two hours walk
inland . . . south . . . a five hours walk from the Centre. One teacher, also a
former Cultural Centre student, was trained. In September . . . another former student . . . was hired. . . . About 20 students attend school at B, including . . . several female students. . . .

Material . . . typed, and printed on the Centre's stencil duplicator, . . . [in-
cluded] several small books . . . produced for use in the school, and also for
purchase by non-students at cost. I trained two counterparts in the gathering
and transcribing of material, tape recorder and cassette maintenance, and
cataloguing. This . . . provided literacy materials for education, and it contributed towards recording and preserving Kwaio culture. An effort was made
to gather material [amounting to some 70 cassettes] that might otherwise have
been lost in the coming years.

On the art front, too, the achievements were impressive. Akin's report
notes that

almost 100 lost or almost lost art forms were revived and documented. Kwaio
artists learned to make traditional art forms and students learned about them in
school. I organized crafts classes taught at the school by knowledgeable artists.

Over $20,000 was brought into the Kwaio area through sales of new art work in
Honiara and overseas. . . . The Kwaio Arts business is now run by two Kwaio
men trained . . . in quality control, book-keeping, transport and sales tech-
niques. . . . The object of the arts business is to give as much money as possible to the producers.

Kate Gillogly, in addition to teaching in the school, took on the challenge of working with the women who would otherwise have been pushed
into the background. She organized a flourishing Women's Club, which
generated considerable productive enterprise, including a successful bakery. Jonathan Fifi'i (1989:154) reflects on their achievements.

All those things went really well. Lots and lots of young people—well over
a hundred—learned how to read and write, and do arithmetic. They learned
about new ways, but they also learned about their customs and old ways. Our
elders had always been afraid of the kind of education young people were being
given around the Solomons, which turned them against the old customs and
led them to lose respect for old people. In our school, old people taught young
ones about the past and the ancestors, while they learned new skills as well.
Young people who had learned to write wrote down stories of old wars and battles, our epic chants, and other stories. Those were made into books that were
used in the school.

After the Akins returned to the U.S. to do graduate work in anthropology, they arranged and found funding for two young Kwaio pagan
men to visit the East-West Center in Hawaii, giving demonstrations of
Kwaio art and music and raising funds to support the schools.

The breakdown of the school complex at Ngarinaasuru was physically
caused by Cyclone Namu in 1986. But its social breakdown had come
from Folofo'u's interventions and political activities. Jonathan Fifi'i's autobiographical account (1989:160–61) recounts what happened after
the Akins' departure.

As soon as David and Kate finished their three years and went home,
Folofo'u started to wreck the work of the school and the things that had been
built up. First, he announced that girls and women who came down to
Ngarinaasuru couldn't wear skirts. He put a ritual injunction against it,[1] so
that anyone who violated his word would have to pay him compensation.
Well, it's true that according to our custom, unmarried girls and women go
completely nude. But nowadays, girls from the bush have learned to be

1. He *kwaigoongae*, a kind of injunction whereby an important man curses his own head, with
the curse only becoming operative if the injunction is violated.

ashamed to go nude in areas where outsiders often visit. It's not that they are
ashamed of their bodies, or afraid of their own people seeing them nude. They
do that every day, in their own settlements. What they ashamed of is going
nude in front of people who don't understand their customs, and will stare at
them or make fun of them. "Ngarinaasuru is a meeting place people come to
from all over—mission people, Europeans, Government people. It's not good
for us to be there without any clothes on. When we go there, we have to put
our best skirts on, and dress up and be seen. We wash and put our best ornaments on and do ourselves up and put our best skirts on. Going nude is for
our own place. If someone comes up there, that's all right. We're not going to
be ashamed of following our own customs in our own homes." But Folofo'u
wouldn't listen, and swore by his own head against their putting skirts on.
From that time on, the women started to stay away from Ngarinaasuru.

When David and Kate had left, after three years, they had told everyone to
carry on. But after Folofo'u swore that way, the women gave it all up. Women
stopped coming, and the bakery was closed. Even Moruka,[2] who had been in
charge of the bakery, didn't want to go nude at Ngarinaasuru. Anyway, how
could she run the bakery all by herself?

. . . It was Folofo'u who broke down all the things we had built at
Ngarinaasuru. The cyclone of 1986 broke some of the buildings down. But it
was really Folofo'u who broke things down. Ngarinaasuru was abandoned and
overgrown.[3]

There were more dramatic confrontations going on as well.

2. The oldest surviving daughter of the great feastgiver 'Elota. See Keesing 1978b, and especially
the epilogue to the 1983 edition.
3. Five years later, in makeshift school buildings, virtually unequipped and with teachers working for token wages, two schools are transmitting literacy and customary knowledge to children in
the mountains. Although the marketing side of the craft industry has disintegrated, a number of
enterprising individuals in the mountains are still producing beautiful combs, ritual batons, clubs,
bags, and other craft items from which they can derive a small but sustaining cash income.

18 Kwaio Fadanga and Confrontation

Folofo'u's vision of the Kwaio future represented a synthesis of political
autonomy, hence freedom to follow customary law, and economic prosperity that would come from development assistance from overseas, especially "Marika"—the U.S., still remembered by older Kwaio pagans for

wartime generosity and comradeship. The contradictions between the following of ancestral ways and the prosperity "development" would bring were pushed beneath the surface.

From 1980 onward, Folofo'u's position became progressively strengthened by the recognition he was getting from the Province and central government as "Paramount Chief," hence legitimate spokesman for the Kwaio people. In dealing with these two levels of government, in the name of Kwaio Fadanga, Folofo'u was helped—but also manipulated and misled—by opportunistic Christian assistants variously called "secretaries" or "clerks." First, a young man named Lee Siilamo, who returned to Kwaio with political ambitions after being fired from his job with Solomon Islands Planned Parenthood, worked with Folofo'u and the "chiefs." But he was accused of appropriating Fadanga valuables for his personal use, then fired when he stopped turning up to teach at the Centre or work with the "chiefs." He was replaced by Silas Wanebeni, an equally ambitious young man who had taught faithfully in the Cultural Centre.

It is difficult to assess just what role these two men played in formulating the political demands of Kwaio Fadanga, but it seems to have been considerable. At this point, Fifi'i had narrowly lost his parliamentary seat to a young Christian named Daniel Fa'asifoaba'e. That name means "cause the ancestral shrines to lose their power," and the name was apt: he was intent on extending Christian evangelism as well as development through the district, and he had little sympathy for the pagans or their political aspirations. Hence, the pagans of Kwaio Fadanga felt increasingly alienated from national as well as provincial politics, further heightening the oppositional situation.

In this situation, Folofo'u—who had an old personal feud with Fifi'i that went back to their parents' generation—sought to marginalize and neutralize Fifi'i's still strong influence in mediating between the pagans and the powers outside. Fifi'i's autobiographical account recalls (1989:156) the conflicts of the time:

Folofo'u, acting as Paramount Chief, announced that Kwaio Fadanga didn't want me to work with them any more. I said that was all right. So after that, I had to stay out of what they were doing. In 1978 and 1979, I had been working with the leaders in the bush trying to work out compromises so people could follow their customs and use traditional ways of settling disputes through compensation, and at the same time work within the laws of our new country.

Meanwhile, relations between Kwaio Fadanga and Premier Stephen Tonafalea had totally disintegrated. Tonafalea refused to visit any of the Kwaio "passages" or to meet with the Fadanga leaders. In February 1983, when I was in Honiara briefly, the Minister for Malaita Provincial Affairs asked me to meet with Tonafalea, with Jonathan Fifi'i, to try to sort out the breaches of communication—and to persuade Tonafalea that, contrary to his suspicions, I was in no way responsible for the secessionist demands of Kwaio Fadanga. The Ministry arranged a meeting in 'Aoke. But when Fifi'i and I flew in from Honiara for the meeting, Tonafalea refused to meet with us: in fact, he fled from his office and hid all day behind the Province garage.

By this time, Kwaio Fadanga demands had incorporated a new and dramatic element: a claim for a staggering sum as compensation for the destruction of lives and property by the 1927 punitive expedition. The idea had been in the air for several years. In 1978, Siilamo had mentioned to me in a letter his idea of claiming compensation for the devastation of 1927. Jonathan Fifi'i had sought to pursue the question in 1977 and 1978 constitutional talks in London. In 1982, with Wanebeni acting as catalyst and spokesman, lists were compiled of the deaths caused by the punitive expedition, and of women raped, property destroyed, and shrines desecrated. Although by then *Lightning Meets the West Wind* (Keesing and Corris 1980) had been in print and for sale in the Solomons for two years, what took shape as a demand for massive compensation emerged without reference to the book; and the devastation assigned to the punitive expedition massively exceeded what Corris and I had documented. Jonathan Fifi'i's autobiographical account (1989:157–58) reflects his view:

Folofo'u and Silas Wanebeni were working together. They started recording all the bad things the Government force had done in 1927, when they came and destroyed our area after Mr. Bell was killed. I was away. I didn't know about what they were doing. I didn't have any part in it. Anyway, you can't give Folofo'u any advice. When he makes up his mind about something, nobody can change it. There's no way to stop him or talk him out of something once he's made up his mind. Nobody can budge him. Nobody can get a word in. Whatever he says he's going to do, he goes ahead and does it.

They worked on that and then they announced that they were demanding death compensation[1] for the people killed by the Government force in 1927. . . .

Folofo'u went about that in the wrong way. If I had been working with

1. *Firitaa*, or compensation by those held responsible for a death made to the bereaved kin. A closely related category of compensation (see chap. 9) is *firiadalongaa*, where the ancestors of the victim are given compensation for the death of their descendant.

them, I'd have told them so. The British Government refused the claim on grounds of a statute of limitations. But if I'd been advising them, I would have said, "How can you invoke a statute of limitations when we weren't allowed to make our claims right after it happened?" When Mr. King was at Gwee'abe in 1928, when he was getting ready to go back to 'Aoke, he summoned all the Kwaio Headmen: Tafugenimauri from 'Oloburi, Maenaa'adi from Uru, Silifa and Braun Kwarialaena from Sinalagu. He announced to them, "I'm serving you notice that you can't talk any more about the things that happened after Mr. Bell was killed: not the six men who were hanged, not the men who died in prison, not the men sentenced to life in prison, not the people who were killed in the bush. It's all finished. Nobody can say anything more about it. From now on, if anyone talks about what happened, I'll send him to prison for a year." When the Headmen notified people about this, everyone was afraid to say anything, or make any claims. How could anyone say anything? The government had threatened us that anyone saying anything about it would be put in prison. How can you invoke a statute of limitations saying people didn't make a claim at the time when the same government ordered you not to, and threatened reprisals if you did?

Anyway, who did we have who could have argued our claims? The Headmen didn't represent us. They worked for the government. If they had spoken for our side, the government would have sacked them. When we did put forward leaders to speak for our side and voice our grievances, in Maasina Rule, you know what happened. As soon as we did that, the government arrested us and put us in prison. How can they talk about a statute of limitations? That's what I would have argued if I had been making a claim for compensation. I had talked about that when I went to London with the Constitutional Committee. But when Kwaio Fadanga, led by Folofo'u, made their claim, they didn't ask me for my advice.

Late in 1983, when I was again in Honiara, Premier Tonafalea issued a statement to Solomon Islands Broadcasting Corporation (SIBC), broadcast on the national news, demanding that *Lightning Meets the West Wind* be banned from the Solomons, on grounds that the book was stirring up old conflicts. He then arrived in Honiara, and in a meeting with the Ministry of Education and Training, demanded that I be deported, and that all copies of the book in the Solomons be burned. His grievances against the book, which had been publicly expressed in terms of fanning conflict, were in this context made more explicit: he objected to the chapter on the punitive expedition, which documented in detail the shooting of prisoners in cold blood by the punitive expedition, naming the north

Malaita police Sergeants who led the patrols (whose sons and close kin were among his closest political supporters and allies in the Provincial Assembly). He justified his demand that I be deported by claiming that I had previously been deported: either pure fabrication on his part, or a mistaken identity in which he confused me with a historian working in Fataleka who had been forced to leave some years earlier.

At this inopportune moment—on a trip long delayed by transportation difficulties—Folofo'u and a delegation of Kwaio "chiefs" arrived in Honiara to press the compensation claim on the Prime Minister. I sought to persuade them to stay out of town for the short period until my scheduled departure; but instead, they surfaced immediately by issuing a radio press statement about their claim. Given the Premier's conviction that I was behind the compensation claim (even though it was subverted by the account in *Lightning Meets the West Wind*) as well as the separatist demands, my position was precarious to say the least. I had one opportunity to meet with Folofo'u and his fellow "chiefs" at the house of Fifi'i's son, and attempted to dissuade them from pressing the compensation claim. I argued that under international law, there were no legal grounds for such a claim (at that time, no figure had been announced). "I don't care about *their* laws," Folofo'u pronounced in his usual rhetorical style. "According to *our* laws we have a right to compensation." The claim was being cast as *firitaa*, the Kwaio category of compensation paid by those responsible for a death to the bereaved kin (although elements of it entailed other forms of damages, such as *totonga*, compensation for a sexual invasion).

I issued a press statement dissociating myself from the demands of Kwaio Fadanga, and beat a retreat to Australia. It was to be almost three years before I was allowed to return—and then only grudgingly. In that period, the compensation claim was put to writing by Silas Wanebeni. Fifi'i (1989:158–60) recalls:

The money they demanded was ridiculous, something like $294,612,630,000. Too much even to count or to think about. I didn't know anything about a number like that. When I went to America, I heard people talking about millions. But I'd never even heard of a billion. But that's what the two of them came up with, Folofo'u and Silas Wanebeni.

How could you take a claim like that seriously? Even the people Folofo'u claimed to represent couldn't make any sense out of it. The people in the bush said, "That can't be right. Folofo'u claimed an unthinkably large amount, just out of his imagination." In the Kwaio language, we call some amount like that *abuidumia*—'impossible to count'. "What government would have an amount like that?" they asked. "It's like one of us having hundreds and hundreds and hundreds of important shell valuables: out of the realm of possibility. Could any country have that much money?" I told them they were right: no country has money like that to pay compensation with. Silas Wanebeni took the numbers Folofo'u gave him—2,000 people killed, and so forth—and did the multiplication: so much per life, so much per rape, so much per desecrated shrine. He added it all up and that's how they got that silly total. They just made all the numbers up, anyway.

Folofo'u started to talk against me really strongly then. He was angry because I wasn't supporting them. He cursed me. It's not right to curse against a senior man. We're both senior men, he and I. It's all right to swear at a young boy. It's all right to swear against someone who's done something really bad. But Folofo'u—my own 'father', and a man only a little older than I am—cursed against me. . . .

When I [went] up to Ngarinaasuru, they didn't talk to me. Folofo'u and his advisors kept to themselves, as if he were a dictator. . . . I tried to talk to them, and calm down the trouble they were stirring up. "If the government sends you some kind of paper, let me look at it and make clear what it means. I've worked in the government for years. I know how the government operates, and I would know the implications of what they might write to you. I understand the thinking of the government, and the kinds of things they write. They might have quite good intentions; but you could misunderstand what it is about, and go off in the wrong direction. You might get angry about something the government has written when there is no reason to. You might tell the people, "Oh, the government says such-and-such," or "The government is doing such-and-such," and stir up a lot of hostility, when that's not what it's about at all. Even if they do send you something that goes against you, you might misinterpret it. Before you make any pronouncements, let me have a look at the papers and check up." They refused. "If you send anything to them, give me a copy so I can see what's happening." They refused that as well.

The amount demanded, according to a copy of the correspondence Silas Wanebeni sent me in 1986, was even higher than the one Fifi'i gives. I note in a recent paper (Keesing 1990:292–93) that

framed by Christian scribes, the claim lists the number of people, pigs, and houses whose destruction is attributed to the punitive expedition. Using a formula of the value of each life, and each act of rape or destruction, the claim totals up damages sought, arriving at the amount of $341,941,000,000. Exactly which government Kwaio Fadanga expects to pay the claim is not fully clear: for the the postcolonial state is a continuation of the colonial state, and "gafamanu" is "gafamanu." The Solomons Government passed the claim to the British High Commissioner, who promptly rejected it on grounds both that no claim had been made at the time and that the number of victims claimed was fanciful. . . .

Kwaio Fadanga claims that 1,246 deaths were caused by the punitive expedition. . . . This total of deaths was based not on the number supposed to have been shot (although that total was extremely inflated) and to have died from exposure and in prison, but added to this a total of those Kwaio pagans whose deaths since 1927 have been attributed to the anger of the ancestral spirits whose shrines had been desecrated by the punitive expedition.

I note that "the matter is slightly more complex than meets the eye, since the north Malaita police who committed the acts of desecration did so with the intention of causing Kwaio ancestors to kill and abandon their descendants" (ibid., 293).

The view of Kwaio pagan participants in three delegations that went to Honiara—marching en masse, in warrior finery, to the Prime Minister's office (and to his house, on another occasion)—is reflected in the recollections of Dangeabe'u of Furisi'ina I recorded in 1990:

Nothing happened—just talk. We talked about the *firitaa*. We talked about it and [Prime Minister Solomon] Mamaloni said, "That's fine." We went twice. First, we talked with Mamaloni and he said "fine." We waited, but nothing happened. So we came back a second time. Saelasi discussed what we wanted to do with the police and they gave us permission. So we staged a march. we marched to Mamaloni's office. Again we presented our demands for *firitaa*. He said, "That's all right. We'll put your claims forward, and we the government will see what happens. Maybe they'll agree to it. It's good that you've come to me."

I asked Dangeabe'u how they had arrived at the amount of the *firitaa* claim.

I don't know about that. Those foreign things—I don't understand them. . . . Saelasi Wanebeni put the claim together—the *firitaa* they demanded. All the "chiefs" tallied up the damages [from the punitive expedition]. They counted *fanua* [kin group territories], people dead, pigs, all the things that were destroyed. They reported their damages and Wanebeni put the claim together. The *alafa* worked with him [to compile it].

I asked Dangeabe'u how the amount was calculated.

They were such big numbers I couldn't understand them. Lots of money. All that went on the paper Wanebeni put together, but we didn't understand it. The amount for a single [dead] person was really big. And for the houses and gardens and pigs and shrines and bundles of saved valuables—there was an amount for each. All that was read out over the radio. They named a total of something like 7,000 people—people who have died because of the Gwee'abe fight.

I asked him what they had intended to do with the compensation if they had received it. "Well, it would compensate people for the loss of all those people whose lives were lost even though they and their groups had nothing to do with the fight or with planning it."

The demands of Kwaio Fadanga had been passed to the British High Commissioner. Eventually, the predictable response of an ever-legalistic former colonial government, and one with so many historical sins of so many colonial frontiers to keep buried, came back: a statute of limitations for pressing the claim had long since passed. (While dissociating myself from the claim, I pointed out to the British High Commissioner in correspondence the same irony on which Fifi'i commented: that when the Kwaio did attempt to express their grievances, immediately after the punitive expedition and during Maasina Rule, they were subjected to massive repression by the colonial state and a denial of the legitimacy of the leaders making the demands.) However, the British expressed willingness to consider funding an appropriate aid project—a medical clinic for the bush, for instance—as an expression of retrospective regret over the events of 1927, and (implicitly) as redress for years of neglect. Fifi'i (1989:163–64) recounts what happened when the message came back to Kwaio Fadanga.

Sir Peter Kenilorea and Andrew Nori, the son of my old friend and prison companion, who is Minister of Home Affairs and Provincial Government, went to Sinalagu to talk to Folofo'u. Kenilorea said, "I've had a reply from the British High Commission about your claim for compensation. It has been too long. The period for making a claim under international law has run out— what they call the "statute of limitations." After the six years you have to make a claim have passed, no one can put a claim forward. The British High Commissioner said he was sorry, but it had gone past the time limit. But I think if you asked for some money for some form of development, they would help you."

Folofo'u said, "Impossible! Give us our money! Put the money in my hand!" Sir Peter said, "That's impossible. The amount you're talking about doesn't exist. It would be impossible for England to pay that much, or any other country. Nobody has heard of that much money. Maybe some people can count that high, but nobody can really imagine how much it would be."

Folofo'u said, "Impossible! We don't want development! We want our
money! Hand it over! If you gave us money for development, how long would
that last?" "That would depend on how much money was available, and what
you want to use it for." Folofo'u said, "If you're going to give us money for development, you have to give it to us for 99 years." Sir Peter said, "You go off
and think about it. I want to do something to help you, but you have to be reasonable. Go off and discuss it."

After thirty minutes, Kenilorea called them back. "You've been discussing
it. What have you decided?" Folofo'u said, "Impossible! Give us our compensation!" Kenilorea said, "There's nothing more I can do. But if you think about it
and decide you want some form of development, you have to send word to me.
You have to decide what you want—a clinic in the bush, or whatever it's going
to be—and I'll try to find the means to do it. I think the British Government
will help you." But Folofo'u and his Kwaio Fadanga supporters didn't pursue it.

Dangeabe'u recalls Folofo'u's response:

But the government didn't do it. The government didn't want to give us the
firitaa. After a long time, Folofo'u said, "They're not going to give it. They just
lied to us. . . . "

Kenilorea said that [although the *firitaa* wouldn't be paid] the Government
would build us a clinic, and that the Government would give money for whatever kind of development we wanted. But not the money. That's what led to
the boycott and the teargassing. [Folofo'u said] "If they won't pay the compensation, we won't allow the Member to represent us." That's when he imposed
the boycott. "You lied to us, you the Government, so we won't allow a Member to represent us."

19 Confrontations and Dangers

When *gafamanu* failed to produce the compensation Folofo'u demanded—
he seems to have been unconcerned with the question of which government, the British or the Solomons, might be responsible—he again dramatically turned his back on the participation of Kwaio Fadanga and the
Kwaio people in the affairs of the country. The most dramatic way to express this withdrawal and rejection was to "boycott" the national parlia-

mentary election that would have sent a Kwaio[1] Member to Parliament. Since the standing member, Daniel Fa'asifoaba'e, was recontesting the election of November 1985—and with the strong support of the Prime Minister was likely to win—in fact this represented both a general and diffuse political protest and a sharply focused one: a rejection of the Kenilorea government and of Fa'asifoaba'e as its representative. There was an alternative strategy: Silas Wanebeni, representing Folofo'u, demanded that he, Silas, be made Member to replace Fa'asifoaba'e. Busumae remembers that

Saelasi Wanebeni went to Honiara. He wanted to replace Fa'asifoaba'e [as Parliament Member]. [Home Minister Andrew] Nori told him that he would have to win an election, according to the law. Saelasi came back and he and Folofo'u imposed a boycott. At that time Saelasi was secretary to ["Paramount Chief"] Folofo'u. Folofo'u imposed the boycott because the claim had not been paid. "If you won't meet our demands, we won't have Fa'asifoaba'e, we won't allow a [Parliamentary] Member to represent us. Because you have refused my claim, and the King [Kini] hasn't firi [paid death compensation] for me."

Folofo'u dramatically put a ritual injunction—a kind of curse by the sanctity of his head (kwaiabuingaa)—against the election being held in Kwaio, and against anyone voting if the government forced an election.

By this time Sir Peter Kenilorea and his Minister of Home Affairs Andrew Nori were thoroughly fed up with Folofo'u's rejection of what seemed reasonable compromise. Nori later confided to me[2] that up until this point, Folofo'u and Kwaio Fadanga had been politically brilliant in using the compensation issue to force recognition by both the British and Solomons governments that East Kwaio had been systematically left out of the country's development and that redress was just and needed. In fact, the last British Governor of the Solomons (whose experience went back to his days as District Commissioner of Malaita in 1947 presiding over "Operation De-Louse") told me in Government House in 1977 that it had been unwritten BSIP policy for the fifty years since the Bell massacre to leave the east Kwaio interior and adjacent 'Are'are forever undeveloped as a reservoir of cheap labor. If this was indeed a matter of

---

1. In all this, "Kwaio" can be taken to mean the eastern side of the island, and East Kwaio as an electoral district. "West Kwaio" is mainly Christian and relatively developed economically; those communities have been only indirectly and marginally affected by Kwaio Fadanga and separatist politics.

2. Personal communication 1988.

policy, and not merely geography—and the deployment of Protectorate resources points in this direction—then the confrontations with Kwaio Fadanga and the present situation whereby Kwaio pagans constitute an angry underclass, the main perpetrators of crimes of theft and violence in the country, are its fruit.

But in rejecting offers of massive redress, Folofo'u and his Christian advisers had lost their moment and such sympathy as they commanded in Honiara. The government resolved to hold the 1985 election in the face of the boycott. The boycott was solidly maintained at Sinalagu and 'Oloburi. But in the Christian villages around Uru Harbor, substantial numbers of voters cast their ballots; and at the Atoifi Hospital, most of the nurses apparently voted.

This challenge to his authority as "Paramount Chief" and to the sanctity of his head enraged Folofo'u and his followers, and he sent word down to the Atoifi Hospital that he was coming to exact his due. (The accounts I have give conflicting versions of what threats of violence, if any, were used to back up demands for massive compensation to "purify"[3] the defilement the ignoring of his ritual injunction entailed.) Confrontation seemed about to reach the violence that had long been feared. Busumae recalls that

we boycotted it [the election]. Just the people at Uru, the people at Atoifi Hospital and the mission people, voted. They elected Fa'asifoaba'e. He won. Folofo'u said, "All the Sinalagu people didn't vote—only the people at Atoifi." He heard that those people had ignored his boycott. He sent word down: "I'm going to come down to claim my purification compensation [siulaa] for all you Atoifi nurses, and you mission people. You're going to purify me! I'll come down at such-and-such a time."

The government's response was to ready the Field Force, a mobile quasi-army unit of some sixty men, to deploy them in protection of the hospital. The Australian High Commissioner Trevor Sofield, with a special interest in the protection of the Australian staff of the hospital, persuaded the government, with Australian logistical assistance, to evacuate the staff. Busumae's account continues:

Folofo'u and his sons and Saelasi [Wanebeni] went down to Atoifi. The people down there had all run away and taken refuge in 'Aoke and Honiara, in the face of the warning threats. [Kwaio Fadanga] had threatened to dig up the airstrip. Only three men, Mousisi and Seda and the driver from Langalanga,

3. *Siufia*, lit. "wash."

had stayed at Atoifi. The rest had all run away, saying "the Kwaio people are
going to come down and kill us. Let's take refuge." They all left, and the police
came from 'Aoke . . . to keep anyone from coming in and destroying things.

The police waited for two days, but Folofo'u and his men didn't come down.
The police went to Folofo'u. The AAO [Provincial Administrative Officer]
came. I think the important people from the Provincial Government came.
Folofo'u came down and met with them. They straightened things out.
Folofo'u told them, "We weren't really going to dig up the airfield or destroy
anything. We weren't going to kill anyone. That was just a threat. But you,
the government, and the people who voted, have to give me money as purificatory compensation. You have to purify me, and I'll be satisfied." The police
and the Province leaders went back . . . to discuss it. People had thought they
were going to be killed; they were relieved that nothing was going to happen.
"That's good. We'll straighten it all out."

"We're going to pay to purificatory compensation. Even I [Fa'asifoaba'e] am
going to pay you compensation for having voted." They brought $1000 as pu-
rificatory compensation. Even the government, the Member and Provincial
Members, contributed money. They paid purificatory compensation, down at
Gelebasi. I was there.

Then Samusoni Sikumia took Fa'asifoaba'e to court [challenging his election on the grounds that too few people had voted]. They considered the case
for two months or so, then Sukumia won. Daniel [Fa'asifoaba'e] was stood
down as Member [his selection was declared void]. For six months or so—I
don't know, we don't keep track with a calendar—Fa'asifoaba'e didn't represent us. There was no Member representing us.

But having paid compensation the Government wanted Daniel's election to
be validated. But Folofo'u still wasn't satisfied. The compensation [for the 1927
post-massacre-massacre] still hadn't been paid.

A new election would have to be held; and until the obstacle of
Folofo'u's boycott could be effectively cleared, the matter lay in suspense.

Further storms, climatic and political, were building. In June 1986 a
devastating cyclone, Cyclone Namu, struck the Solomons. Along the
eastern coast of Malaita the damage was massive: whole villages of
thatched houses were totally destroyed, on the coast and in the mountains; and in the bush, huge forest trees torn away as if mowed down.
Tens of thousands on Malaita and elsewhere in the Solomons were left
homeless, and without the sago thatch for roofs and walls needed for re-
placement houses. Gardens were devasted, paths were blocked; in the
central Malaita mountains, the thin forest and soil cover was torn away
down to bare basalt.

Relief efforts from overseas were swift and substantial, but they were to generate more discontent in the region. In the weeks that followed the cyclone, thousands of sheets of corrugated metal roofing were delivered along the Malaita coast and sold at low cost; and sacks of rice were distributed. But given their advantages of patronage, local politics, access to cash, and geography, all the metal roofing and most of the rice ended up in the hands of the coastal Christians. As usual, the pagans in the bush were mainly ignored, heightening their bitterness and cynicism about the benign rhetoric of the postcolonial state.

In the immediate wake of the cyclone, more storms—this time political ones—were brewing in Honiara. Prime Minister Sir Peter Kenilorea, already frustrated by the blocking of the election and the departure of Daniel Fa'asifoaba'e from the government's ranks, was threatened by a vote of no confidence; and the numbers looked ominously as though without his East Kwaio Member, Sir Peter would lose out and fall from power.

The government resolved to force a new election to fill the vacant seat. Busumae recalls the events that could have led to massive bloodshed, hearkening back again to the refusal of the compensation claim as the beginning of it all.

The beginning of it was when Folofo'u's claim for *firitaa* from the Gwee'abe fight was rejected. We went to Honiara. Folofo'u demanded *firitaa* but it was rejected. He was angry about it. He *kwaigongae* [swore by his head] against their holding the [parliamentary] election. "I Folofo'u demanded our compensation, and you the Government didn't fix it up, you rejected it." He swore by his head that people couldn't vote. The Government insisted that the election go ahead. They insisted that a Member be elected to represent us. But Folofo'u stood against it.

So the government brought the army. Sixty of the field force came, in two ships—the *Belama* and the *Tulagi*. They sent a message: "Go to Folofo'u and summon him here." The police went to his place.

In the morning, they went to Nunubilau, and we gathered there. There were 50 or 60 of us. We gathered there and the Government said: "You are to vote." Folofo'u replied: "There won't be any voting. Even though people have gathered here, they can't vote."

They brought the voting boxes into the house, and two clerks with the voting papers stood at the door. We sent two of our "soldiers"[4] with them: Diake

---

4. Kwaio Fadanga have maintained a set of "police" or "soldiers" since the early 1980s, a modern equivalent to the "Duties" of Maasina Rule (see Laracy 1983).

Futageni and Bati—to make sure no one voted. The "soldiers" of Kwaio
Fadanga. No one could vote without their seeing it.

Nothing happened until around noon, Maaten Akomae went, took a ballot, and voted. He put his ballot in the case, and Bati and Diake called out.
We were a long way away. "Maaten Akomae has cast his vote. He has broken
your law, gone against your ritual injunction." Folofo'u and his sons 'Ubuni
and Kwa'ilamo jumped to their feet. "Why did you vote? Who said you could
vote? You've violated my injunction!" Folofo'u called out, and his sons grabbed
their machetes and went forward with him. "You have to *siufinau* [ritually purify me]!" They stepped forward with him. They weren't going to attack him,
but to quarrel, to impose their claim. "You have to purify me."

The Field Force had gone into formation, one line facing in this direction
and the other line facing them. They pointed their guns at us—tear gas guns
and real guns. We all surged forward in a body, challenging them. Folofo'u
and 'Ubuni and Kwa'ilamo may have had it in their minds to beat up Maaten.
When we all surged forward, the soldiers let loose their teargas. They shot at
Folofo'u—shot the teargas into the ground. Sgt. 'Abaiata, from West Kwaio,
fired first. And Sgt. Nau'ania—I don't know the third sergeant's name. They
raised their hands and then threw their teargas canisters.

Some of the teargas was thrown, like a hand grenade when you pull the pin;
and some of it was fired from guns. Two different kinds of teargas. They shot
real bullets too, but over our heads. We picked up the empty cartridges afterwards—after the Field Force had gone back to their ships.

Basiitau[5] called out, "They're shooting at us! What are they shooting with?"
"They're shooting teargas," I called out. Basiitau thought they were shooting
real bullets, and he was about to invoke his ancestors. If he'd invoked the *adalo*
there would have been no turning back—it would have been a real battle, like
the one at Gwee'abe. Because if you've invoked your *adalo* you go into a state
of craziness [*kaku*]. The *adalo* would press you to fight. Basiitau wasn't the only
one. All of us would had done it.

We lunged at Sgt. 'Abaiata—Fa'afusia and I and others—and knocked him
down and stood over him. If anyone of our men had fallen, we would have
killed 'Abaiata. Fa'afusia and I stood over him with our machetes raised like
this. The others lunged for the Field Force soldiers. They didn't stay in their
formation: they scattered in the face of our men. Four of the soldiers from the
Shortlands ran away into the sea. They scrambled ashore down the coast, and
came upon an old woman named 'Asu. She was so frightened she tried to run,

---

5. A man in his sixties from Furi'ilai, whose father had taken a prominent part in the Bell massacre and had been killed by the punitive expedition.

and fell down, hitting her torso on a stone. She was in great pain for a week, then died.

We faced off with them, and 'Abaiata called out[6], "Nothing is going to happen—it was only teargas." "You're not going to shoot at us? If you do any-thing more we'll go for you and it will be just like Gwee'abe. Even though you have the guns, we're not afraid of you!" We all challenged them. We'd have fought them to the end, even if we'd all been killed—it would have been just like Gwee'abe.

The mission people came running down with steel pipes and knives. "What happened? Have they killed anyone?" "No, they just shot us with tear gas." But the teargas gassed young children who were being held in arms up in the vil-lage, and they were really sick. The old men from the mission were brandishing their war clubs, and we had to restrain them to keep them from attacking the police.

We thought that when the people from [the mission village at] Gounaabusu got there, they *would* attack the Field Force. So I told 'Abaiata to get his men out to the ships. X.[7] knew about machine guns. He had gone aboard the *Tulagi*, where they had the machine gun trained on us. The police com-mander, David Silheti, was there on the machine gun. X. was right next to him, ready to bash him if he had opened fire, and use the machine gun to si-lence the ships.

The police took all their stuff, including the ballot boxes, back to the ships. We told them if they stayed on shore, people would get killed. They took the ballot boxes onto the ships, and the people who wanted to vote cast their votes there.

If they had tried to hold the election at Gelebasi [which would have been the normal place, and the place that had apparently been announced as the polling station] there really would have been a fight. Because that's where people had expected a confrontation, and men were hiding in the bush with lots of guns. There were lots of men concealed in the bush. It was like the time in Maasina Rule when they came to arrest Fifi'i. There were two fifteen rounders. If they had tried to do the voting at Gelebasi, it really would have been like the attack at Gwee'abe all over again.

The election at gunpoint attracted just enough votes to get Fa'asi-foaba'e reelected. (The cynicism of the election as a political exercise was underlined by the fact that a day or two after being declared elected,

6. In Kwaio language: the east and west coast dialects are close and mutually intelligible.
7. A Kwaio man from Sinalagu who had retired as one of the most senior officers in the Solomons police force.

Fa'asifoaba'e cast the deciding vote in an eighteen to seventeen defeat of the motion of no confidence against the Kenilorea government.) It left further bitterness—and a further claim for purificatory compensation by Folofo'u—in its wake.

The following year, Fa'asifoaba'e died: was it a liver ailment, as the doctors claimed, or the ancestors? But by that time, Folofo'u's pagan supporters were losing their enthusiasm for his confrontationist policies and angry rhetoric and dictatorial style, and were staying away from his political meetings. The Cultural Centre complex at Ngarinaasuru had been largely destroyed by Cyclone Namu, and Folofo'u's ancestral curses had done the rest of the damage. Fifi'i, Folofo'u's longtime political rival, reflected (1989:164–65) that

now it's probably too late, Folofo'u has decided he wants "development." He has no idea what that means. Folofo'u says, "You have to give me money for 'development'." The Government told him that he had to have a plan. The Kwaio leaders had to decide what they wanted and plan how it was going to work. Then the Government would try to find aid money to pay for it. Then they would have to form a committee that would negotiate an agreement with the Government about the funds. Once all that had been done, the work could go ahead. But Folofo'u just imagines that the Government is going to come up and hand him a big bundle of money, so he can do whatever he likes with it.

Folofo'u claims he wants "development." But he doesn't know what that means. Development is very complicated. There are lots of different sides to it—health, education, agriculture. Kwaio people ask Folofo'u, "What kind of development are you talking about? What is the government supposed to give you money for?" He doesn't know. He just wants the government to hand over a lot of money, so all we'd have to do is sign for it. He wants it to be for 99 years, so money would keep on coming for generations. People down on the coast, people with some education, don't know what he has in mind. People in the bush don't know what he has in mind. Folofo'u is now giving the government three months to meet his demands for money for "development." If they don't, he says he'll be "finished with the government." I wish we were finished with him. People want to replace him, but he has put a curse against that.

The Kwaio people are angry about the way they've been ignored by the government. They say, "The British government forgot about us for 50 years, and never did anything for us but take our taxes. Now we're independent, and we Solomon Islanders are in charge of our own government, things are just the same. The new leaders are black on the outside, but they're just like the white men on the inside. We're still forgotten." That's why people from the bush were ready to listen to Folofo'u for a while. He seemed to be standing up to the government and demanding that they listen to the Kwaio people. But he was leading them in the wrong direction. It's not anyone from outside who has destroyed the work we were doing. It's Folofo'u, in our own midst, who has destroyed Ngarinaasuru.

People have demanded that he be replaced. But he cursed against that, too. He cursed saying, "A man shits on the tip of my knife blade and replaces me." That's a threat to kill [his successor], as well as a curse: a threat that Folofo'u will cut him in half. Whatever happens that runs against Folofo'u's will, he makes some curse or another. He curses and curses and curses. Those are matters of life and death. "Folofo'u has defiled us.[8] That's not a proper way of cursing."

Folofo'u's physical powers declined in the late 1980s, and walking is difficult for him now. The pagans regard him as a spent force, but bide their time until he can be replaced. Moves were afoot in May 1990 to rebuild the *bungu 'ifi* at Ngarinaasuru. A half hour of talking with Folofo'u on my way down the hill left me doubting that we had heard the last of him as "Paramount Chief" and charismatic antigovernment leader. He was talking of again summoning meetings at Ngarinaasuru, of forcing the issues of compensation and legal jurisdiction yet again. And again, his political rhetoric was brilliant and logical in its own terms, though its vision was quite incompatible with the *realpolitik* of a post-colonial state:

Who are you, the government, to come here and tell me that I can't follow the customs of my ancestors, live on the land of my ancestors, follow the laws of my ancestors? Who gave England the right to come here and rule us according to their laws and against ours? And now we are supposed to be independent, what gives a black government the right to force those laws on us, living in our own ways on our own land with our own ancestors?

Until death stills his anger and his charisma, Folofo'u's voice will be heard, his powers will bend events around him. If Ngarinaasuru is to rise from the ruins, the time is not yet here. Nor is there clarity, among the Kwaio pagans or Christians, about what a rebuilt Ngarinaasuru is to be. It is envisioned as headquarters for a curious conceptual and political hybrid: Kwaio Fadanga and a reconstituted East Kwaio Area Council.[9]

8. *Fa'atafua*, lit. "made trash out of us."
9. The Province had proposed that the headquarters be located at Atori, at the head of the trans-Malaita road; but this is twenty miles by sea from Kwaio country, on the Kwara'ae-Fataleka border, and could not possibly serve Kwaio interests.

(From one context to the next, and one person's categorization to the next, the two entities are either separate or two names for the same thing; the government hopes to coopt separatist politics, the pagans to maintain an oppositional stance.) Ngarinaasuru is also variously envisioned both as a focus of Kwaio relations with the outside world and as the political heart of regional cultural and legal autonomy.

The pagans are still committed to codifying *kastomu* and using a written form of customary law to demand the right to cultural autonomy. We will come back to the contemporary forms of an old vision of a *kastomu* committed to writing, and hence both sanctified and legitimated. But first, we need to look at the Kwaio pagans outside their homeland, in a rapidly modernizing, Westernizing, and urbanizing young country.

20 Beyond the Mountains

Young Kwaio men continue to leave their home mountains, as they have for more than a century, to seek adventure and to acquire Western goods and cash. Like their fathers and grandfathers, they have nothing to sell but their musclepower. But the world to which they go has changed strikingly. Until the mid-1960s, the government centers of Honiara, Gizo, "Auki" and Tulagi were small, and commerce was entirely in the hands of Chinese and a few expatriates. The plantations where employment for Malaitans lay were mainly in the Russell Islands, the Western Solomons, and Guadalcanal. Most of them operated their own recruiting vessels or obtained labor under contract from recruiters. Hence to *leka naa faka*, 'go abroad, go to a plantation', meant signing aboard a recruiting ship, being conveyed to a plantation where quarters and rations were provided, obtaining trade goods through a company store or Chinese store, and then being brought back home when two or more years had expired. The plantation recruit could expect to return with a box of trade goods—axes, knives, cloth, mirror, spoon, cigarette lighter, a pipe, earrings and beads for a sister or girlfriend, some twist tobacco—and some cash. (With their proclivity to gamble, with dice or cards, some recruits returned home empty-handed, but otherwise a predictable return was guaranteed.)

In the mid-1960s, Lever's Pacific Plantations Ltd. made a policy decision (catalyzed at the time partly by Kwaio cattle rustling, when the company tried an alternative and more profitable means of keeping undergrowth cleared in the plantation paddocks) not to recruit contract labor from Malaita, but to settle permanent plantation workers and their families. Although in the years since some short-term jobs have been available at the Lever's Yandina Plantation in the Russells (and at other Lever's operations), aspiring workers must now find their own way to the plantations, and with no certainty of work. The recruiters and recruiting ships have long since disappeared from Solomons waters.

To get to Guadalcanal or Western Solomons plantations, young Kwaio men must find and pay their own way, by commercial or government ship (at a cost of $10 to $50 or more, depending on the destination), or take the SDA plane from Atoifi (now $64 one way to Honiara). A similar cost must be incurred to get home. Thus a young man going "abroad" to seek adventure and cash must now go substantially into debt simply to get there. If passing through Honiara or Auki or Gizo, he will then be dependent on networks of *wantoks*—Kwaio settled in town or already on plantations, such as Lavuro Plantation at the western end of Guadalcanal or the oil palm plantations on the Guadalcanal plains—for food and shelter. There is no guarantee of work, although Kwaio men working as plantation managers or as entrepreneurs may provide jobs. (In the Western Solomons, many Kwaio men are married to local women who own the land; and they hire young kin as laborers.) Other jobs are available, often on a casual basis, in the rapidly expanding towns; but there, the workers must usually find their own shelter and rations. (There, the position of Kwaio pagans in the workforce is precarious; a few years ago, the Honiara Town Council hired mostly young pagan men, mainly Kwaio, to "brush" the grass along the roads; but now these jobs go mainly to women, increasingly pressured to get paid employment, and more likely to be committed workers.)

Until the late 1960s, virtually all Malaitans who worked in the cash economy did the same labor, in the same conditions, as the Kwaio pagans. Only a small handful were involved in serious cash crop production or were working as clerks, teachers, or functionaries for government or missions. Nowadays, Solomon Islanders are sharply stratified by class, education, and mode of life. The Kwaio pagans are at the very bottom of an indigenous class system, working for wages no others (other than "unskilled" women) would accept, under uncertain conditions, with less certain rewards than their fathers had received. They are surrounded by comparative prosperity: Solomon Islanders driving their own cars, watching videos at home, drinking beer. They walk the streets of Chinatown, hang around the markets, with no cash; or they work on plantations, and come into town when they can.

At any given time, several hundred young Kwaio pagan men are working on plantations and drifting around the towns. The disruptions they
cause to law and order far exceed their numbers. With ancestrally supported and culturally reinforced skills of theft—at home, of pigs and
valuables—they are well equipped as well as motivated to redistribute
the wealth they see around them. With a reputation for toughness and
bravado, and the support of warlike ancestors, the young men seek out
confrontations and violence. When fights break out or a killing is reported, suspicion inevitably first points to Kwaio thugs, and most often,
with good cause.

In 1989, I got lengthy accounts of urban theft—shoplifting, safecracking, and housebreaking—from several Kwaio men, including the
most famous thief of his generation. A few fragments of a long and rich
text will give glimpses of Kwaio predation: what I have called "foraging in
the urban jungle" (Keesing n.d. 5). L, the archthief, recalled:

When I first came to Honiara, I had been working at Niusamo. It was three
months or so after I arrived in town that I ran out of money. One day I was
standing in front of this store in Chinatown, and I said to myself, "I haven't got
even a dollar, not even fifty cents." I turned it over and over in my mind. And
then I got an idea. In those days, the Chinamen didn't stick the bills they got
under the counter, the way they do nowadays. They just set them out in a line
on the counter—all the two dollar notes, all the tens, all the twenties. I got an
idea. I went and got a stick, and put a nail in the end [at right angles to it]. I
went in the store. I reached over with the stick and stuck [the nail] into [the
pile of bills] and swept them up. I got maybe fifty dollars in one try. I went into
another store and did it again. And then another. I had started at nine o'clock
in the morning, and by eleven I had about five or six hundred. I said to myself,
"Hey, luck is with me."[1] So I went off with the money. I used it for food, and
beer, and in a week it was all gone. So I went and did it again. . . .

I said to myself, "Well, why not take a sewing machine?" So I picked one up
and walked out of the store with it. But once I got outside, I wondered to myself, "What am I going to do with a big, heavy thing like this?" I got out to the
street and flagged a taxi. So I took it off and sold it. A Kwara'ae man bought it,
for four hundred. So then, before the week was out I took an outboard motor
and sold it. I took it from this place where they sell outboard motors. I just
went in . . . in the middle of the day. There was only one man inside. He went
into the room [office] and I just carried it out. I went outside with it and put
it down. I said to myself, "What am I going to do with such a big and heavy

1. He uses Kwaio Pijin *baoa* ("power"), as a calque on *nanamangaa*, which here can be glossed
'ancestrally conferred luck [in the sense of efficacy]'.

thing?" I stood there and a taxi came by, driven by a *wantok*. I flagged him down. He asked me, "What about that thing? Did you pay for it?" "Hey, man, what do you think?" I was already getting a reputation. They'd say, "Oh, he's a larriken!"[2] They'd know that whatever I came up with, I'd stolen. And so it went on. I'd go into a store and walk out with a tape recorder or a mattress or a bolt of cloth or a radio. Whatever was in the store that I wanted.

K, L's boyhood accomplice in theft of pigs and shell valuables, and now a plantation foreman, recalled that

his stealing went on and on. He'd get tape recorders—I'd see them. He'd take anything at all—tape recorders, chainsaws. He'd show me the loot. "I've got a chainsaw." So I'd go and see, and sure enough, he'd have one. I'd say, "What did you steal that for? I don't want to know about it." "That's OK, it's mine. I'll take it and sell it." "How are you going to sell something like that?" "Oh, everyone knows about [the quality of my merchandise]." That was his way. Watches, whatever you wanted. Sometimes you'd look and he'd have put a whole row of watches all the way up his arm. His bag was like his store. You'd look inside that big bag of his, and you'd find whatever you were looking for. It was practically a suitcase.

L reminisced that

in those days I used to take the things I'd stolen back home, and sell them. I used to steal things from vehicles in the market. One time a taxi was backing into a space and I just opened the door and made off with this thing. If I'd see a car with money or a tape recorder in it, I'd lift it in no time; when they'd come back they'd find it gone. But they'd never see me. . . . Word did get around. In the end the Chinese would stare at me when I'd come past and then call to one another in their own language. "Oh, there's that guy!" They knew my name, too.

I asked L if he prayed to his ancestors, as Kwaio thieves do at home. "I didn't pray to the *adalo*. . . . It wasn't that I'd invoke my *adalo* to steal. I don't know—maybe the spirits were there in my body. As though I had the power of the *adalo* in me. . . . One 'boy' saw me stealing and asked me, 'How do you do it? Do you know some magic?'[3] I told him, 'No, I don't know how I do it.' I could just do it. Not by praying, not by using

---

2. I use the Australian colloquialism, which has implications of a troublemaking tough guy but also a rogue, a system-beater with a sense of style combing bravado with humor. The Pijin expression L uses is *man baa*, lit. "a steel rod of a man."

3. Solomons Pijin *meresin* 'medicine'.

magic." K added his views about the *adalo* and the powers to steal in town without being caught. "My feeling is that because from the time we were kids we had asked our ancestors to help us in stealing, he [L] had acquired a kind of power from that. So he didn't have to pray specially to be able to pick something up and get away with it. I didn't either—I didn't pray. We both had that kind of power, but it was as though mine started to cool down, and his got hotter and hotter."

L went on to tell me about his stealing of safes and his housebreaking.

I know all about stealing safes. . . . I've stolen two or three of them. I didn't ask my *adalo* to help, but other people do. Because sometimes even a small safe is too heavy to lift unless the *adalo* helps you. But I still don't think it's right to do that. One of the ones we got—there were only two of us—was really big, up to here. But the two of us just picked up the bottom and carried it outside. . . . I opened it with an axe. I just broke it open and took the money. . . . I think it was twenty thousand dollars. Not too bad. And fifteen thousand in the other two I got. They were bigger, and it took four of us to lift them. But when we got them outside, it took us no time at all to break them open.

L went on to detail his successes in housebreaking (and his methods for turning watchdogs into friends) and his burglaries of shops and offices at night. I asked L and K about whether theft by Kwaio was common in the Western Solomons as well.

It's a great place for Kwaio thieves. The houses are no good. People leave their money inside and don't shut the houses properly. They're like pig houses. Sometimes they sleep inside without even locking the doors. So you can just go in and help yourself to whatever you want, take the box of money. But even where the money is in a safe, and it's a strong house made of iron, you can still get in and take the whole lot, every penny. . . .

Malaita people can steal those Western people blind. Those people don't understand those ways. They just leave their houses wide open. The Guadalcanal people are the same way. Lots of them don't watch over their houses carefully, and just leave their money and shell money lying around any old way. So we Kwaio people come to Honiara. Suppose we just hang around and don't work. We can just go around and rob people. People who steal can get rich from it. The ones who work don't get rich they way the ones who steal do. Everyone is getting rich from stealing. Some people say that stealing is no good, but others see that the thieves are getting rich, so it must be OK.

Two teen-aged Kwaio boys were working on the plantation, and I asked them about stealing. One of them told me,

Sure, when we were young kids at home, we used to steal. Pigs and shell money and cash and any old stuff, like knives and pieces of cloth. We knew all about stealing that stuff. [When we came to town and then the plantation] of course, we tried stealing. When we came, it was just like they talked about— we did the same. We wanted to steal other people's good stuff . . .—in houses, in stores. We saw the stuff in the Chinese shops and wanted to get our hands on it. So we had to find money. We went ahead and stole it. . . . If it was to steal something big, you'd ask your *adalo* to help. But not for any old thing, something not worth very much. You just go ahead and do it. . . . We stole from people's houses too. Everyone tries that. Because at home, we all go around stealing pigs and shell money and good stuff other people have. So when we come here we have to try the same thing.

 . . . [Stealing is] something that came from the olden days, from our fathers and our ancestors. So we're just following our customs and the ways of our fore-fathers. [RMK: But is it different when you come here to town?] Well, in some ways we look at it as just the same, but in some ways, it's different. It's not such a big deal at home. At home, you take shell money or cash or pigs. If you get caught, they have to pay compensation, but it's not a big thing, and they don't take you away. But here, you steal some trivial little thing, and if they catch you, they send you to prison.

If the predation by Kwaio thieves wreaks havoc among the more pros-perous Melanesians, the shopkeepers and companies, and particularly the expatriate community, recent killings have been vastly more disrup-tive. Strong resentment and hostility have been building up for years among the people of the Guadalcanal coastal zone who are faced with increasing numbers of Malaita squatters, Malaita dominance of Honiara and its Town Council, and the depredations and violence of the Malaita riff-raff, especially the Kwaio. Fights in town, and on and around planta-tions, have regularly been attributed to Malaitan wildness. (Although nowadays Polynesians from Bellona are rivaling the Malaitans for tough-ness and violence in town.)

A string of unsolved and seemingly unmotivated murders on Guadalcanal[4] in the 1980s brought matters toward a crisis. The crisis erupted when, in February 1988, three villagers from Barana, on Mt. Austen near Honiara, were hacked to death with axes as they slept. Three young Kwaio pagans were arrested soon afterwards, and brought to trial.

I have elsewhere (Keesing n.d.4) written of the extraordinary disjunc-

4. And in the Western Solomons.

ture between the account of the murders constructed by the Western legal machinery of the Solomons and the event as culturally constructed by the Kwaio protagonists. What was in legal terms virtually unmotivated represented, from the Kwaio side, an unfolding of ancestrally enjoined violence and vengeance that ultimately went back to the 1927 massacre. The most immediate provocation from the Kwaio point of view was an incident a year earlier in which, after a fight that broke out at a party following a wedding at a Guadalcanal village, a young Kwaio man was killed, and his body hidden. Two Kwaio men, agnatic first cousins connected to two of the three descent groups whose leaders plotted the killing of Bell in 1927, empowered by prayer and sacrifice, took an SDA flight to Honiara to kill Guadalcanal people in vengeance. They killed the sleeping villagers in cold blood—victims chosen almost randomly on the basis of a minor grievance—and then flew back to Atoifi. They were joined in the attack by a young Kwara'ae man they had apparently met on the margins of the victims' village, who had been intimidated into accompanying them.[5]

Frighteningly, the killing was partly triggered by the fact that a blood bounty had been put up, with any Guadalcanal person as a suitable vengeance victim, for the death of the Kwaio man after the wedding. There is some hint in the tangled and largely hidden web of accounts regarding the killings that that victim may himself have been trying to collect a blood bounty secretly offered earlier. It seems that a strong element in these ostensibly unmotivated killings by young Kwaio men has been incitement by fathers who, though descended from warlike ancestors and coming from warrior kin groups centrally implicated in the 1927 massacre and earlier blood feuding, have themselves been immobilized by forced pacification. Among those who have incited their sons to acts of homicide and blood vengeance we find men whose own fathers were at Gwee'abe and who were themselves ready to fight against the government in 1947. Fathers who were forbidden to kill, and satisfy their ancestors and their pride, are encouraging sons to do what they could not. Independence can be construed, in the rhetoric of Folofo'u and Laefiwane, to mean autonomy to live according to custom; and this provides a context in which clandestine murder and blood vengeance can be constructed as assertions of freedom.

---

5. The transcripts indicate that the Kwara'ae man attacked and gravely wounded a young boy, who identified him. But he testified for the prosecution, and charges were dropped.

The third Kwaio man tried for the murder was not involved but was implicated by the Kwara'ae attacker so as to be able to clear himself. (The innocent Kwaio man accused offered an alibi that caused some vibration in the legal machinery: he testified that at the time he was hiding outside the Honiara Hotel waiting to steal the cash box.) In the end, one of the two men who committed the murder was acquitted on grounds of inconclusive identification, and the innocent man and the other murderer were sentenced to life imprisonment. (Fortunately, the innocent man was acquitted on appeal; by that time, the murderer who had been convicted had hanged himself in his cell.)[6]

A storm of anti-Malaita hostility broke loose on Guadalcanal. A petition was submitted to the Prime Minister and his government on behalf of "the indigenous people of Guadalcanal," signed by a long list of Guadalcanal leaders, demanding that the government "take immediate steps to halt the brutal killing of the innocent indigenous people of Guadalcanal and we want state government." The petition claims that fifteen Guadalcanal people were killed by "non-indigenous persons" over the past twenty years, and lists in an appendix many cases of murder and serious wounding. Where the assailants are identified, most are "Koio" people. Noting that "our island is the only island that has been invaded by squatters and other uninvited guests," the petition demands that "your good government . . . deliver us from our predicaments," attributing the violence in part to "a well calculated plan, tailored by Politicians and Senior Civil Servants, to systematically deplete, if not eradicate, the indigenous peoples of Guadalcanal." The petition then demands that the government address the problem by "finding ways and means of repatriating all non-indigenous unemployed illegal squatters, who squat on our lands," so that "immediate steps be taken to reduce the pressure of internal migration" and that a death penalty be reinstituted.[7]

We can well pause to ask what the Kwaio women back in the mountains—mothers, sisters, girlfriends, wives—think of the depredation and violence men engage in away from home. A first point is that they are squarely situated in the same world of ancestral powers and cultural values as the men, even though they—like women everywhere—may have good reason for ambivalence regarding male violence and destructiveness. When boys and men steal pigs or valuables at home,

6. The Kwaio man acquitted on appeal is a notorious urban tough and thief. Shortly after he was freed, he was arrested while housebreaking; and he confessed to a string of burglaries. He is now serving a seven-year sentence in Rove Prison, along with a substantial number of his *wantoks*.

7. I am grateful to David Roe for providing me with a copy of this document.

mothers and sisters may worry, but it is more a concern that they may be caught or forced to take a false oath of denial (bringing disaster on themselves and their own kin) than it is a moral concern about stealing. They bask in pride in successful deeds by their menfolk, and they know as the men do that their ancestors enjoin, demand, and support such predation. But what about predation and violence in the urban context, where it can lead to long imprisonment? I have recently recorded two brief texts that provide some insight.

One comes from the famous thief who recounted his mother's reaction to his conviction for breaking into a house at the Atoifi Adventist Hospital.

I broke into a house at Atoifi. Some crazy guy had told me there was money in there. I broke in, but three people witnessed the break-in and turned me in. I was tried in Auki and sentenced to eighteen months in prison, at Rove. I said, "No way!" So I appealed. After four months in prison my appeal came back from Fiji. They said, "You're free! You won!" [RMK: What were your grounds for appealing?] I said that it had been a case of mistaken identity—I said it had been someone else. [RMK: But it was you!] Of course! The appeal came back, and I had won. [RMK: How did that happen?] It was my ancestor. When I lost, it was because the girls who had been the witnesses had used the same toilet as I had, there in Auki. That's the reason I lost. Because of the *adalo.* [RMK: Then did you straighten it out?] Yes, I fixed it up. One man saw what it was [that had made the ancestors angry, through divination]. He said, "Oh, your *adalo* said, "We want this man to lose. Because he went to the place the women have used." So then I talked to my *adalo,* and after I'd fixed it up, I appealed. That's why I won my appeal.

[RMK: What did your mother think about your stealing and your going to jail?] My mother? When I was in prison, she sacrificed pigs to her ancestors so I'd win my appeal. So I'd come home. She raised pigs for sacrifice, and told the priests how to appeal to the ancestors. So they talked to the *adalo.* That's why, even though I'd been convicted and was in prison, I won my appeal and got out.

The second text is a letter I received from a woman closely related to the Mount Austen killer who had hanged himself in prison. She wrote to ask me to intervene on her behalf with the government to help her claim compensation for the death of her "son":

My "son" [her FBSS] A has died for no good reason. He was tried and convicted, and they put him in a cell; and he just died to no purpose.[8]

8. The Kwaio expression I have glossed 'for no good reason' and 'to no purpose' is *tagonimaenga,* which implies uselessness, lack of good reason or cause.

I want to claim compensation for it. I am asking you [RMK] to notify the government that I am claiming death compensation [*firitaa*] for that. I am asking you to make this representation on my behalf because I am a woman. . . . I am so upset thinking about my "son" that I have been unable to eat and unable to sleep, in the house down below [my dead "son's"] men's house.

Kwaio violence and predation took a different form in December of 1989. A young Kwaio man, B—a Christian from Sinalagu—plotted to steal the payroll of the R. C. Symes plantations at the western end of Guadalcanal. Inciting a young pagan man, a fellow urban hoodlum, to join him, B took a taxi to the point where he planned to ambush the white plantation manager, Jimmy Symes. His accomplice stood watch and alerted him to the vehicle's approach, while B waited in hiding beside the tree he had felled across the road. When Symes stopped, B killed him—to the surprise and horror of his accomplice, who had intended theft but not murder—and seized the payroll. The police were aided in their investigations by the Kwaio pagans working at Lavuro Plantation: it was their payroll that had been stolen. As of July 1990, B was at large in the bush around Sinalagu, presumably having hidden the missing $9000 payroll, with the police afraid to go in and look for him. In May 1990 his accomplice was sentenced to life imprisonment.

Relations between Malaita plantation workers and urban drifters and Guadalcanal villagers remain tense; the Kwaio remain an angry, frustrated, and predatory underclass. It would seem that this situation can only get worse, given the unequal access to the country's (very limited) wealth and the cultural sanctioning and ancestral support of theft and violence in Kwaio custom.

21 Resistance in the Nineties

At the onset of the 1990s, Kwaio pagans face a slow erosion of their power and an ever-widening gulf between the ancestral way of life they follow defiantly in the mountains and the ways that prevail in other parts of the Solomons, especially in the towns.

The gulf would be wider, economically, if the country were prospering. But the Solomon Islands totters on the brink of economic ruin, sustained only by growing injections of foreign aid. This in turn generates a series of contradictions. A Westernized Solomons elite is increasingly caught up in the global culture of consumerism; yet rising living costs, a worsening balance of trade and a faltering Solomons dollar have pushed most salaried workers into economic difficulty—with the demands from village kin and unemployed *wantoks* draining off wages that in real terms are falling. Moreover, the infrastructure of government medical and educational services is showing signs of crumbling.

It is in many ways a good time to be relatively self-sufficient economically, able to produce one's own food, build one's own house, and pursue status and prosperity not through imported goods but through strung shell beads and the production of pigs and taro. Kwaio traditionalists see the pressures and frustrations, as well as the material rewards, of Western-style participation in the cash economy; and they know that if they opted for change in this direction, their geographic isolation, the difficult terrain, and their lack of education would make them very marginal participants in the cash economy. It is further clear that a government that has never provided them with the medical, educational, and transportation facilities available in other parts of Malaita cannot afford to do so now.

Either Kwaio pagans will have to go their own way, defiantly following the ways of the ancestors, or they will have to get "development" from some other direction. There are hopes in the air still that the Americans—or *someone*—will come and help them. But in contrast to the millenarian visions of Folofo'u and some of his followers, the realists in the bush—and there are many of them—know that elsewhere in the Solomons, when outside companies have come in search of wealth—timber in particular—they have despoiled environments, leaving erosion, ruined soil, and denuded hills behind. The Kwaio know, from their experience in places like Kolombangara and parts of New Georgia and Guadalcanal (and even across the mountains in West Kwaio), that outside companies have ruthlessly extracted profits at the expense of local communities, disregarding sacred places and customs.

In May 1990 I spent two weeks in the Kwaio mountains. A good deal of my talk, especially with my hosts from Uka and Furisi'ina, concerned the threat posed by the breakdown of custom elsewhere in the Solomons, and the destructiveness of "development" as they have seen it. Maena'adi told me,

> You the government have brought the missions here under your protection. They've come and made us peaceful. The whites brought Christianity to destroy our customs. So you can steal our timber and steal our land and all our things. Those are the lies you white people brought. You've lied, pacifying us,

telling us that when we die we'll go to Heaven. "Come down, come down. The *adalo* are deceiving you." That's what the mission people say. But we hold fast to our land, to our ways of living, to our ways of sharing.

His older brother Dangeabe'u gave a remarkably astute analysis of Solomons political economy—if we make provision for the fact that he classes as part of the "government" the multinational corporations visibly allied with the state machinery in pursuing "development":

The government has brought the ways of business, the ways of money. The people at the coast believe that's what's important, and tell us we should join in. Now the government is controlling the whole world. The side of the Bible is withering away. When that's finished, the government will rule unchallenged. It will hold all the land. All the money will go to the government to feed its power. Once everything—our lands, too—are in their hands, that will be it.

I've seen the people from other islands who have all become Christians. They knew nothing about their land. The white people have gotten their hands on their lands. The whites led them to forget all the knowledge of their land, separated them from it. And when the people knew nothing about their land, the whites bought it from them and made their enterprises. . . .

That's close upon us too. If we all follow the side of the Bible, the government will become powerful here too, and will take control of our land. We won't be attached to our land, as we are now, holding our connections to our past. If the government had control of our land, then if we wanted to do anything on it, we'd have to pay them. If we wanted to start a business—a store, say—we'd have to pay the government. We reject all that. We want to keep hold of our land, in the ways passed down to us.

Not long before my arrival, a group of militant evangelists (who have been arriving in the Solomons in droves), some from other parts of the Pacific, had arrived on the Kwaio coast. They had enlisted SSEC villagers to lead them into the bush to confront the "heathen," pray for them, and try to convert them on the spot. Big delegations invaded the mountains, from which they normally keep their distance, seeking to enlist the pagans into their prayers; rebuffed but undaunted, the evangelists left behind pamphlets—of the wonder of God's love, miraculously healing a New Guinea child and hence converting skeptical parents. They also left behind bitterness and anger. Dangeabe'u told me,

The things the mission has brought aren't things passed down from our ancestors: we don't know about them. The 'teachers' brought papers and things into the bush. Just now, they came up here and gave out little books to people—small children, old people. We don't know what those things are all about. We understand about our own ways, things handed down to us from ancient times—but not things that came from some outside place, brought by outsiders into our midst. We don't want their things. And we don't want them coming up here, bringing them.

We don't want the mission people to come up here. We don't want to have to listen to their preaching, to turn our minds.

We know all about *sukuru* [Christianity—the old Pidgin word 'school']. But it's for us to choose. If someone wants to go there [and become a Christian] he follows his own mind and goes. If he is living in his own place, the place that's his from olden times, and his living is too hard—then he'll make up his own mind to go down to the mission.

But nowadays, all the people down in the Christian villages direct their prayers against us. They pray for the pigs to die, all of them. They pray for our shell money to be all gone. They pray for our taro to be finished. They pray for our priests, the priests who sacrifice crematory pigs in the shrines, to die. So that we'll give up our shrines and go down to the mission and all be Christians.

But we reject that. Even though we are no longer strong, even though the Christians outnumber us, we want to stay and follow the ways passed down to us. But they pray against us. They say, "Wait for tomorrow, wait for tomorrow. Then come down and join us in *sukuru.*" But we don't want that.

But now they try to come up here, bringing their pictures, praying here in the bush. And that really defiles us. We're defiled because of the bags and the clothing they bring up here. We don't want those things up here defiling us— not even their knives. If we buy those foreign things ourselves in a store, that's all right. But those things they bring from their houses—we don't want them up here in our homeland. The *adalo* visit death on us because of it. The *adalo* are disgusted by the people from the mission. "Oh [the ancestors say], the mission people have come, with their bags, and sleep in your place. That's no good." So the *adalo* visit death on us. And our pigs and our money are used [in atonement] for the *adalo.*

If the things handed down to us, the way of living from ancient times, had all disappeared, then we could replace them with something new. But those things they have brought have forced us to use our pigs and all our resources for purification to the *adalo.* We're not going to allow it any more.

I complained about that down at Atoifi. "That's all right," they said. "You're just kicking against iron. You'll come down and join us soon." Well, it's not [the existence of] *sukuru* I object to. If I want to go down there someday, I will. But as long as I choose to stay here I reject them.

If we were all to become Christian, we'd no longer know our genealogical histories. I wouldn't know even the man who fathered my father. Or my mother's mother. If I followed the Bible, I'd forget my genealogy; I wouldn't be able to talk about my ancestral heritage. I wouldn't know the things to do with my ancestors and my shrines. I couldn't talk about my land. If I went and became a Christian, I'd have to abandon it all.

If you live away from your own place, you forget about your origins. The young people down there don't know who their grandparents or great-grandparents were. It's impossible for them to keep that knowledge. And if we don't know about our genealogical origins, we can't know about our lands either. It will be finished. So when they come to ask, "How are you connected to this piece of land?" How are you going to know? You'll have forgotten it all.

The young people who don't know about their connections to the past can be easily tempted by the things down there in the mission. So a young kid who goes down there, attracted by the lies and the playing around will go down there and leave the important things behind. And they'll know nothing. They'll live blindly.

. . . The mission people call us 'people in darkness'. But we, the ones in the darkness, are the ones who know things—who know their genealogical connections back to ancient origins. If a [pagan] man goes down to the seacoast, he'll know nothing—none of the important things of his place. He won't give mortuary feasts. He won't do the rituals for crematory sacrifice. He won't do the rituals for the death of an important person. Those are the real things, the important things, handed down to us from ancient times.

It's what's down in the *sukuru* that's worthless—but that's what they tell us is important. As far as I can see, all they really want to do is make money. They talk about Jesus, they talk about God. But even the Church is just trying to get money: that's not what's important.

Here, on my own land, following the ways of my ancestors, I can live the way we have always lived, even though by their standards I'm poor. But if I went down there to the *sukuru*, they'd make fun of me because our clothes are old and dirty, because I don't have nice new clothes for my children. But living without [material] things, living dirty but in the way of old—that's what's good for me.

If they want to criticize me and make fun of me down at the market—well, that's up to them. But we people who are still following the ways of our ancestors don't want them to bring their talk up into the bush. Not any of these three passages, 'Oloburi, Uru or Sinalagu. We don't want it. We want their talk to be confined to the coast. We don't come down there and preach about our ways. Why can't they stay down there and leave us alone?

We don't want to listen to their lies. They tell us we should leave the things that bring death behind, and come down and join them. But the Christians die just the same way we do. The white people die just the way we do. It's all the same. People who don't steal die just the same. People who kill and steal die; people who don't kill and don't steal die just the same. Anyway, we see that no matter what they say, people down there in the mission villages steal. And they claim sexual compensation and death compensation. They're supposed to be following the Bible, but they don't. They just lie to us. They want to bring their mistaken ways to us and make us the same way.

Another day, I sat with Dangeabe'u's wife Maato'o while she voiced her complaints about the mission villages and what Christianity had brought to the Kwaio:

The reason I'm angry with the Christians is that they've destroyed the things passed down to us from olden times. In the olden days, everything was good in our living. Then the mission came—not long ago, only recently, when my father and mother were already grown up. It came at the time they killed Mr Bell. Up until that time, our living had been good. People lived to a ripe old age, and there were lots and lots of people. People weren't all dying, and they lived until they were bent with age. But since the missions came, people have been dying out.

Now the mission people say to us, "You come down and live here with Jesus, a really good man, and with God. Saetana was thrown down—God's son. He has no *fanua* [territory], no land; he has nothing good to live with. Because God threw him down and he stays here on earth." They talk like that; and I see them spoiling the things from our custom. I see people dying from it. They destroy things with their defilement. They shit in streams, down there at the mission villages. They shit there, and [pagan] men walk through the streams. They die because of it; that's something taboo for us.

In the olden days, fresh water and sea were like land. They were handed down to us with the land. People fished in the sea. For a crematory sacrifice or the death of a priest, they'd go [initially] to the sea to get fish. They got fish from the sea for the desacralization [rituals] of the dead and for desacralization after a crematory sacrifice. But now the mission people just shit in the sea. I see it, and I see our people dying from it, and I get very, very angry. Even when they dig a pit latrine, it pollutes the streams. Our menfolk go down there, to fell trees, and they die from it.

The mission people pray and pray every day for our pigs to die and our valuables to disappear and our fishing to be bad. I reply to them, "We're not trying to take over anyone else's place. We just stay in our own land—and if we're poor and dirty, that's our choice. We don't pray for your living to be bad. Why do you pray against us day after day after day? That causes sickness and dying, forces us to use our pigs and valuables in purification. That's not what our living used to be like."

They reply, "God is powerful, Saetana is weak. All the things your ancestors passed down to you are lies. They said you were descended from a bird. But if people were descended from birds, they'd look birds. [They said] we're descended from a snake. But if people were descended from a snake they'd look like snakes.[1] Those are the lies Saetana foisted on you, and you believe them. The land is God's land."

I reply to them, "How is it that though you say this is God's land, when someone in the mission forbids you to work on a piece of land, you come running up to us 'heathens' to find out how you're related to it? You say 'Where is my kinship connection to such-and-such land?' If it's God's land why don't you trace your connections back to God to lay claim to it? It was people, our ancestors, who founded the land." They have nothing to say to that.

I get angry about it. I say to myself, "Here we are living on our own land, and you mission people just come and intrude on us." In the old days, five generations of people would be alive in a place at the same time, before the old people, bent with age, finally died. But now, because the mission people shit in the sea, and shit in the streams, when we go down and bring back shellfish and fish from there, then eat them, we get sick; the *adalo* afflict us because of it. I'm fed up with it.

So I went to my husband [Dangeabe'u] and said, "Those people down there pray against us every day. Why can't you do something about it? Why don't you go down and put a ritual injunction against it? Why don't you, or someone who speaks really well, swear against it? Against people down there praying for our ruin—I'm fed up with hearing [about] it." So he went down to Atoifi and put a ritual injunction against it and swore against it.

People down there got angry with me. "You went down and saw our latrines and then you complained to the men about it." I said, "That's not what was passed down to us in our [and your] custom. You're killing us by what you're doing. We're dying from it!" They were angry and said they wouldn't let me eat with them there or use any of their things.

I said "I don't care. We who are still living on our own lands and following our own customs just want to be left alone, even though we may be poor and unimportant, and not be exposed to death this way. The things that you're

---

1. Here she is responding to the arguments against evolution promulgated by fundamentalists in the Solomons, as understood by the local Christians.

doing are causing us to die. Someone will die and the surviving spouse will be left alone and will go down to *sukuru*. That's what I'm fed up with."

In the olden days our living was good. People would live to a great age. The taro was good—the corms big and fat no matter what soil they were grown in. But not now. The mission people have destroyed the forest—eating coconuts there, eating taboo taro there. And so the taro is bad nowadays. Everything is bad. But what can we do about it?

Maena'adi, too, talked with anger about the Christian encroachments.

The Christians came and we were told we had to follow them. "You are to follow their ways. You have to give up your old ways. You come down [to the coast]. Give up your *'otofono*; give up that *baru*; give up that *kwalafaafingaa*; give up your sacrifice of pigs; give up your *mamu* you take up for a death; give up crematory sacrifice; give up your ritual puddings. You come down here and live by the coast. Let's follow the ways of Jesus."

They try to uproot us with the white people's ways they brought. From our way of living. But our way of living has been handed down from ancient times, two or three or four thousand years ago—handed down to us today. We say metaphorically that our ways began in the earth, began with ashes.

The Christians—the *sikosi* [SSEC], the SDA [Seventh Day Adventists], the Anglicans, the Jehovahs—have brought different ways, under the protection of the government. Under the protection of the white people. They try to force us out of our way of life. . . . And now they've come up bringing their prayers and their books, trying to drag us off to Christianity [*sukuru*].

But we resist. Because there's no land down there. Because there's no kindness down there. Because even if they catch a huge fish, all of it will get eaten by just one household. Even if they buy a pig worth a *banii'au*, only a single household will eat it all. We see that there is no sharing, even though they try to bring their ways up here.

We see that if a man has sex with a girl, nobody contributes to a compensation payment on his behalf. They say that kind of compensation is taboo for them, that if they contribute Jesus will strike them down and they'll die because of it. What we think is that it's all lies. It's not true.

And we see that land is scarce, and the Christians are always fighting over it. They give first fruits to God, and pray, saying that it's God that created it. But I see that's not true. Those ways aren't right.

Another thing is that down at Atoifi [Hospital] they burn the afterbirth [from the maternity ward] and the smoke blows all over the place. From the olden days, you can't even burn women's sitting mats because the smoke would blow around and the *adalo* would be angry and visit death upon people. In the old days the only way you could purify the place that had been defiled was by a killing. That would finish it. You couldn't even purify it with a pig, in the old days, if smoke from a woman's sitting mat had blown across the place. But the SDA's paid no attention to that, and burned the afterbirth [from the maternity ward] and the smoke has blown far and wide. Our living has been bad because of it. The things we plant in the land aren't growing well.

The Christians have brought giant lies. The hospital is something else— bringing medicine to save our lives. That's a good thing for us Kwaio people. But the Christianity they have brought is no good. They're lying. It's not true.

The old issues remain unresolved. Even though the pagans have withdrawn support from Folofo'u, they are once again busy compiling lists of people killed by the 1927 punitive expedition, of women raped, valuables stolen, shrines despoiled, property destroyed. The new Parliamentary Member, a Christian from a coastal village near the Kwara'ae border, has encouraged them to expect that some more reasonably calculated claim for compensation might be met. I played devil's advocate in discussing the question with Maena'adi, suggesting that if they wanted a medical clinic in the bush, they might get one; and warning them that Mr. Bell's family and others who lost kin in the Gwee'abe massacre might levy a claim against *them*. Maena'adi took the bait with gusto:

In the old days, our Kwaio people had their own laws—about women, about land, about shrines. In those days they had their taboos and their customs, and they held strongly to them.

When Mr. Bell came and brought the tax, he forbade their getting blood money. "The killing is finished." And that intruded on their eating pigs, on their getting valuables, on their living. It's true that some of the killings, some of the customs, were no good. The government forbade old ways and they demanded a tax. The Kwaio people weren't stupid. They saw what that meant. "Here we are living on our own land, gaining the fruits of our own land; how can Mr. Bell come and demand a tax from us? We haven't come to live on the white people's land!"

They were angry, and some of the senior men refused. Then some of the people who had come under the government's aegis, under Mr. Bell, swore at the important men, saying that *ta'a i busi* were *ta'a i bisi*,[2] saying that they re-

---

2. A malicious Pijin-Kwaio pun, in which "bush people" was recast as "bisi people"—'menstrual hut people'.

fused to pay the tax and they cleaned up pigshit. And so they killed Bell and Lillies. That killing down at Gwee'abe—they wouldn't have killed the men from north [Malaita] who came with Mr. Bell if they hadn't come with their sashes and their rifles. Our people said, "Oh, they've come with the rifles Mr. Bell gave them. They're wearing red sashes and police belts. They're bringing the things Mr. Bell gave them, representing the power of England. To break down our gaining of valuables, our living, our taboos. So they killed those police who had come with Mr. Bell, men from To'abaita and Agia [Baegu] with their sashes in place. They didn't kill indiscriminately. They didn't kill men with rattan belts, the men with bows and clubs. They singled out the men with European things.

After that the British government force climbed up and destroyed everything in Kwaio country. They destroyed the pigs, they destroyed the taro, they destroyed gardens, they raped girls and women, they chopped down all the sago palms and coconut palms and betel palms. They did terrible things here in Kwaio.

So many of the things they did weren't right. If they had destroyed Basiana's place, and Fuufu'e's and Tagailamo's and Tolea's place, and 'Ulasia's and Alefo's and Kwai'ime's place—maybe that would have been justice. Because they planned the battle and carried it out. But the destruction [the punitive expedition] visited upon the interior behind 'Oloburi, Sinalagu, and Uru—the overturning of shrines, the throwing of ancestral skulls into the clearings, the throwing of the things from houses into menstrual huts—the devastation and death from that will afflict the Kwaio for five generations before it is finished.

For a hundred years, or two hundred, the dying will go on. That's what I learned from the elders—from 'Eda and Fungu'i—when I was a little boy. And it's true. I know. I've seen . . . the dying because of that has gone on. . . .

The killing brought by the government extended from Wadawada to Anoano (W. Kwaio) and Gule'ekafu [south of 'Oloburi] to Kwaiba'ina [the Kwaio-Kwara'ae border]. We know what the laws of England say about killing: the person who kills is taken off to prison. But that's what they did. They killed indiscriminately.

The British say that if we had a claim to make, we should have made it at the time. But our leaders tried to voice their grievances, and the British said, "If you talk about that, we'll shoot you. If you talk about that we'll send you to prison." They threatened them. So nothing could be voiced at the time. And now years later, when some people are educated enough to understand how they could make a claim, the British Government says, "You had to make your claim within ten years. It's all over and done with: it's too late for a claim."

But when they did try to voice their grievances at the time they were threatened with prison, with life imprisonment. I think England is just lying. How can you, England, say it is too late for a claim when you wouldn't let us make one at the time? When you threatened us with prison and with rifles, threatened us into silence? And now you tell us it's too late. . . .

If we're going to settle things and be friends, it will have to be with pigs, and with money. If we get no satisfaction—well, that's the way it is. But you, England, don't expect us to forget, when we're still dying from it. And we will be, for a hundred years, or two hundred.

There was one thing, England, that you brought that we benefitted from. That was your stopping the killing. It's true that the killing was a bad thing. You stopped the killing and that's a good thing. The 'Are'are people and the Anoano people and the To'abaita people aren't our enemies any more. That was a good thing you brought.

But the dying you've brought upon us goes on from generation to generation. The ruin you bring on a place can go on and on and on. Let me compare it with something you from England will understand. It's like the poison bomb the Americans dropped on Japan. The Japanese are bitter because that poison stays, and even now children are born deformed. That poison is terrible, and it will affect them for generations.

And for us, and the dying caused by our *adalo,* it's the same. It goes on and on. People say that that poison bomb affects plants, too, for a long time, so they don't grow properly. It gives off emanations that destroy whatever's growing. Pigs, even ants, will die. You can't eat the things that do grow there.

Well, the Americans and the Japanese seem to be friends again. Maybe their customs are different. Maybe death compensation was paid. Maybe the Americans built a clinic for Japan [an ironic commentary on my suggestion that the British might pay for a clinic in the Kwaio mountains]. We don't know why the Japanese are no longer angry about that.

Well, you [RMK] said that if we claim compensation for damages, maybe England will claim compensation for the death of Bell and Lillies. But we didn't go to England to kill Bell and Lillies. You, Mr. Bell, you came here in the name of the Government of England. You came and your men cursed the Kwaio people. You came and stepped all over the customs of the Kwaio people, their earning of valuables, their good living. So they killed you. And then Basiana was hanged, and Tolea, and Fairi'ia—and they shot Maenaafo'oa and 'Iiba'e at Gwee'abe.

And all those people were shot. I've counted them myself. I know all about the ones at my mother's place at 'Auagama. There were 1,130 people killed after the fight at Gwee'abe. The ones who were hanged and shot were enough to pay back the killing of Mr. Bell and Lillies and Makasi and Lausa'o and Teloa. *So what's to* balance all the other ones from our side who were shot?

What about the sacred valuables they destroyed, the shell money, the taro, the coconuts, the settlements, the shrines they destroyed? What's to be balanced against that? My mother's people had no part in the fight. They killed them all. Two big bags of shell money, belonging to Teeruma and Kwalata, were thrown in the fire there at 'Auagama and burned. Sufaboo and Maefa'afuru and Riofane and Ngiri and Ru'ufiamae were all shot. And forty valuables of Teeruma's, and forty of Kwalata's, destroyed. Only the women escaped, from my mother's place. But those people had done nothing wrong. They hadn't incited the killing, they hadn't put up a blood bounty, they hadn't been there. They had nothing to do with it.

The ancestral skulls in Kwaleo were tossed out on the ground and smashed. But you, England, you're supposed to follow laws. The skulls of the dead didn't go to the battle at Gwee'abe. The skulls of the dead didn't kill Mr. Bell. The skulls of the dead didn't kill your police, Mr. Bell. They just sat in their places. For a hundred years those ancestral skulls had been kept there at Kwaleo. By what law did you come and smash them? They did nothing. They said nothing. They didn't get up and walk. They just rested where they were. They just sat there—like the hibiscus outside the [British] High Commissioner's place in Honiara.

The sacrificial ovenstones in the shrine didn't do anything. So why did the police, and the white men who came up with them, throw them around and destroy them? The coconut palms and betel palms and sago palms didn't walk down to Gwee'abe and take part in the fight.

Under what laws, England, did you cut them down? Coconuts are our life, and taro. What gave you the right, England, to come and destroy them? Food is the breath of life for us. It was as though you were cutting down our lives. The food that was the stuff of life, you destroyed it all.

Your laws, England, are not true because you didn't follow them yourselves. We don't want a clinic and some medicines. We want pigs and money. We'll use them following our Kwaio customary laws, and after that, people will live, not die. We'll use them to give atonenment and purification to the *adalo*, and then we'll live, not die. When the *adalo* have been compensated, people will live and the taro will prosper.

And another thing. The *'otofono* medicinal shrubs at my father's place—they just chopped them all down. They told that white man Captain King, "This *'otofono* is planted to keep away malevolent spirits, and to keep fighting away. And that *ma'ufitafita* cordyline at the path-entrance at Saua." They just chopped them down. But the *'otofono* and *ma'ufitafita* didn't do anything. They didn't kill anyone in the battle. They didn't pray to the ancestors for Mr. Bell's death. So why did you cut it down? It was just growing there.

The sacred things from the *adalo* in the men's houses—if they'd seen them

march down to the seacoast, then they'd have had the right to burn them and
smash them. According to your law, England, if a man was seen to kill someone with his own hand, you could take him off and hang him. But by what laws
did you come and destroy things that were just there, inert?

    . . . It was only Basiana and Fuufu'e and Tagailamo and Tolea and
Maenaafo'oa and 'Iiba'e and Kwai'ime and Fuitaa and I'aforia and Si'owane
and 'Ulasia and Alefo and Toonia and Maeto'o and Farimae and Tagi'au and
'Eda—they were the ones who were there at Gwee'abe, the ones who launched
the attack. Those were the ones they saw at Gwee'abe. There were only a few
of them. Those sacred things of ours and important property—the *bibi* [sacred
shrubs], the pigs, the coconut palms, the betel palms, the *maa'e adalo* [sacred
men's house objects], the ancestral skulls, the sacred valuables, the houses, the
menstrual huts—who saw them down at the battle at Gwee'abe? The things
Basiana left behind when he went into hiding—that would have been just. He
started the fight.

    But all those other places, the home places of so many people who had
nothing to do with the fight at Gwee'abe—they were just destroyed. The plan-
tains at our place were cut down. But they didn't go anywhere. They don't
have arms and legs. Why did you cut them down?

    What made the police and the whites who came up into our homeland so
angry that they destroyed everything? They destroyed the skull of Kwauka at
Furinudu. What enraged them to the point of doing that? Kwauka's skull
wasn't running around killing people at Gwee'abe. Ancestor Lafusua's skull is
supposed [according to a myth] to have gone around killing people. If they'd
seen that, there would have been a good reason to smash it. But Kauka's skull
was just sitting there in its bark wrapping in a tree fork. What reason did they
have to shoot it and smash it?

    The Suriauo people didn't take part in the fight. They weren't there. The
police went up there and destroyed the shrine at Susufane. They dismantled it
into the clearing. They shot up the bamboos in the shrine. What was in their
heads to attack a shrine? People didn't sacrifice these for the killing of Mr.
Bell.

    Why did they shoot the people there? Why did they arrest the people there?
They didn't do anything. The laws of England don't allow the deliberate killing of little children, even in a battle. Why did they kill Daulamo's child? A
little child, still in its mother's arms. What law was that? What I want to ask
England about is this. At the time they killed Mr. Bell, wasn't there a King
yet? Maybe there weren't any laws in those days—maybe that's just something
recent. Maybe England didn't have a government yet, back then.

    Kwagiinamae was just an infant, not yet toilet trained. When people ran

away, when the police came, she was left behind. All that was left behind were
her little bones. Even babies so young they were still in arms were snatched
away and killed. That's what happened at 'Auagama, my mother's place. Sufaboo's two children—when he was shot, they just threw the two babies into a
house and set fire to it. But a baby in arms doesn't do any harm in the world.
Your own law says it's a terrible thing to kill a little child, but you just allowed
it to happen. What kind of fight was that, waged against little babies? Was
there no law in those days?

During my 1990 visit, talk turned often to the old project of "writing
down *kastomu,*" in its latest form. In the second half of the 1980s, when
the pagans became disillusioned with Folofo'u's leadership, they had
again sought Jonathan Fifi'i's assistance in the project that had occupied
their political energies for almost half a century. In his autobiographical
account (Fifi'i 1989:165–66), he recalled that

two important leaders from the bush, Ma'aanamae and Ngiri'a, . . . asked,
"What can we do about it? In the old days we used to meet all the time to discuss what's happening and straighten out whatever is going wrong. But now we
all just go our separate ways. We don't work together anymore. We just are
wandering around lost. Let's meet up at Fanuariri to try to get started in working together again."

So I climbed up the hill to meet them there. . . . They said to me, "What
about all the work we did together, from the time of Maasina Rule? Why don't
we talk about those things any more? We see our customs getting messed up
nowadays." I just played dumb, and asked, "What do you mean, your customs
are messed up? It looks as though everyone is still following them." "We see
things going wrong. In the old days, when an unmarried girl and an unmarried
man had an affair, and it was discovered, the compensation wasn't very much.[3]
But now people are demanding ten or twenty valuables for that. That's what
the compensation should be for committing adultery with a married woman.
That's the kind of thing that's getting messed up. It isn't just trouble about sexual affairs. If someone steals just a little pig, and it's discovered, people claim so
much compensation no one could afford it."

"Why are people doing that nowadays?" I asked them. "It's the influence of
town.[4] If a man has an affair with someone's daughter, her relatives will demand $500 or $600 or $1000 from us as compensation. People see those bad

3. Something of a misrepresentation, since so often the girl was killed, and a bounty put up
against her seducer.
4. I.e., Honiara.

customs from town and try to bring them back home. Another thing that is
messed up is the rising cost of things that have always had values set according
to custom. A hundred taro corms are supposed to cost a *lousu'u*.[5] If they're big
ones, you should get fifty for a *lousu'u*. But now, people are trying to charge a
dollar for a single big taro corm. They're trying to charge a dollar for four sweet
potatoes. Those are the bad ways from town, that people are bringing back
here. That's messing up our custom. Only people who have dollars can afford
to buy food for feasts.

"We need to start working to straighten out our customs. We don't want to
hide what we're doing from the Government. We want our customs to be recognized as if they were laws, so that people in our area have to follow them.
We want to be able to settle disputes according to custom."

The codification of the customs the pagan leaders envisioned was once
again an emulation of a colonial law book, although political changes of
the independence period have brought new concepts and labels. Now,
they talk either about *baeloa*—in emulation of the Province's "by-
laws"—or "constitution" (the latter carries separatist connotations to
them, as to us). So Fifi'i worked with the Kwaio leaders in trying to draft a
kind of legal charter for the ancestrally constituted society. As in earlier
decades, the benefits that were supposed to flow from such an eventual
codification of *kastomu* were a combination of the squarely political and
the mystical. On the one hand, being able to present the provincial and
central governments with Kwaio customary law set out in the style of the
old Protectorate lawbooks and their modern equivalents would, they
imagine, give them a more solid base on which to claim jurisdiction and
the right to settle disputes according to *their* law, not the alien laws
brought by the British and bequeathed to the post-independence Solomons. More immediately, if the customary laws relating to the sanctity
of lands and shrines, and pollution taboos, were accepted by the Province
as binding within Kwaio country, then that would give the pagans a powerful legal and political instrument with which to resist Christian incur-
sions into the mountains and defilement of sacred things and places.

To these envisioned political benefits are added the diffuse mystical
notions about power and sanctity attributed to the written word during
the colonial period, the symbolic force of a shared *kastomu* objectified
and externalized. *Kastomu*—as "culture" externalized, idealized, hypo-
statized, reified, fetishized[6]—acquires a symbolic power that transcends
its contents (Keesing 1982a, 1989b).

5. The standard measure of length of strung shell beads, a length from fingertip to bicep.
6. In Marx's sense.

When Fifi'i died of throat cancer in October 1989, there was dismay among the pagans at the loss of a leader who, though (offically) Christian, had had a genuine sympathy for the pagans and their ancestral culture, and who had represented their interests powerfully for four decades. Heightening the dismay was a realization that without him as their scribe, all their collective work to codify the "by-laws" would be lost. In his house at the coast, when I visited to mourn the death of a dear old friend and colleague, I searched through his papers and rescued the papers on which bits and pieces of the intended "by-laws" had been written (in Kwaio and Fifi'i's limited English). The papers would otherwise probably have been lost; and last year and this year, I assured the pagans that they were in safe-keeping and that once I had finished making copies, the originals would come back to them.[7]

What about the project? Could I finish it for them? That was, after all, what they imagined I had been working on all these years: my books and many articles were seen as some kind of by-product for consumption by the outside world (though the Kwaio are pleased that any money that comes from what I write comes back to them). It was for an American to come and write down their customs—in the form of "laws"—that they had prayed thirty years before. Senses of irony and frustration loom large here. The scraps left by Fifi'i illustrate what the Kwaio pagans have in mind. First, there are passages that make clear the continuities back to Maasina Rule and frame the goals of the project of codification:

> When the Council of Chiefs form, they decided to draw Kwaio Customary Laws, Common Laws, and By Laws, which Waiparo and Harisimae of 'Are'are calls Fuamae and 'Elota of Kwaio 1945 to draw, and Colonial Government arrested all leader chiefs from Maasina Ruru 1946–47.

> 1. This is Kwaio Customs I was required by the Kwaio Communities Chieves to writing Kwaio Unwritten Customs: as are Customary Laws, Common Laws, and By Laws.
> 2. Kwaio Communities Chieves, wants customs must deals similar of the law, that only special groups to work themselves and to give decision, by themselves. . . .
> 4. The Community of Chieves wishes and express to writing customs (1) that Kwaio customs to work similar of laws besides National Laws. (2) that to choices some experience bodies hearing and sits given decision similar lawyer for instance

---

7. They have since been returned, by way of Fifi'i's son.

Kwaio Religious Ceremonious to burying pig opposite the face of the previous old doer's at his grave, and shall bind them live taboos for period of 30 days or 60 days, cannot talk with other people neither visiting other vilages. Even other people cannot cometh to reagion area. That if any girl or woman entries in same area all about where are prohibited and forbiden by customary laws, any man entries in region area, the court shall make up its decision to pay compensation of two pigs up to 30 pigs with 4 string shell money, and liable to find $50 up to $100.

If woman entries the same region area, was the altar of *bibiboonga,* court shall determinedly to reach certain decision it shall saying for compensation of 2 pigs up to 30 pigs with one *fa'afa'a* or six string shell money and liable fine of $5 up to $200.

2. No step over women's legs.
3. No suspect women as accuracy of a report, or conjectured her to steal or any other ways.
4. Any religion bodies no use swearing against anything, to imitating heathen, or to heathen tombs or tombstones or anythings of alike manners.
5. Women though from heathen no swearing of any tombs or tombstones.

With these fragments in hand, with new resolution to build *bungu 'ifi* meeting villages and again commit time and energy to "writing down the custom," and with substantial numbers of Kwaio now able to read and write in their own language, it might prove possible to produce something like the *buka fofo'afu,* 'complete book', of *kastomu* they have envisioned for years. I have promised to help as best I can. But I have warned them that I have grave doubts that customary law can be codified in the way they envision and preserve its flexibility; and I have warned that my continuing political access to Kwaio country is precarious, and could be jeopardized by activities the government could interpret to be political.

With or without me, the Kwaio pagans face the onset of the 1990s and the approach of the twenty-first century with continuing commitment to the ways of their ancestors and to their struggle for cultural autonomy.[8]

8. Folofo'u's death at the end of 1991, just as this book was going to press, may help clear the way for a constructive compromise with the national and provincial governments. It is worth pausing to reflect that although Folofo'u's vision was local and millenarian, his challenge to the sovereignty of the state vis-à-vis the cultural autonomy of regional minorities interestingly parallels those being played out in what was the Soviet Union and Yugoslavia, in Czechoslovakia, even in Canada.

22 Discourses of Resistance, Structures of Culture

As evening falls at Saua, where the panpipes were playing as we first entered the Kwaio mountains, the daily regime of domestic work is in full swing. Maato'o and her oldest daughter have come back from the gardens with sweet potatoes and taro, carried in woven bags. The second daughter, after chopping firewood, has brought in a dozen bamboos of water, carefully marked and separated for men's and women's use. The pigs have been fed, their droppings swept. The fires in the dwelling houses have been built up to roast the tubers; smoke sears eyes and lungs. Dangeabe'u has returned after spending the afternoon mending fences and looking for a young pig that has strayed—or been stolen. Tagi'au is dead and buried, his mortuary feast given. In Dangeabe'u's clearing, in the saddle below the one where Tagi'au lived his eighty years, and died, the daily round goes on.

That round of daily life is strikingly like the one Dangeabe'u had seen in his boyhood; and it has not changed dramatically since Tagi'au's childhood. The things that now strike the eye of a cultural purist as alien—the steel knives and axes, the pipes, the cloth,[1] the beads—were visible then. This is the background against which the dramas of resistance that have unfolded in these chapters have taken place. In this lies a real key to the nature of Kwaio resistance that could be overlooked if we focus on these dramatic moments and contexts of political rhetoric.

The critical strategy of Kwaio resistance has lain not in confrontation but in compartmentalization. The ways of the ancestors endure because of the invisible fences built around them, policed and tended. Before turning to these strategies of containment through compartmentalization, their significance must be underlined. One theme in recent historical anthropology of the Pacific, particularly in the work of Sahlins (1981, 1985), has been the way invading Europeans have been culturally encapsulated or conceptually incorporated by Islanders: interpreted in terms of indigenous cosmological structures, myths, and symbols. In the scenarios Sahlins has reconstructed for Hawaii, Fiji, and New Zealand, resistance was manifest as much at the level of cultural symbols as of po-

---

1. Laplaps, a fathom of cloth wrapped around the waist, were de rigeur for men until the 1960s, and have mainly been replaced by shorts since then—but many senior men still wear laplaps, and some revert frequently to nudity, in the prevailing style of Tagi'au's day.

litical confrontation. Even where indigenous peoples resisted the invaders with what seemed to be warfare, as with Hone Heke's rebellion in New Zealand (Sahlins 1985:60–67), they were pursuing symbolic goals defined in their own cultural terms: the flagpole Hone Heke repeatedly attacked acquired its meaning through Maori ritual symbolism, not European symbols of sovereignty. The British were defending the flag. The Maori warriors were attacking the pole, which, embedded in the earth, represented a crucial symbol both of power and of attachment to place: the pole became *putake o te riri*, 'root cause of the war'. Elsewhere, as with Hawaiian construction of Captain Cook in terms of Lono, the aliens were seen as actors in mythic heroic history and cosmology.

There are elements of a similar symbolic incorporation in Kwaio resistance, particularly in the early decades, and I shall underline some of them in the pages to follow. In first encounters, aliens and their behavior can hardly be construed other than in indigenous terms—conceptions of otherness, of power, of history. But first encounters are transitory, and where there are drastic imbalances of technology, it is local interpretation that soon must bend to accommodate political realities. What is more striking in the texts we have examined is how pervasively, particularly from the 1930s onward, European symbols (including Noto'i's flagpole, as well as the paramilitarism of Maasina Rule and the conceptions of "custom" and "law") have been adopted and emulated, how resistance has been expressed in terms of European categories. This oppositional structuring of Kwaio discourses will be the theme of chapter 23.

There is no direct evidence on how the Kwaio interpreted their earliest encounters with the Europeans in their ships. Kwaio ideas about the ultimate nature and origin of things are relatively undeveloped and inchoate. There are few myths; and most accounts of the past, especially in epic chants, assume a world of pigs, taro, feasts, feuds, shell valuables, and communities organized in small, local descent groups and structured in terms of gender. Without an extensively developed cosmology, without political hierarchy traced back to the gods, the Kwaio do not conceptualize the kind of heroic history that provided the backdrop for Polynesian interpretations of Europeans, as Sahlins (1981, 1985) has reconstructed them. There was no mythic place or cosmological realm in which powerful aliens could be situated. There are traditions of powerful outsiders in some of the epic chants; but they were fellow Malaitans, from the north or south, who came as outcasts or refugees to Kwaio country, but brought with them great magical powers and special knowledge. This was no scenario into which the first sailing ships that passed on the horizons, or those that kidnapped or lured the first Kwaio to Queensland, could be incorporated, no drama in which they could be cast as protagonists.

And when Afio and Toobebe and other early Kwaio came back from Queensland with axes, adzes, knives, plane blades, cloth, mirrors, and other trade goods, and brought stories of a wondrous land far across the sea, there was no way to encapsulate conceptually that land or the powers that prevailed in it. The Kwaio learned quickly enough from the early encounters that these were fellow humans, ruthless, dangerous, and treacherous; that firearms could kill suddenly from long distances; and hence that this represented a formidable enemy. But the steel tools and other trade goods, and eventually the firearms, were irresistibly tempting as targets for a plunder that could be cast as revenge as well. The early ship attacks by Maeasuaa, scarcely a decade after the first Kwaio were taken to Queensland and Fiji, show how quickly the aliens had been accommodated into the Malaita scheme of things and how shrewdly their powers and their vulnerabilities vis-à-vis warriors with greater numbers but much more limited fighting technology had been assessed.

We have in the early skirmishes of the labor trade the beginnings of a bifurcation in Kwaio experiences with Europeans. Along the coast, on their home turf, the Kwaio could sacrifice to their ancestors, read the omens, perform their magic, and use long-established strategies of ambush and treachery. If a leader was prepared to *dii'aia*, 'try', the aliens, he could trust his ancestors to protect and empower him. (If he failed, as 'Arumae did, retrospective interpretations were fashioned through divination.)

But on the ships and the overseas plantations, the balance was entirely shifted. Kwaio were away from the shrines and their priests, subjected to the brutality and exploitation of overseers but dependent for rations, without means of escape or return to their homeland, and in the early years, virtually unprotected. In these alien settings, whites held almost all the power, the Malaitans almost none. They could pray to the ancestors, use their magic; but far from home, the efficacy of cultural powers could not be counted on. Moreover, the Europeans who on the ships were a mere handful, seemingly vulnerable, were in Queensland totally dominant numerically, as well as awesomely powerful technologically. This domination precluded a sustained cultural incorporation of the whites within a Kwaio cosmos even if the cosmology had offered them a place.

It is this bifurcation between the world inside, defensible through skirmishes along the margins from which one could retreat up the formidable mountain wall, and the world outside, where cultural powers melted away, that established the foundations for the terms of Kwaio resistance. The world inside and the world outside had to be conceptually walled off from one another, and the world inside defended and preserved.

The nineteenth-century labor trade established as well a strategy of containment economically. The new tools, and the firearms, were desperately coveted; so the walls had to be permeable by physical objects. The contradiction in this situation was one of age and power. The young men who went overseas were marginal in terms of the power structure at home, subordinated to their elders. It was the physically strong, young men who were wanted by the whites for plantation work; and in Kwaio terms it was urgent that these be unmarried men who could be spared by the community and sacrificed if need be. Young men, then, were sent by their elders to work on the distant plantations; and most of what they brought back was appropriated by the elders. The "beach payment" of early recruiting, where trade goods were paid in advance in exchange for the consignment of a strong young man to the recruiters on the ships, established the pattern.

After the labor trade was well established, and especially in this century when overseas recruiting ended and an internal plantation system was created in the Solomons, it became impossible for the elders to continue appropriating the trade goods brought back by young men. What they *could* do was insure that young men could not use the trade goods, or particularly the cash, to buy their way into independence, in the form of feasting and marriage. Had young men returning from plantations with cash been able to use it to finance their own marriages, or convert it into shell valuables effectively, the basis of the control of senior men over junior would have been eroded. So one wall built around a realm where traditional ways could be preserved was a barrier isolating cash from shell valuables, preventing cash from being used in the prestige economy of exchange, and militating against conversion from one medium to the other, from cash to shell. It is a wall that remains remarkably—though not completely—impermeable, a century later, at the onset of the 1990s.

A second wall was established to compartmentalize the Christian villages being established on the coast. In the Christian villages, menstrual and childbirth taboos—the very pillars of ancestrally imposed rules—were systematically flouted. The Kwaio response was to define an entire mission village as categorically equivalent to the menstrual areas of settlements living by ancestral rules.

The other side of this process of containment, categorical and geographical, has been to keep the mission villages from climbing the mountain wall. By and large, it remains successful in the Kwaio heartland, the mountains above Sinalagu on the east coast. A few Catholic villages have been established in the hills up the Kwaiba'ita valley to the northwest; and Naanakinimae, a large SSEC village, perches on the mountain rim between Sinalagu and 'Oloburi to the south. But the wall preserving a spatial realm where ancestral rules can prevail and ancestral ways can be followed has been fiercely defended for eighty years, and endures unbreached in the critical central area.

This separation of the Christian settlements from ancestrally governed ones, and their classification with menstrual areas, underlines the way that in compartmentalizing external dangers, the Kwaio in fact have been building on cultural models of separation and containment. The Kwaio cosmological scheme depends centrally on the separation and compartmentalization of powers and dangers, on the invisible lines and rules that separate male from female, sacred from ordinary, mundane from defiled. Culturally defined dangers are controlled by being walled off categorically and behaviorally.

The plantation areas have also been separated categorically from the world at home. Once out of their mountains, Kwaio men can no longer maintain the pollution taboos and strict rules separating the sexes enjoined at home. From the moment they set foot on a ship, Kwaio were potentially exposed to the pollution of menstruation or even of childbirth. The rules have had to be, in effect, held in abeyance where their practice is impossible. Kwaio do maintain a ritual life as best they can away from home, through prayer and magic and, where possible, sacrifice; but connections to ancestors are precarious, their support and its efficacy always in doubt. Still, the protection of one's ancestors is one's best hope when disaster threatens. An incident shortly before my arrival in 1962 will serve to illustrate. Two Kwaio men returning from a Lever's plantation on their recruiting ship miscalculated in stealing a bag of money from an elderly South Malaita man on the ship, since the ship went first to his village. The thieves denied their guilt, but threatened by all the men of the Small (South) Malaita village, they were forced to undergo a ritual ordeal to seek to establish (falsely) their innocence: they were required to swim a shark-infested estuary.[2] Praying to their ances-

---

2. On South Malaita (Malamasike, 'Small Malaita', an island separated from Malaita proper by a narrow channel), the dead were traditionally disposed of by being thrown to the sharks (construed to be spirits). The waters where the sharks were fed human remains were particularly dangerous.

tors and invoking their protection, the two Kwaio men dived into the water and swam safely across the estuary.

One way to maintain both the strict categorical divide between the world of plantations and mountains where ancestral rules prevailed was to keep girls and women at home. This made plantations and plantation experiences a male preserve, and helped to insure that women were kept jurally subordinated as well as subject to strict ancestral rules. In my 1963 census, I found only one adult woman out of about a hundred who had been out of her home mountains—and she, only unwillingly, to testify in a court case in Auki. This helped as well to ensure that the linguistic medium of the plantations and dealings with the world outside of the mountains, Solomons Pidgin English, was accessible only to males. This closure of the world of women remains substantially intact almost thirty years later, although women from the mountains now experience some elements of Western technology and European ways around the Atoifi Adventist Hospital.

The compartmentalization of the realm of plantation experience from the realm of ancestors emerges in the account by the most famous thief of his generation we glimpsed in chapter 20. Recall his comments about how, although he called on the support of his ancestors for thefts of pigs and valuables at home, he did not pray to them when stealing in town. Even when talking about success or failure in urban thefts, he used the Pidgin English terms *lake* and *batalake* ('good luck' and 'bad luck') in place of the Kwaio term *nanamangaa* ('efficacy, ancestral support'; the nominalized form of the reflex of Oceanic *mana*). He went on to talk about the power (Kwaio *tegelangaa* 'strength') conveyed by the ancestors, in this urban context, as *baoa* (the Kwaio rendering of Pidgin English 'power'). The point is that even when, in the urban setting, ancestral powers are invoked or perceived, in this setting they are characterized using Pidgin rather than Kwaio labels.

The one point in the history of Kwaio resistance where the boundaries compartmentalizing Christianity and alien ways and institutions were seriously breached was during the height of Maasina Rule. The movement's ideologues insisted that divisions between Christians and those practicing the ancestral religion be transcended so as to forge unity in confrontation and collective bargaining with the colonial government. Pagan men started mixing more freely with Christians, and ignoring these pollution taboos. As Oloi'a put it, "When Maasina Rule came, the men said, 'We have to work close to the coast now, mixing up with mission people. And those mission people have to mix up with us. . . . And so bags were taken back and forth, people asked for tobacco back and forth, and for fire. Even men ate things from the bags of the mission people." Oloi'a and other the women with whom Schreiner and I talked attributed the traditionalists' declining power and numbers in recent decades to the moral laxity that came with this mixing up of pagan men with Christians.

Another partial breach of the walls protecting ancestral ways from outside dangers and alien forces came with the establishment of large Maasina Rule communal villages. In most parts of Kwaio country, however, such larger settlements were continuously occupied only briefly at the height of the movement, if at all. Through most of the movement, and in subsequent decades, the large clearings where people from a region gather to discuss political matters and *kastomu* have not been domestic settlements at all. These *bungu 'ifi*, 'conch shell villages', are outside regular settlements, are not permanently occupied at all and serve only sporadically as the sites for meetings (often ones lasting a day or two). This is another walling-off strategy. In coming together to 'work on *kastomu*', the Kwaio traditionalists are stepping outside the boundaries of everyday life. It is the *bungu 'ifi*, particularly Ngarinaasuru (since it was established in 1963), that have been the loci for Kwaio pagan interactions with representatives of government, the missions, and other outsiders (such as a doctor on tour, a once-in-a-decade sight in the mountains).

This, then, establishes the crucial categorical and geographical contexts for discourses of resistance. Kwaio resistance can be structured in terms of the categories and concepts of colonial domination, pervasively oppositional in structure, precisely *because* it is carried on on the margins. The Kwaio discourses of resistance are articulated in defending the invisible walls that compartmentalize and hence preserve and defend the ancestral way of life. Talk and action directed toward representatives of the colonial, or now postcolonial, state is cast in alien categories, and articulated mainly in Pidgin. Talk of *kastomu* or resistance by the pagans among themselves is expressed in a Kwaio heavily laced with Pidgin lexicon; more important, its logic is pervasively oppositional, as we will see in the next chapter.

In an early paper after my initial fieldwork, I pointed out the irony that the Kwaio had 'chiefs' only on Tuesdays, and only when at the *bungu 'ifi*. And it was there, on Tuesdays, that talk was directed to 'straightening out' and 'writing down' *kastomu*. The 'chiefs' of the "Sub-District Committee" (as we will see, organized in terms of the governments old tax "lines") would hear litigation, and settle cases in the light of customary law (*loa*). While the *sifi*, the 'chiefs', discussed matters of momentous import, the *koomani fiifuru* 'common people' (other men, as well as women and young people) occupied themselves with lesser matters.

The compartmentalization that preserves the ways of the ancestors—the realm within which women stay, rules are kept, shell valuables hold their value—has as its concomitants striking transitions of personae for the men moving from one compartment to the other, as well as striking disjunctures of context and meaning. The two Kwaio murderers who underwent the rituals and magic of war and in their liminal state took the mission plane to Honiara to kill their victims will serve to exemplify. But the same disjuncture goes back many decades, even though the transitions are now more sudden. In 1969, I sat with blind octogenarian 'Ulasia, wise priest of his descent group and epitome of cultural conservatism—who had been a famed warrior in his prime[3]—as he told me about his ten years in Fiji, talking with excitement about the railroad trains in the cane fields, and producing phrases in Fijian he still remembered.

The Kwaio have confronted the forces that have threatened them and their ancestors, then, not by culturally incorporating or encapsulating them but by marginalizing them, building walls and fighting to preserve them against breaches. It has been a cultural fencing operation, to keep the enemy without rather than encapsulating him within. The fencing has been possible only because—unlike the Maori, the Hawaiians, the Fijians—the Kwaio have lived in an isolated, mountainous terrain of no economic value to whites. Without the mountain wall there could have been no cultural fences.

3. Under his previous name I'alamo (see Keesing 1978b:61, 67).

23 Continuity and Change in Kwaio Resistance

Having followed Kwaio resistance across the span of 120 years, articulated where possible through their own voices and from their own perspectives, it is time to step back and pose more theoretical questions. First, I will examine continuities and changes in Kwaio resistance through the decades. I will use these processes of change and continuity to reflect, then, on current debates with regard to the nature and conceptualization of "resistance." Before examining the striking continuities in Kwaio resistance, some general observations about representation and interpretation are in order.

Theoretical Problems in Historical Interpretation

Reading historical events as moments in a struggle sustained over many decades tempts us to see individual acts and scenes as part of the design of a continuous tapestry. One danger here is interpreting events in the light of the subsequently unfolding history, or attributing motives and meanings that could only have crystalized much later. When the testimony comes from protagonists in this history who themselves read the past in terms of the present, the dangers and complexities are multiplied. The interpretation Talaunga'i placed on events of 1880 was heavily shaped by his retrospective interpretation of events in 1927, 1947, and since. There is a dangerous temptation to situate long past events in a context of subsequent political struggles rather in the context of their unfolding.

There is also a danger of attributing meanings and motives to protagonists in terms of the historical sweep of the whole tapestry. There undoubtedly were elements of "resistance" in the early ship attacks or in the assassination of Daniels in 1911. But there were other motives, of plunder, vengeance, self-aggrandizement, satisfaction of the ancestors. Reading events in terms of a tapestry of historical struggle tempts us to pull out of such complexities of individual meaning and motive the elements that fit best into the longer design. Where the story has a romantic cast, as resistance clearly has, the temptations to emphasize political motives and leave elements of greed and pride in the background are themselves hard to resist. I will come back to this problem.

But situating events and motives in their own historical context and situating representations of them in the contexts of their telling is by no means a simple and transparent process. I have recently (Keesing 1990) examined the paradoxes and contradictions involved in representations of the 1927 massacre. Even in the moments immediately after the battle around the tax house at Gwee'abe, as Kwaio warriors surveyed the carnage they had wrought, their own diverse and conflicting interests, motives, and interpretations broke to the surface: the three groups most centrally involved came to the brink of internecine battle. In the weeks to follow, kin groups not involved in the massacre were to be wiped out and plundered and desecrated. Still, in 1990, the descendants of the Kwaio of 1927 have very different and conflicting interests in these events and representations of them. The warrior leaders at the time—

Basiana, Tagailamo, Fuufu'e, Maenaafo'oa—and their followers had diverse personal and often hidden motives. The legal machinery of the colonial state constructed an interpretation of these events entirely predicated on the legitimacy of their own rule, and hence cast in terms of misunderstandings and misreadings of the benign intentions of Bell and the government.

The multitude of retrospective interpretations by descendants of the north Malaita police who devastated and decimated the Kwaio interior, by politicians in Honiara and Auki, by British diplomats, by Kwaio Christians and pagans with diverse and conflicting interests precludes any single and definitive reading of these events. I have pointed out (ibid.) the irony that whereas Corris and I imagined that in our book (Keesing and Corris 1980) we were in some sense expressing the previously unarticulated Kwaio perspective on these events, the subsequent demands for compensation by Kwaio Fadanga are based on a radically different construction of them. Any Kwaio oral account of these events, whether those I recorded from warriors like Kwai'ime and Alefo who took part in the councils of war and in the assault on the tax house or those of men of their children's or grandchildren's generation, is not simply situated in the time of its telling and framed in terms of subsequent events and experiences, but it is also situated in these tangled webs of interest.

But we, too, are situated. However radicalized politically and sharpened by training in critical theory we might be, we are also deeply steeped in imperialist discourses we have imbued since childhood—in books, films, and even in our language. The assumption that European invasions of the New World, Africa, and the Pacific were in some sense natural, their legitimacy unquestioned—that Columbus and Captain Cook "discovered" something, that the Cowboys are the Good Guys and the Indians are the Bad Guys—is deeply programmed in our consciousness. Our own attempts at counterimperialist historiographic interventions always swim against the stream of these implicit understandings. To resurrect a quote from the introductory chapter, "We are products of an imperialist discourse that irresistibly shapes our language and our perceptions."

I have been as careful as I know how not to read modern political meanings uncritically into the past, and to place the Kwaio representations in these chapters in the contexts of their telling. But the processes at play are enormously complex, and our own readings are part of the complexity.

Continuities in Kwaio Resistance

All that said, we can scarcely fail to note the striking continuities across the decades, both in terms of the ideologies of resistance and of the cast of characters. The stance toward taxation, as an instrument of subjugation and as a one-sided tribute rather than an exchange, has been a continuous theme for almost seventy years. In it we find a reluctance to be taxed that we all share, heightened by a realization that they, the Kwaio, are least able in the Solomons to pay what is asked of them. To that is added an astute understanding of the political aspect of the tax as an instrument of subjugation, an assertion of sovereignty and power on the part of a government whose hegemony the Kwaio continue to challenge. The resistance to taxation also expresses a Melanesian perspective on exchange: a transaction, with the government as with any other, ultimately should represent a balanced exchange. The reciprocation in some transactions is to be in kind and exact (as in mortuary feast prestations). In other transactions, such as sacrifice, an asymmetry of power is explicit, but reciprocation in the form of ancestral protection and succourance is axiomatic. What, the Kwaio ask, is the reciprocation for their tax?

The theme of "writing down *kastomu*," producing a codified analogue of colonial legal statutes, has similarly been a continuous theme, across decades of struggle, for some forty-five years (Keesing 1982b). The ideological warfare between the Christians and the pagans, the depictions of the ancestors as Saetana and the counter-depictions of the white Jesus as interloper on ancestral lands, goes on in 1990 much as it must have gone on in 1920.

We find curious senses of reenactment and déjà vu, as where in 1947, twenty years after the Gwee'abe massacre, the government party that had come to arrest the Maasina Rule chief faced hidden guns, and massive bloodshed was imminent (Fifi'i 1989); and where, in 1986, another government party faced hidden guns and the police and Kwaio warriors again came right to the brink of another massacre. Even the geometrical progression of the intervals, twenty years and then forty, gives an eerie feeling. The killing of Dunn in 1965 shows eerie parallels, too, with the killing of Daniels in 1911.

If we look at Kwaio resistance across the decades, striking continuities in the cast of characters emerge as well. We have seen how the leading Maasina Rule chiefs of the 1940s included 'Alakwale'a, co-assassin of missionary Fred Daniels in 1911, and Anifelo, whose father had smashed

Bell's skull in 1927. Forty years later, Basiana's younger son Laefiwane led Kwaio Fadanga demonstrations on the Prime Minister's lawn in Honiara. We encounter Alefo of Ngudu (whose oldest brother was one of the three leading warrior strongmen of the 1920s) as warrior in the Bell massacre in 1927; and we encounter him again at the 1947 confrontation, after his release from prison, urging an attack on the government force. In the 1960s, he was centrally involved in the politics of *kastomu*. We find men whose fathers took part in the 1927 assault on the police in the tax house at Gwee'abe in the 1947 confrontation and again at the 1986 teargassing. There is an eerie continuity between the cast of characters from Furi'ilai, the warriors Fuufu'e and Lamotalau, and those involved in the 1988 killings at Mt. Austen.[1]

It would be simplistic to gloss the life of an Alefo, an 'Alakwale'a, an Anifelo, or a Laefiwane as a text of continued resistance through the deades, to see opposition to *gafamanu* and *sukuru* as the dominant theme and motive of actions over many years. The meanings and motives that move and shape and color a life are far too multi-stranded and complex to be reduced into such a cardboard political stance.

Yet for the older Kwaio pagans I have known well, the historical theme of struggle looms more centrally than we might expect. They have lived through decades in which the proud independence and ancestral power they experienced in childhood have been progressively reduced. Christianity on the one hand, alien law on the other, have bit by bit reduced autonomy and immobilized ancestral power, seemingly irresistibly despite the dramatic confrontations. Listening to middle-aged and elderly Kwaio women and men construct their lives in retrospect, I have over and over again been struck by the way personal tragedies are interpreted as consequences of this invasion, desecration, and loss of power. If we remember that virtually every untimely death and misfortune since 1927 has been interpreted in terms of the devastating pollution by the punitive expedition and the consequent withdrawing of ancestral support, we begin to understand more deeply.

To begin to understand the way tragedy wrought more directly by the punitive expedition hangs over individual lives, one need only listen to an old Talaunga'i recall with tears in his eyes how his parents and siblings were shot down in a dawn attack; or his sister Fa'aoria speak of how she grew up like a wild animal, without a mother to teach her; or a Basiitau

---

1. For legal reasons, I cannot make them fully explicit. See Keesing n.d.4 for an account of the Mt. Austen killings and their interpretation.

recount how as a little boy he saw his father beaten and shot by police; or old Gisuni, whose elderly father had been shot by the soldiers, who told me with an air of tragedy how her whole life had been blighted by the desecration of 1927: "When they destroyed our shrines and villages, they destroyed all the good things in our lives."[2] Alefo and Kwai'ime spent years in a colonial prison for their part in the 1927 massacre. Tolonga'i, who as a boy in 1927 had killed a policeman who had taunted him,[3] escaped from prison and spent most of his adult life as a fugitive in the mountains. These and many others had their lives woven out of skeins of defiance and repression.

That the bitterness and anger smoulders deep, and that it has surfaced recurrently through the years in contexts of political confrontation should not, then, surprise us. Nor should the continuities in the symbols of sovereignty and subjugation, opposition and capitulation. It was by intervening in blood feuding with alien laws that Bell first sought to force acceptance of colonial rule; and over and over again, it has been law that has provided a field of struggle. Taxation, too, has been a kind of annual reenactment of the drama of tribute and defiance that began in the 1920s. There are recurrent symbolic themes, as well. The King as distant symbol of colonial authority is juxtaposed against the ancestors as source of customary authority. That Kwaio defying the government have regularly used ritual injunctions—Folofo'u's curses are only the most recent—has been a recurrent strategy of countering the power of the King with the power of the ancestors, and demanding that the government recognize the legal force of custom.

Historical Phases in Kwaio Resistance

If we counterpose to these striking continuities the *changes in* Kwaio resistance across the decades, other perspectives emerge. I have no faith in periodization—dividing a history into time slices with labels—as an analytical or even expositional strategy. But there might be some value in distinguishing three major phases of Kwaio resistance, each characterized by a dominant mode of opposition. First, from the early ship attacks until 1927, armed struggle and violent confrontation constituted the dominant mode of resistance. Second, through the 1930s, ancestral revelation and religious (though not quite millenarian) cultism seems to have

2. For her full text and a series of others expressing a similar sense of tragic doom and a pall cast over the decades since the punitive expedition, see Keesing and Corris 1980, 201–204.

3. About having killed his classificatory father.

been the dominant mode. Third, from the mid-1940s to the present, political confrontation has become a dominant mode. Such a periodization adds some enlightenment, in that the successively dominant modes of struggle have a kind of logical and even philosophical coherence: armed struggle as long as keeping the invading forces at bay was militarily feasible; a retreat into religious and mystical resistance, in the face of massive defeat and overwhelming force; and, finally, political confrontation and a kind of collective bargaining, as that colonial force visibly lost its potency in World War II, and the instruments of domination, legal and political, were understood to be negotiable and could be turned back on those who wielded them. For the Kwaio, in comparison to most peoples subjected to British colonial rule, full political subjugation was to come very late, and hence to last only briefly. It was only during the 1930s, the period when overt resistance had been smashed, that the Kwaio were placed in the position of colonized subordination; and significantly, it was in this period that their struggle was displaced into religious forms, so canonical a manifestation of subalternity (Guha 1983, 1984; Comaroff 1985).

In parallel with political confrontation and collective bargaining, other modes of Kwaio resistance have emerged in the postcolonial Solomons. As an indigenous class system has developed in urban areas, Malaita pagans have found themselves at the very bottom. Young men still go to work on plantations far from home, as their fathers and grandfathers did; but now they form a predatory underclass, many engaging in theft and violence. Ancestrally conferred powers and culturally sharpened skills in stealing pigs and valuables are deployed in shoplifting, housebreaking, safecracking—and clandestine murder (see Keesing n.d.4). Such acts of violence and urban predation constitute another mode of Kwaio resistance in the modern period.

But the enlightenment added by this periodization carries some cost. First, for the Kwaio pagans, the "religious" is an inseparable component of everyday life, and of "political" action—and of armed violence. When the warriors confronted Bell and his police at Gwee'abe in 1927, they had sacrificed to the ancestors, prayed for support, read the omens; and when twenty years later, they confronted Cameron and his police at Gelebasi, they had sacrificed to the ancestors, prayed for support, and read the omens. The Mt. Austen murders were committed by two young men who had sacrificed to the ancestors and read the omens, and were in an ancestrally empowered state of liminality. From the early ship attacks onwards, engaging the colonial enemy—by whatever means—has been possible only with the ancestors' support. Outside their home mountains, as well as in them, the Kwaio have depended on and invoked their ancestors for the powers to steal, kill, fight, and survive the malign and polluting forces to which they are exposed. At a mortuary feast high in the bush, in 1990, Susu Fa'ari, a man once tried for murdering Brother Dunn, told me, "Those people out there from other parts of the Solomons are much bigger and stronger than we Kwaio people are; if we didn't have our *adalo* to pray to, they'd pound us to pieces."

Second, in each period, the other modes of resistance have been important subsidiary themes. There clearly was much political confrontation in the early engagements with colonial power and missionaries, as well as sporadic violent attacks; and in the recent epoque I have characterized in terms of political confrontation, actual or threatened violence has been a recurrent though subsidiary theme. As I have shown, "religious" resistance runs through the entire period (recall that in Kwaio eyes it was the ancestors, responding to their sacrifices and prayers, who brought to them the American who was to write down their customs).

While millenarian cultism was a much less important element in Maasina Rule than European accounts of the time would suggest, ideas that to us seem fantastic were unquestionably widely circulated and widely "believed"; and such ideas are a continuing theme of Kwaio politics. Folofo'u is thought, especially by his SSEC supporters, to have a magical telephone with which he communicates with "America." When, in 1986, I was refused permission to come to Malaita, but I issued a statement broadcast over SIBC dissociating myself from Folofo'u's secessionism, some of the latter's followers spread claims that this was a smokescreen on my part to deceive the government, and that I had secretly met with Folofo'u on an American submarine.

The forms of submerged resistance of the sort Scott (1986) calls "Brechtian," in the contemporary predation of young Kwaio in the urban jungle, again show continuities with the past. For a century, Kwaio plantation workers have resisted abuse and exploitation with violence and predation when they could, and with more indirect strategies reminiscent of Scott's Malaysian peasants when they could not.

The Conceptualization of Resistance

Seeing a single and continuous historical struggle manifest in varying outward forms illuminates contemporary debates about the relationship between the subtle and often covert strategies described by Willis (1977) and Scott and overt acts of confrontation. We can use the Kwaio case to pull apart some of the strands of recent debate about resistance.

The manifestations of resistance by the Kwaio across 120 years do not push us to the outermost and most problematic margins of the category of "resistance" now being debated: whether, for example, microscopic challenges to a patriarchically imposed code of costume or demeanor by wives or daughters (fingernail polish, going bra-less, or their equivalents in another cultural universe) can usefully be viewed as everyday acts of resistance.

Scott's Malaysian case suggests that one crucial element distinguishing modes of resistance we might call "political" in a broad sense from individual acts of self-assertion or rebellion is the existence of a *subculture* of subalternity, a collective code in which strategies for opposing domination and exploitation are communicated, shared, themselves represented ideologically.[4] (The distinction I am seeking to draw parallels Marx's discussions of whether peasants constitute a *class*: what matters, he argued [particularly in the *Eighteenth Brumaire of Louis Bonaparte*], was a shared consciousness of class-position—in effect, an oppositional, counterhegemonic subaltern ideology.) If we take such a stance, then one element that distinguishes resistance (in the collective sense that is at issue) is communication among subalterns regarding their common situation of subordination and regarding modes and strategies of opposition to it (bold and overt or subtle and covert, depending on the mode of domination and the nature of sanctions).

We might here usefully think of the prewar Solomons plantations, and the various modes of opposition used by Malaita workers. The opposition took forms ranging from work slowdowns and prolonged smoking or betel-chewing breaks to killing the foreman. (In the mid-1960s, when Lever's Pacific Plantations Ltd. threatened the livelihood of those who "brushed"—cut down the undergrowth in the paddocks—by introducing cattle to graze between the coconut palms, the Kwaio stole the cattle and ate them.) What makes the work slowdowns—and the occasional beatings and murders when they were seen as possible—acts of "resistance" was, I think, a subcultural tradition of how and when to fight back that was widely communicated among the workers and imparted to young recruits as part of their introduction to the plantation world. (Half a century later, elderly Malaitans regale me[5] with stories of how they fought back against an oppressive plantation system.) We find similar subcul-

---

4. I am indebted to Igor Kopytoff for raising this question in regard to Kwaio acts of violence on plantations when I presented a lecture on Kwaio resistance to the Philadelphia Anthropological Society on Feb. 1, 1991.

5. As they did Judith Bennett (1987).

tures of resistance among the young Kwaio men around Honiara today, for whom acts of shoplifting, housebreaking, and violence are not mere sporadic and individual acts of predation but moves in a quite conscious game of class warfare.

In this light, whether painting fingernails constitutes an act of resistance is not a question of polish but a question of politics. The same distinction can be expressed from a different perspective. As I will go on to suggest below, it is crucial whether individuals see their own actions in terms of their own membership in a category subjected to common forms of oppression, and see the individuals toward whom they act as similarly representing a wider category.

While the existence of a counterhegemonic consciousness and political awareness, an oppositional subculture for resisting domination by whatever means are strategically available, may define part of the territory of "resistance," it seems not to define all of it. Two further forms of expansion have been explored in recent literature.

First, Jean Comaroff's analysis (1985) of the Tswana, locked into the South African state and its ruthless political economy, suggests that we may not want to define resistance solely in terms of conscious and collective subaltern strategies of confrontation and covert opposition. The Zionist cults among the Tswana and other Bantu-speaking peoples may be viewed by their adherents as quite separate from the political strategies they use to resist the exploitation of labor and the inhumanities and oppression of apartheid, the pass system, and other institutions of a racist colonial-settler state. Resistance, Comaroff argues, may be deflected into religious forms—such as the Zionist cults—whose political force is at least partly hidden from the consciousness of adherents. So, too, the "Devil" worship of the Bolivian miners examined by Taussig (1980) and Nash (1979) would seem to express a resistance against the oppressive terms of capitalist wage labor whether or not this is perceived by the miners themselves. The spirit possession among Malaysian women factory workers described by Ong (1987:207) may represent "a mode of unconscious retaliation against male authority," and yet at the same time constitute "the . . . beginnings of an idiom of protest against labor discipline and male control in the modern industrial situation."

There are some theoretical difficulties in broadening the category of "resistance" in this direction. We need, at least, to note that when resistance is more in the eye of the observer than the eye of the actor, its character is changed considerably. In the Kwaio cases I have discussed where resistance took millenarian forms—as in Noto'i's cult movement in the 1930s—the political ideology remained transparently clear: the cult prophecies were all about the violent overthrow of the colonial state, and the envisioned millenium was very much an earthly one, presided over by long-established ancestors, restored to their former powers.

Finally, under some circumstances of extreme domination that render a subjugated population powerless to resist in any overt ways, it may in the end be useful to see accommodation—even though it appears passive—as a kind of latent phase of resistance. Such a position has been plausibly argued by Genovese (1974:597–98) in regard to plantation slavery in the Americas.

Accommodation itself breathed a critical spirit and disguised subversive actions and often embraced its apparent opposite—resistance. In fact, accommodation might best be understood as accepting what could not be helped without falling prey to the pressures for dehumanization, emasculation, and self-hatred. In particular, the slaves' accommodation to paternalism enabled them to assert rights, which by their very nature not only set limits to their surrender of self but actually constituted an implicit rejection of slavery.

There is a two-sided problem here. On the one hand, if we define resistance so flexibly and broadly that subalterns are resisting when they are not aware of it, or when outwardly they are passively accepting the terms of their domination, we have taken a term that—in its common uses at least—implies conscious agency and intentionality and so bleached it that these qualities disappear. On the other hand, if we insist on a more strict definition, and observe a subordinated population through time, we find overt resistance bursting forth at historical moments when circumstances allow (slaves rising in revolt, peasants at the barricades). Resistance seemingly then emerges out of apparent quiescent acceptance, consciousness bursts out of apparent unconsciousness. This problem has been discussed at length by Scott in his latest study of *Domination and the Arts of Resistance* (1990), where he proposes that we attend closely to "hidden transcripts."

There is another set of problems on which I have touched in the introductory chapter, at several points in the historical narrative, and in my methodological cautions at the beginning of this chapter. The concept of resistance prototypically conjures up images of collective struggle, a standing together in a common cause, as well as of intentional agency. It is easy on the one hand to idealize and romanticize acts and stances that have an oppositional element. More closely examined, such stances and acts may themselves hide *other* transcripts—personal motives of self-aggrandizement or political ambition, fantasy or psychological instability, projections of unconscious conflicts and hostilities. What appears as a collective stance, even when prototypically (and romantically) it is at the barricades, may hide a multitude of private, diverse, and more complex "transcripts." We have seen in the narratives of Kwaio history how an attack by Maeasuaa or 'Arumae on a recruiting ship or Basiana's assassination of Bell has a large element of "resistance": but it would be simplistic to read only these strands of meaning in a complex, multi-sided web of motives; and more simplistic still to see the warriors that joined them simply as engaged in collective struggle against invasion.

Resistance and Metaphoric Categorization

Some unpacking of resistance as a category in terms of recent studies in cognitive linguistics seems worthwhile. Academics seeking to define their analytical terms precisely and unambiguously are, it would seem, swimming against the stream of human mentation, the logics of the mind. Recent research on cognition (see, e.g., Lakoff 1987) suggests that humans do not categorize the world into things and events and acts the way logicians since Aristotle's day have imagined: in terms of the necessary and sufficient conditions for being an x or a y. Rather, categorization is based heavily on prototypic images, often themselves representing the confluence of several conceptual elements. The prototypic patterns, characteristically iconic, abstract, and relational, then serve as the basis for a radial extension of the category. The extensions of categories rest on what Lakoff calls "image-schema transformations," based on topological transformations of iconic images,[6] many of them metaphoric.

This conceptual framework, technical language, and perspective will be unfamiliar to many readers. An illustration from the semantics of English may give needed clarification and insight. Consider the semantics of "run" in "the man ran through the woods" and "the road ran through the woods." Here an iconic image of physical movement is transmuted into an image of a path, resting on a metaphor of what Leonard Talmy (n.d.) calls "fictive motion." If we add to this "the theme ran through his speech" we see an iconic image metaphorically extended and transformed, with a path of continuity through time metaphorically treated as continuity in space; we see it further permuted in "the ad ran all week in the newspaper." Consider further the image of "run" as a movement of a

---

6. Here Lakoff (1987) draws heavily on the work of Leonard Talmy, who in 1978 introduced the concept of "rubber sheet cognition." See Talmy 1978, 1988a, 1988b.

liquid, as in "the stream ran dry," or of a substance that flows like a liquid, in "the rice ran out of the hole in the bag." The image of something running out of a container is metaphorically transformed into the supply of something being exhausted, as in "our water had run out." The substance that runs out can itself be metaphoric, as in "his luck had run out" or "our time had run out." Finally, this image of a container emptying to represent the dwindling of some substance or quasi-substance is further reversed with "we had run out of water" or "he had run out of luck." We find permutations of the image of the agitated physical movement of running in such compound verbal expressions as "run wild," "run roughshod," "run scared," "run amok." The metaphor-based transformations of a prototypic image—in all directions—begin to emerge.

One implication of this mode of prototype-based categorization, resting heavily on iconic images and their topological, metaphor-based transformation, is that not all members of categories have common features. All are related in some image-based/metaphoric/metonymic way to some element(s) in the cluster that forms the prototype of the category. Very often, the conceptual core of categories is not only iconic but related directly to bodily experience and orientation, especially spatial orientation. "Run" will serve to exemplify. The physical act of running is deeply grounded in human bodily experience, of the kinesics of movement and musculature, and the rapid transformations of the visual field and change in location that accompany running. But as we have seen, running has other conceptual elements, since it implies a trajectory, a path, a destination (or a direction of flight). By a spatial transformation we can see a direction of movement as if it were a two dimensional space with a path through it. The running can be conceptualized from the perspective of the runner moving through space or a stationary observer past whom the runner is moving. What is running is prototypically animate, but metaphorically it can be inanimate and traversing or pervading what is conceptualized metaphorically as if it were a space (an argument, a book, an organization). The prototypic image of running thus is formed of clustered elements—a path of movement, movement as a flow, the physical motion of running, continuity along a trajectory, the kinesics and visual field of the moving runner. Each element in this cluster can be separately developed metaphorically.

A further implication is that categories are not neatly bounded: they have fuzzy edges, and overlap—some objects made to sit on are not really chairs and not really couches. Another implication is that because one sense of a term is metaphorically based on one element in the cluster that forms the prototype, and another sense is metaphorically based on another element, the two senses may be conceptually very far from one another and have no clear element in common.

Here, then, is the paradox that confronts tidy-minded social scientists trying to define "political" or "family" or "kinship" or "power" or "marriage"—or "resistance." As humans speaking natural languages and equipped with *Homo sapiens* brains, we have no difficulty understanding (more or less) what we mean when we say something is "political." When we attempt to define what we mean in such a way that everything we want to call "political" has some set of criterial defining features, we are paralyzed. Our canons of rigorous scientific discourse tell us that categories should have neat and precise edges, and that one instance of the family or politics should be just as familial or just as political as any other instance. As human speakers of human languages, we social scientists talk and think in terms of categories with fuzzy edges and clear (but abstract, iconically defined) centers. As human speakers of human languages, we have no way to talk and think other than metaphorically.

What, if anything, does all this tell us about *resistance?* First of all, resistance is image-based and deeply metaphoric. The conceptual prototype of resistance is of a physical force, experienced as impinging or pushing against the body; and of a pushing back against or obstruction of that force. The force itself is uncontrollable; the pushing back against it is prototypically a deliberately applied, kinesically experienced counterforce, a pushing back against the impinging force.[7]

This prototypic image allows of multiple permutations. The force that is impinging can be metaphorically constructed in many ways. What is perhaps most important here is that the impinging force need not be clearly conceptualized, need not imply an agency, need not be personified as animate. There is an implication of a direction in which the impinging force is applied. But the force can be (and most often is) general,

7. Shortly after writing this and what follows, I received from Leonard Talmy a copy of a recent paper (Talmy 1988b) in which he characterizes an imagery he calls "force dynamics," which he shows to be pervasive and fundamental in language and cognition: "how entities interact with respect to . . . the exertion of force, resistance to such exertion and the overcoming of such resistance, blockage of a force and the resistance of such blockage, etc." (ibid., 49). Talmy suggests that the attribution of force dynamics (of force or inertia) to opposing elements (what he calls Agonist and Antagonist) is central to the grammatical representation of causality and modals, as well as to the semantics of lexical forms (such as "resist") and the conceptualization of intra-psychological and social psychological (and we could here add, political) processes. Talmy's general and theoretical analysis fits well with the less general and formal one I offer for "resistance."

abstract, inchoate. It is, prototypically, stronger but also more global than the force that can be applied against it.

The resistance against the force can entail a conscious agency; but it can (as with electrical or physical resistance) simply be a slowing or obstruction, metaphorically conceived as if it were a counterforce. One metaphoric representation of the impinging force would see it as if it were a flowing liquid in a channel that can be impeded, dammed, slowed, diverted; the resistance is passive, an obstruction of flow. However, in many of the metaphoric uses of resistance, there is an implication of conscious agency, a deliberate, energetic physical pushing back against the impinging force (the pushing back allowing of multiple physical and metaphorical imageries).

In some contexts the image of resistance against an impinging force is flip-flopped by changing the perspective from that of the entity doing the resisting to that of the entity conceived as applying the force.[8] You can be resisted, as well as resisting yourself. Here, the images are of frustration, of being blocked in moving in a direction or attaining a goal.

A further image flip-flop is based on a model of *attraction* toward a source or vortex, from the perception of an entity being pulled unwillingly by an overpowering force. Here the image of resisting, again strongly kinesthetically based, is of bracing the body and desperately trying to hold a position against a force too strong to fight against. This metaphorized image of force and resistance is used when one is being pulled against one's will toward some situation or outcome. Models from the physical world (e.g., magnetism) and the biological world (e.g., the irresistible power of scent to attract) may be developed around this permutation of the image of force and resistance. This image of irresistible attraction is also used, in conjunction with folk models of psychology, to conceptualize temptation. Such metaphoric conceptualizations depend on folk models of psychology that depict the experiencer as having inner and more or less unconscious urges and a regimen-following, discipline-maintaining consciousness. Hence we cannot "resist" doing something—

8. We have already encountered such an image reversal with luck running out and someone running out of luck. Lakoff (1990) has pointed out that metaphors of time entail a similar splitting or image-reversal: time is metaphorized in terms of space both in terms of an observer moving through space and in terms of a stationary observer with time moving past. Leonard Talmy (n.d.) has shown that metaphors of perception have a similar splitting or reversal of image in many languages, where perceiving something is represented both as rays or emanations impinging on a fixed observer and by perception *as* emanation—that is, where the perceiving agent is metaphorically cast as emanating outward to impinge on the object perceived.

succumbing to the lure of chocolate or the adventure of a destructive sexual attraction—even though we may try.

All this at least helps us to recognize, first of all, that when we talk about resistance in a political sense, our talk is deeply metaphorical. The metaphoric permutations of the prototypical image-cluster of resisting in relation to human agency need to be more closely examined. First, resistance may be used both in senses of individual (usually physical) efforts to fight against aggression or control or capture, and in political senses. It is the latter set with which we are concerned. We need to remember, however, that when an individual fights against police officers or struggles against a potential rapist, we speak of "resisting arrest" or "resisting a rapist."

The senses of resistance which concern us here differ from these characteristically physical struggles against aggression or coercion in their conceptualization. Resistance when we use it in a political sense, in contrast to resisting arrest or resisting a rapist, requires a particular kind of metaphoric reading of the events in question. Although it may be an individual who is "resisting" (against a "force," whatever it is), characteristically it is a group or collectivity or category of persons which is conceptualized as the entity on which the force is impinging. Prototypically, the counterforce they exert (by their actions or their holding to a fixed position in the face of pressures that would displace them) is conscious; and prototypically it is applied as a direct counter to this impinging force. The image of the impinging force is that it is stronger, or more global, than the counterforce that can be applied against it: so resistance is always an arduous, and by implication often a dangerous or hopeless, effort. But when we use resistance in these political senses, the struggle characteristically is not directly physical—although it may be—but some mode of counteraction metaphorized in physical terms.

Note that to develop the image of resistance in these political senses also requires that the acts of individuals on the *other* side, the side where greater power lies, have themselves to be metaphorically developed as manifestations of some greater and more general force: "the state," "colonialism," "the government," "communism." As a metaphoric characterization, it may itself rely on a metonymy in which the individual person or act serves to represent the whole: Mr. Bell *was* the *gafamanu*.[9]

9. George Lakoff, in discussion of his plenary address to the Second International Conference on Cognitive Linguistics (1991), brilliantly developed an argument about the complex interplay between metaphor and metonymy, suggesting that metonyms are most commonly encapsulated within metaphors in this way.

To characterize acts as resistance (rather than as murder or assault or malingering) implies that the observer impute to the actors precisely this kind of reading. In the historical texts we have examined, there is ample evidence that the Kwaio were interpreting those against whom they fought not simply as individuals, but as representatives of institutional forces. Daniels was assassinated not as an individual but as representing *sukuru* as an institution threatening the ancestors; so, apparently, was Dunn half a century later—he had just arrived and was scarcely known locally. Bell was killed as an individual, but above all, like his policemen, he was killed for the position he held and the force he represented. Kwaio political rhetoric has for decades been directed not against individuals, whatever their faults and foibles and deeds, but against *gafamanu* and *sukuru*. The individual planter or recruiting ship against whom hatred was harbored or vengeance was sought was the prime target—but in the end, *any* white man, or *any* ship would do.

That such political interpretations have motivated action makes the metaphor of resistance apt; but it need not imply that the forces of which individual planters or recruiters or missionaries or government officers were seen as manifestations be clearly perceived or understood. In our metaphoric usages of "resistance" those subalterns who are doing the resisting need not clearly or aptly comprehend the forces arrayed against them. They have a local and partial view of a wider, more global pressure that would move or transform them. In the Solomons case, the complexities and cleavages of class and gender and interest that divided Europeans one against the other were as best possible hidden from the view of "the natives": that the latter oversimplified their adversary in acts of struggle is scarcely surprising.

I find it helpful to raise here a conceptual point that emerged in my discussions with Fredrik Barth regarding the nature and conceptualization of power.[10] I advanced a parallel argument with regard to the metaphoric core of the concept of power. Barth added the interesting perspective that experientially, we all know (from our frustrations as infants onward) what it is to be *powerless*; but experientially, none of us knows—really—what it is to be powerful (although we all have our moments of control and authority). He suggests that our ideas of power have an inchoate and underconceptualized nature because our experiences have this asymmetry: power is the vague, diffuse imagined force, whose

10. During a national teaching seminar for Norwegian graduate students in anthropology Prof. Barth and I conducted at the University of Bergen in May 1991.

agency and form is unclear, which is the assumed complement of our experientially rich powerlessness. I believe he is right; and I think this helps us to understand resistance as a category. Resistance again is experience-rich; but what it is that presses against us, compels us, is experience-thin, abstractly and generally conceived. If personified, it is, like power, personified in abstract, metaphoric ways.

Seeing resistance as a metaphor, and analyzing the image-transformations developed around its conceptual core, is useful in other ways in helping us see why it comfortably characterizes a wide range of phenomena. As with electrical or physical resistance one can impede an impinging force by immobility or slowing down; or, by invoking the image of a force drawing the experiencing entity irresistibly toward a vortex, resistance may lie in digging one's heels in and holding one's position.

We may usefully here come back to the question recently raised of whether wearing fingernail polish or going without a bra may be construed as a form of resistance. If we consider this in the light of the discussion of resistance as a metaphor, the points at issue are highlighted. It is not so much the *act* that matters as the actor's reading of its context and meaning (Abu-Lughod 1990). If painting the fingernails is directed at attracting a lover or making a husband jealous, we strain our analysis in construing this as resistance; if it is intended as an expression of independence, and if the woman who paints her nails sees herself as representing (in some sense) A Woman and her act as directed toward Control By Men, then it becomes political—and the metaphor of resistance becomes apt. If one woman goes without her bra, it may or may not be a political act. If ten women burn their bras, it can scarcely be otherwise.

This highlights the reasons that the aptness of resistance as a characterization becomes uncomfortable in cases where the actors seem to have no conscious awareness of a political motivation—when they think they are following God's word or hearing voices. Again, it is not the action that matters: the classic Melanesian "cargo cults" such as the Vailala Madness (Williams 1976) were millenarian in content and doctrine, yet at their heart lay a political analysis of European wealth and power. The political analysis that underlay the Kwaio cult movements of the 1930s is unmistakable. Where there seems to be no such political analysis, perhaps we more aptly characterize religious cultism as a *displacement* of resistance.

Need resistance be overt? Humans have the capacity to imagine scenarios they do not or cannot enact. Here we can come back to Scott's notion (1990) of "hidden transcripts." A galley slave in chains is likely to have harbored fantasies of vengeful violence against those who chained, whipped, and coerced him or fed him with slop. The capacity to imagine retribution in specific images and fantasies is again experience-rich, something we all have done in the face of discipline, punishment, or constraint. It is this mode of hiding transcripts in imagination, as well as covert networks of communication among even the most oppressed, that makes it possible for overt acts of defiance and retaliation to burst forth when the situation allows. The brooding galley slave instantly becomes a warrior battling for escape and freedom and retribution if the chains are loosed and the moment comes. In the meantime, he will row as slowly as he can and rest as often as he can and grumble as defiantly as he dares: and those, too, are modes of resisting, as Scott tells us so vividly.

I would urge that we understand that "resistance" is a useful metaphor to characterize a range of phenomena, but that we cannot expect or demand that it be precisely definable or that it fit all situations equally aptly. Like all metaphoric, image-based conceptualizations, it fits prototypical cases better than marginal ones (not in any prescriptive sense, but because there is a more coherent metaphoric mapping from one domain to another). Where those whose lives we are describing imagine that they are communicating with God and following His messages, rather than fighting colonial domination, the fit will be less comfortable—the metaphor of resistance less prototypically apt—than were they to go on strike or attack the police. Yet if the consequence of their religious movement is to withdraw from the labor force, this may frustrate the capitalist interests seeking to exploit them—hence, changing the image to the perspective of those applying the impinging force may have the consequence of resistance in the way a dam resists a flow of water. Or they may hold their position, refusing to be drawn into a vortex of temptation. A people may resist capitalism simply by being satisfied to eat sweet potatoes instead of rice.

Images and metaphors may be more or less apt, more or less useful; they can scarcely be incorrect. If we expect our technical terms to be precise, resistance will not serve us well in theoretical analyses. If we see our theoretical discourse as inevitably cast in everyday language, then we will abandon false hopes for precision and prescriptive definitions.

The difficulties with regard to conceptualizing resistance suggest to me, however, that a much more extensive and effective theorization of this field is needed. I agree with Ong (1987:221) that "human struggles for morality" among the historically subordinated must be interpreted "in their own terms and in the constitution of their own subjectivities." We move in this direction by attending to the "marginal . . . [and] divergent voices and innovative practices of subjected peoples" (ibid.). The marginal voices of the Kwaio pagans, beleaguered but never fully subjugated through colonial invasion, express through the decades a resistance that has changed its character but never changed its ultimate vision. These voices have much to teach us if we listen carefully.

24 Oppositional Structures in Kwaio Discourse

To attend to these voices, we must seek in them pervasive logics of counterhegemonic discourse. I will argue that the circumstances of domination generate a dynamic whereby the voices of resistance are expressed through a logic of *opposition*.

Counterhegemonic Discourses as Oppositional

In seeing how counterhegemonic discourses are shaped by and modeled on the very ideological systems they challenge, I take theoretical guidance from Antonio Gramsci and my colleague Ranajit Guha (1983, 1984). Gramsci wrote, in the *Prison Notebooks*, of how "the lower classes, historically on the defensive, can only achieve self-awareness via a series of negations" (1971:273).

This oppositional cast of counterhegemonic discourses is manifest in many ways on many levels. First of all, the categorization of the conceptual field may replicate the categories of domination (even if, as with "Black is Beautiful," the terms are inverted, or the valences reversed). Secondly, the organizational structure of opposition may replicate the structure through which domination is exercised and administered. Thirdly, the identities claimed and subject positions articulated in discourses of resistance may represent categories historically created in the process of colonial domination or subjugation. Fourthly, the semiology of resistance may emulate, imitate, and in the process, consciously or unconsciously parody, the semiology of domination. Kwaio resistance richly exemplifies these modes of oppositional logic.

In examining this oppositional cast of Kwaio antihegemonic discourse, we need to do so against the conceptual background I have laid out in chapter 22. The antihegemonic discourses, incorporating Pidgin terms and colonial categories and concepts, are themselves compartmentalized, deployed, and articulated at the margins of the invisible wall the Kwaio have built to defend and preserve a space within which the ways of the ancestors can be followed. We must see this oppositional cast as characterizing the margins, not the interior, of the world the Kwaio have been defending across the decades. It is a discourse directed at those who would rule and change them, not at the ancestors who give them life and power.

Consider the project of "writing down the custom" that has so occupied and focused Kwaio political energies for almost fifty years. In terms of Melanesian experience of colonial rule, the written word—canonically, in the form of the Bible and the colonial legal statutes—was a powerful instrument of subjugation. Citing chapter and verse, missionaries challenged and condemned ancestral precepts; citing colonial laws, District Officers arrested and hanged men acting according to the ancestral ways, enforcing jural rights and preserving morality. To demand recognition of ancestral ways by the colonial state, it was necessary to provide an indigenous analogue of Bible and lawbook. Kwaio leaders speak of *loa*, 'law', as well as of *kastomu* in their discourse of resistance. It is worth reflecting that the categories of *kastom* and "culture" derive from colonial ideologies, not indigenous ones; and that the hypostatization of "custom" as a political symbol (so prominent in cultural nationalist discourse in the contemporary Pacific; see Keesing 1989b) is only possible in a context of external domination.[1]

European ways of talking about race have been similarly incorporated into the discourses of resistance. Like those who—from the negritude of Senghor to the Black is Beautiful of Cleaver and Carmichael—have adopted the conceptual structures of racism in fighting against it, the Kwaio resist racist domination by counterposing *ta'a bobola'a* 'black people' to *ta'a kwao*, 'white people'.

The identities claimed in Maasina Rule and since—"Malaitans" vs. "Western" (Western Solomons), "Kwaio" and "Kwara'ae"—had no political salience in the precolonial Solomons. These political entities emerged in the context of plantation labor and the administrative machinery of the colonial state.

Similarly, the political structure created in Maasina Rule and subsequent *kastomu* activities and Kwaio Fadanga has been oppositional in the

---

1. Though not necessarily colonial domination. It is possible, for instance, that in the Lau Islands of Fiji, as they were incorporated into the Tongan Empire, indigenous custom became a symbol of local resistance; the same may have happened in places like the Loyalty Islands and southern Vanuatu where Polynesians extended hegemony over indigenous populations.

sense that the leadership roles, the leadership styles, and the units led have all been modeled on their analogues in the colonial state. Maasina Rule leaders organized their political structure to correspond to and counter the structure of colonial control (in the form of Headmen, Districts, and Subdistricts). The Kwaio I worked with in 1963, trying to codify and legitimize their version of *kastomu*, represent a stage in this process. On those Tuesdays at Ngarinaasuru when the Kwaio social landscape was divided into *sifi* and *koomani fifuru* ("chiefs" and "common people"), the "lines" each "chief" was supposed to lead were not the tiny, fragmented descent groups I was studying the rest of the week, but conceptual conglomerates of them—the "lines" organized by the Headmen of the 1920s for tax-paying purposes, to accord with the expectations of the government.

The whole notion of "chiefs," in a society that had no hereditary leaders (see Keesing 1968, 1978b, 1985b), represents an indigenous emulation and embellishment of European expectations about how the "natives" ought to be organized. The roles emulated by leaders in anticolonial struggle (and its continuation vis-à-vis the postcolonial state) continue to have this reactive cast, a process institutionalized in the postcolonial state with the recognition of "Paramount Chiefs." Folofo'u's rise to power was made possible more by European expectations (and European ideas adopted by the indigenous elite) than by his own political charisma. The confrontations between Folofo'u and Silas Wanebeni, leading Kwaio Fadanga, and the government forces were fascinating dramas symbolically as well as politically. After the teargassing, the Gilbert and Sullivan drama of invented customs and non-existent chiefs culminated in a demand that the Christians who voted pay compensation for violating a ritual injunction invoked by a chief: "In Kwaio custom, when the chief taboos something, no commoners can disobey." For a people living at the margins of anarchy, this is heady stuff.

The styles and languages of resistance have had this kind of Black Mass parodic style across the decades. When Maasina Rule leaders presented their demands to the colonial government, when they defended themselves against arrest and trial, the forms and language they used—given their subaltern perspective on European administrative structures and their limited access to education—often emerged as (unconscious or sometimes conscious) parodies of British legalism and Colonel Blimpism. So, too, the styles and structures of leadership and order in Maasina Rule had as their models the plumes and swords and rituals of Empire and the rituals of the American military; scant wonder that Maasina Rule had at times something of the theatrical quality and parodic cast of Chaplin portraying The Great Dictator.

We need to examine this oppositional logic of counterhegemonic discourse more closely, from several directions. A useful starting point is to examine some elements of colonial discourse, as manifest in the British Solomons.

Structures and Premises of Colonial Discourse in the Solomons

We have glimpsed in the Kwaio accounts of their recent history the pervasive racism of British colonial rule. The colonial officialdom centered in Tulagi and scattered through island outposts was organized in a racially constructed "caste" system in which whites did virtually no physical labor, interacted with "natives" in limited situations requiring extreme deference, and expressed contempt for the supposed primitivism, dirtiness, savagery, and ignorance of indigenous Solomon Islanders. (The Chinese traders and shopkeepers were barred from white society but placed on a higher rung than the dark-skinned "natives"; the Polynesians were placed on a lower rung, but still above the Melanesians.)

To the rituals of hierarchy and racial supremacy were added, on the plantations, a brutality and violence and inhumanity on the part of white planters. The missions, too, constituted a different world, but one similarly constructed in racist terms: the option for Solomon Islanders was to be "reborn" as peaceful and passive children, worshipping as second-class citizens in a white God's kingdom. What little education was offered was in Pidgin English, and almost all concerned with Bible teaching.

The ideological edifice and artifice on which British colonialism was built, in the Solomons as in other parts of the world, rested on the premise that a rule of law and order, rationally ordered according to the higher canons of "civilization," was benevolently introduced to replace what had been uncivilized and anarchic and irrational. Indigenous peoples who had been blessed by having a higher and more civilized moral and political order revealed to them should, it was assumed, recognize these benefits and join in their implementation.

Further implicit in this ideology was the premise that the attachments of people to place and of polity to people that had prevailed prior to the colonial order had not constituted sovereignty. Recall that in 1911, two years after the establishment of a Government station on Malaita, the British High Commissioner of the Western Pacific suggested that the cycles of blood feuding in the Malaita interior could be broken if a "combined force" including Panjabi Sikhs or Pathans "visit the villages of the Bushmen" and "explain to them" that the "Government will punish them if they do not desist from their lawless practices" (May 1911). There is a direct conceptual line connecting this 1911 view of customary blood feuds by the indigenous occupants of an island one has invaded and conquered as "lawless practices" and the imprisonment of the leaders of their anticolonial struggle 37 years later for violating British sedition laws of 1798.

Kwaio appropriations of the categories, logics, and semiology of colonial rule progressively stripped away the mystifications of this ideology by portraying the colonial presence as what it was: an act of invasion, an appropriation of lands, an imposition of an alien cultural system, a rule by force and not by law—since the British did not follow their own laws and moral codes—or by consent. We find as signposts along the way, in this process, the early challenges to the tax cast in the terms of British legalism and monarchy (such as those flung by the Kwaio leaders in 1923 to the visiting Resident Commissioner and by Basiana to Bell in presenting a "shilling" with the picture of his ancestor), the invocation of British legalisms by the Maasina Rule chiefs during their trial (and Fifi'i's sardonic observation that their "crime" had been the one Jesus was convicted of), and Maena'adi's 1990 retrospective assessment of how the British had allowed their own most hallowed laws and moral precepts to be broken during the punitive expedition.

The dialectic between British ideologies and indigenous counter-ideologies is illuminating in other ways. By confronting the colonial rulers with counters to their own logics, categories, legalisms, and symbols—as with the "flag" of La'aka, the Maasina Rule chiefs, the codified *kastomu*—the Kwaio were demanding that the British acknowledge their prior sovereignty, their rights under cultural law. Yet, as with the peasant insurgency of the previous century in colonial India as explored by Guha (1983), the British consistently refused to recognize as such the forms of resistance being deployed against them. Acts of armed defense of territory—in the Malaita case, the early attacks on ships—were viewed as "outrages" rather than military operations. When Bell and his entourage were massacred, explanations and motives were sought in specific misunderstandings or provocations: those who investigated the massacre never pondered that it was a challenge to and struggle against invasion and subjugation, a desperate last assertion of *sovereignty*. For to acknowledge *that* would have been to admit the possibility that British rule of the Solomons constituted an act of invasion, that the imposition of colonial law and order was a process of military conquest and domination rather than benign civilizing. When the Maasina Rule chiefs and the tens of thousands who stood solidly behind them confronted the British administration with demands for recognition of customary law, political rights, common humanity, and decent working conditions, the British refused to recognize collective political demands as such. On the one hand, as in the previous century in India (Guha 1983), they portrayed the leaders as scheming despots deceiving and coercing their fellows; on the other, they seized on bits and pieces that could be construed as millenarian to dismiss the movement as a cargo cult fantasy.

We can widen the argument by situating this oppositional process within a broader category of "emulation."[2] Part of the process of colonial domination has been to instill in a stratum of the indigenous population simulacra of the manners, languages, styles, and values of the colonial elite. I say "simulacra" because the "natives" are permitted within certain bounds to emulate, one might say to mimic, the ways of those who rule them: but always with a distance and deference that preserves the bounds of their subalternity. In colonial discourse, such emulation represents the process of "civilizing" (and in many places, Christianizing as well). The semiology and pragmatics of emulation-with-deference by indigenous elites were wondrously intricate, almost a choreographed dance, in the India of the Raj or the Dutch East Indies (Stoler 1985).

But to emulate without this deference, to presume equality, was *transgression*, a challenge to white supremacy and colonial domination. Guha (personal communication) suggests that in the gap between emulation and transgression lies the key to subaltern resistance. The first response of the white rulers was often disbelief, a refusal to interpret a challenge to domination as what it was. It could instead by read as madness, demagoguery, millenarian cultism, or simply uncivilized gaucherie by the natives.

To analyze fully the dialectics of emulation, deference, and transgression would require greater attention, in the preceding chapters, to the Solomon Islanders who served the colonial administration (as Headmen, constables, clerks) and the missions. We get glimpses, in those chapters, of the Solomon Islanders serving in the constabulary and police, with Bell and his successors (such as Cameron at Gelebasi in 1947), and in other capacities within the colonial state and missions; but we see them mainly through the eyes of their Kwaio adversaries. An emulation of

---

2. A perspective for which I am indebted to discussion with Ranajit Guha.

British ways, insofar as this was expressed with suitable deference, runs through the texts of the colonial period, including my own. (In Keesing 1988, for instance, I quote an old Malaita policeman recounting in Pidgin how he and his comrades incorporated European "errors" in Pidgin pronominal usage into their own speech.) Maena'adi's comments about the police killed at Gwee'abe because of their "red sashes" and what they represented further comes to mind.

We must remember how pervasively successful the hegemonic process has been in the Solomons, as in most other colonial situations. Even by the 1920s, Christianity had made dramatic inroads in the Western Solomons, Guadalcanal, Santa Isabel, and other islands, and some parts of Malaita. The Kwaio warriors who killed Bell in 1927 were perceived as wild savages in the clutches of Satan by most of their indigenous contemporaries; the Kwaio pagans of 1990 are despised by the vast majority of Solomon Islanders, staunchly Christian and mainly committed to modernity as well as salvation. As the observations of Dangeabe'u and Maato'o indicate, even the Christian Kwaio living on the coast, who now substantially outnumber the pagans, have deeply internalized European ideologies.

When Malaitans, and most stridently the Kwaio, combined emulation with assertions of equality rather than subordination, the outrage of the British at these transgressions (and their persistent inability to read the messages as what they were) emerge vividly in the preceding chapters. Another illustration will be useful, a story told by Fifi'i (1989:102–3) about his confrontation with a British District Officer:

> I remember a quarrel I had . . . with a District Officer named Lang. When he was on patrol in the bush, he went into someone's taro garden in the middle of the day. According to our customs, you can't go into a garden after eating fish or anything like that, or after mid-morning has passed. His carriers went through the garden too. The owner of the garden claimed a pound in compensation, so he could buy a pig to sacrifice to purify the offense. I went to the District Officer and put forward the man's claim. Mr. Lang got very angry: "It's not taboo for me! It's you who have invented your taboos. They don't apply to me! If he wants to take me to court to claim compensation, let him take me to court!" Of course, he was the Magistrate. I got really angry. "You, the Government, are the ones who brought your laws here, and who are imposing them. And then you think you're above the law yourselves." The District Officer said, "All right, I'll give him the one pound. Here is your compensation. But I'm only doing it out of the goodness of my heart. I don't have to. That's not my custom! It's not taboo for me to go into the garden, it's taboo for him."

"It doesn't matter that it's not your custom. You're the ones who have come to our country. You're the one who has been walking around in the land of my ancestors. You have to pay compensation as purification! You have to do it! If I go to someone else's country and do something that breaks their laws or violates their customs, I'm responsible for what I've done." Later on, he slipped and fell while walking across a waterfall, and broke his arm. I wonder if it was the ancestors.

The Semiology of Domination and the Parodic Cast of Resistance

Fifi'i here illustrates a contestation of meanings, a struggle for a symbolic terrain claimed and defined by the colonizing power.

The legitimacy of British claims to sovereignty was symbolically established with flags and parades and distant King and bewigged magistrates as well as with warships and Winchester rifles. This semiology of domination—and the place of the written word in its imposition—casts important light on Kwaio resistance. Contestation operates at a symbolic as well as a political level. Hegemony operates in part through the imposition of frames of reference, of premises that define universes of discourse, of systems of signs. Counterhegemonic struggle entails a contestation of meanings as well as of political power. In appropriating the conceptual structures and semiology of domination, those who resist it attempt to invert and thus reveal and challenge these premises.

A striking instance of how the semiology of British claims to sovereignty shaped Kwaio counter-claims to *their* continuing sovereignty has been glimpsed in the account of Bell's confrontation with Basiana at the 1926 tax collection. Recall that when Basiana went back up to his settlement, smashed a consecrated shell chest pendant, and ground down a piece into the size and shape of a shilling, he presented it to Bell saying "The other four had your King on them; this one has my ancestor on it!" Recall, too, that when in the late 1930s Noto'i preached resistance to British authority in the name of the ancestress La'aka and foretold the destruction of Tulagi, key symbols of resistance were flags (*fulake*) said to have flown above the palisaded cult centre. Whether the flags actually existed physically is uncertain; it seems that the leaders were arrested before any actual flags were flown. But the flag nonetheless became a symbol of a challenge to colonial authority, again using the semiology of the Europeans.

Considering transgression as emulation without deference illuminates the parodic cast of counterhegemonic discourse.[3] We find a sort of parody

---

3. On these matters, I am indebted to discussion with Nicholas Thomas and Douglas Miles.

at two levels. First, running through the Kwaio texts, we find parody in a strict sense, a more-or-less intentional imitation of the semiology of the rulers, deployed as a sardonic mode of resistance. Basiana with his shell shilling, the pagan priest Bita Saetana ("Peter Satan"), and Fifi'i's conviction for what he called Jesus' crime can serve as tokens. Second, we find what is not really parody in a strict sense, but appears as such only in the eye of the (Western) beholder: as where Malaitans, often Christian scribes acting on behalf of pagans, write documents they intend to be taken with legal seriousness in what they take to be legalistic language. The British have derived endless mirth through the years from what they have taken to be hilarious renderings by Indians of legalese English; the documentary records of Malaita resistance include much that falls in this genre (see Laracy 1983). The sense of parody is heightened when the language is Biblical as well as legalistic, and particularly when the Christian scribes are writing on behalf of the pagans but categorizing the pagans in Manichaean terms. A 1977 document illustrates the parodic cast of Kwaio resistance at both levels. It was written by a Christian scribe on behalf of pagan priests demanding compensation for the pollution brought about when menstruating and postpartum women flew over their heads in the SDA airplane:

Dear Director of S.D.A. and the Pilot of S. Steck [Piper Aztec]

I just want to let you know that I don't want your plain to fly over my village including Ere ere area from now on. I stop in for the following reasonable reasons:

1. The plain carry women with bloody babies.

2. He always fly over our most Holy Alters where we burn offering to our devil.

3. It always cause death to our people because the devil get angry and kill people.

4. Many pigs are kill to mean the plains fly over our devil. . . .

On have of majority of headen people who are living here if you are Christians please don't set your flyth over our area for it cause us death.

> Thank you,
> Yours sincerely Ere ere Devil Priests
> 1. Timikooliu
> 2. Maerora
> 3. Maealea

This parodic cast of the discourse of resistance continues into the present, as with the Kwaio Fadanga claim for compensation. The substance of the claim, resting as it does on premises of ancestral punishment stemming from the 1927 desecration, represents indigenous conceptions of causality and liability. Despite this customary orientation, the form and language in which the demand is framed is—unintentionally—a kind of parody of British legalism. The oppositional nature of Kwaio thought is here transparent. When I advised Folofo'u that the claim was not valid in terms of European or international law, his response was "It's valid in terms of *our* law!": but Kwaio *loa*, so conceptualized, is constructed in opposition and correspondence to the law that has historically been invoked to end Malaitan autonomy.

A final illustration of the oppositional aspect of Kwaio discourses of resistance lies in their adoption of Christian and colonial racist categories. Most contemporary Solomon Islanders have grown up within one of the main versions of Christianity—South Sea Evangelical Church, Uniting Church, Seventh Day Adventist, Catholic, Anglican—and have deeply internalized not only Christian doctrine but Christian representations of their own ancestors and customs. The ancestors are manifestations of the Devil; the past was a time of fear, murder and superstition. Metaphors of light and darkness, of conversion of rebirth, and depictions of Islanders as children are deeply internalized (see Jan-Mohamed 1986). The diehard pagans who have fought for almost a century to keep Christianity out of their mountain fastnesses, and who sacrifice still to their ancestors, who hold sway and enforce their taboos in a shrinking and embattled universe, conceptualize their struggle in the terms of Christian discourse. My friend Bita Saetana (Peter Satan) and his fellow pagans refer to themselves as *wikiti*, 'the wicked', or as *ta'a i 'itini*, 'heathen people'.

Oppositional Thought and Language

As these illustrations show, in contexts of domination and resistance, language itself becomes a politicized field in which oppositional thought is played out. Characteristically, in colonial situations, some lingua franca—a simplified vernacular such as Bazaar Malay in Dutch East Indies or colonial Hindustani in India or a pidgin, as in New Guinea and the Solomons or Nigeria, became the language of domination in which European rule and caste supremacy were enacted. Usually, the white rulers spoke such languages with less than full fluency or with particular twists emphasizing racism, domination, and superiority. Both this language of domination and the vernaculars—to which Europeans seldom had access—used in and shaped by discourses of resistance became politically charged.

Kwaio on the plantations and dealing with colonial police and administrators had to learn and use Solomons Pidgin English, the old lingua franca of the Queensland plantations, expanded and stabilized at the turn of the century. As I have shown (Keesing 1988), pidgin itself embodies evidence of its history both as a language of solidarity among Pacific Islanders on ships and in trade and plantation work and as a medium of plantation economies in which Islanders worked and Europeans gave orders. The grammar is heavily Oceanic Austronesian in many ways; the lexicon comes mainly from English, but with phonology and semantics shaped by indigenous languages. Pidgin is a language Solomon Islanders speak fluently and grammatically, and most Europeans have spoken badly and ungrammatically, imagining it to be a bastardized and simplified form of English one could achieve by inserting "fella" periodically. Yet vernaculars have been heavily shaped as well by the colonial context, in acquiring lexical forms from Pidgin and in acquiring means to characterize engagements with the colonial state and Christianity. Both Pidgin and the vernaculars have been sites of struggle.

The heavily oppositional cast of Kwaio talk about *kastom,* in the special marked contexts of anticolonial politics, should not obscure the fact that unless outsiders are involved, Kwaio is the linguistic medium for such talk. Sprinkled with Pidgin English loan words though it may be in these political contexts, the medium is indigenous and the talk is redolent with culturally salient metaphor and meaning. Kwaio metaphors of resistance come most directly from the physical acts and states of closure common in everyday life. They are metaphors of fencing, of blocking off a path or closing a door with a timber slab. Other elements in Kwaio talk come from the rhetoric of confrontation and challenge in the local politics of threat, intimidation, and feuding: of 'trying', of standing fast. To emphasize the oppositional element in Kwaio discourse without remembering that language itself consititutes a domain of struggle would distort the picture. In speaking one's own language, one preserves a cultural territory and landscape.

Yet in defending this territory, even through one's own language, usage is shaped by the struggle; old forms acquire new meanings. Kwaio rhetoric about land and sovereignty is cast in terms of the symbolic power of *wado,* 'land'—which in contexts of anticolonial struggle and with the alienation of lands elsewhere in the Solomons at issue has acquired a salience it could not have had before European invasion. *Fanua,* 'territory, home place',[4] has acquired in the context of plantation labor migration

4. A common Oceanic variant of an old Austronesian form for a home place (an island, a territory, a village).

meanings it could not have had for the Kwaio before the Europeans came: *fanua ada*, 'our homeland', is a symbol both of a homeland and of the place and ancestral ways Kwaio leave behind when they go away from their mountains. Using Pidgin forms rather than Kwaio ones is a manifestation of oppositional discourse; but even in using their own language, the Kwaio are reacting as well as resisting.

Oppositional Thought and Hegemony

We can well ask, in the light of these contestations, how deeply the thought and experience of a colonized people bears the impress of colonial categories and ideologies.[5] When we find a people articulating their resistance or organizing or characterizing themselves in the terms and categories of the colonialists, does this reflect hegemony in a deep psychological and sociological sense? Or is the political field structured in terms that compel these modes of categorization and representation? The answers are far from simple. As such writers as Fanon (1963, 1965, 1967), Mannoni (1956) and JanMohamed (1986) have argued compellingly, being treated as a despised and subhuman savage and abused physically and psychologically in contexts of forced labor and colonial servitude leaves deep scars.[6] It would falsely romanticize Kwaio resistance to minimize the degree to which the colonial situation has forced experience into reactive molds through hegemonic force, political and psychological. Yet at the same time, the reactive character of countercolonial action is in many ways structured by the political field itself (Goldsmith n.d., Keesing n.d.3). Categories (such as "Malaitaman") that were meaningless in precolonial times acquired a reality in contexts of plantation labor and colonial administration. In Maasina Rule, Malaitans created chiefs to challenge the government headmen who exercised local tyrannies; when the postcolonial state vested legitimate power in "Paramount Chiefs," the Kwaio invented one.

In part, as Stuart Hall[7] has reminded me with regard to the struggles of West Indians in London, the oppositional cast of discourses of resistance reflects a strategic realization that one must meet the enemy on his own turf. The Kwaio case shows how deep and subtle this process is. If one wants to challenge colonial assertions of sovereignty, one must do it in a

---

5. A problem clearly posed by James Howe in his capacity as discussant of the paper when it was presented at MIT.

6. Jonathan Fifi'i's account (1989, chap. 3) of his experiences as a Kwaio boy working in pre-war Tulagi underlines the severity of this scarring on adult orientations.

7. Personal communication, February 1986.

language of flags and ancestors-on-coins in place of Kings. If one wants to challenge colonial legal statutes and Biblical rules by asserting the legitimacy of ancestral rules and customary codes, one must do so through codification, through writing a counter-Bible/counter-lawbook. A recognition that if counterclaims are to be recognized and effective, they must be cast in the terms and categories and semiology of hegemonic discourse, is politically astute, not blindly reactive.

This process is illuminated if we look at the categories in terms of which claims to identity have been framed on Malaita. During and since Maasina Rule, these categories have been those created by the colonial (and now postcolonial) government: "Malaita" (vs. "Western"), "Kwaio" (vs. 'Are'are, To'aba'ita), "Sinalagu" (vs. 'Oloburi and Uru), "Waariu" (vs. Kwailala'e). In each case, the entity in terms of which unity and common interest in proclaimed had no conceptual existence prior to and outside the framework of colonial administration. Yet the framing of countercolonial discourse in terms of such "nonexistent" entities, products of colonial administrative interests and even misunderstandings, cannot lightly be taken as the naïve perpetuation of myths and mistakes by a subjugated population. These non-existent entities *acquired a reality*, both experientially and politically, in a context of plantation labor and colonial rule; and in the postcolonial state, they retain their salience as frameworks and arenas for power and resources.

This picture of the oppositional and reactive cast of antihegemonic discourse calls for two final qualifications. First, to adopt categorical structures patterned on the discourses of domination does not mean that the categories generated oppositionally will be static. It is possible, for example, to adopt a Manichaean categorical structure in which Christian characterizations of light and darkness, good and evil, serve as template; and to change progressively the terms in which the opposition is cast and the meanings structured dualistically. Nicholas Thomas (n.d.2) shows how, in Fiji and other parts of Oceania, oppositions between (e.g.) Christian and heathen and savage and civilized may be recast and inverted as the political field shifts. That is, oppositional thought is not passive or static: the reactive process is a dynamic and creative one. Jukka Siikala[8] observed that in some parts of the Pacific, the latest recasting of a Manichaean opposition depicts the Islanders as Christian and the European tourists and visitors as heathens.

8. In a comment at a Workshop on the Global Anthropology of Oceania at the University of Lund, on October 19, 1991.

Second, the reactive process may generate constructions in which indigenous ways are contrasted with and distanced from alien and invasive ones. Much of the modern ideology of *kastom* has this reactive cast, where an idealized and mythicized ancestral past is celebrated as the antithesis of Western materialism, individualism, and anomie.[9] In some forms and moments of anticolonial struggle, the social order imposed by colonialism has been dismantled or overturned, the categories of colonial rule erased and transgressed, the semiology deliberately rejected, not merely inverted. In the Algerian revolution, for example, ethnic categories defined by the colonial state (e.g., the distinction between "Arabs" and "Berbers") were strategically obliterated in order to forge a united front.[10] A striking example of symbolic resistance through rejection of the semiology of colonial rule was Gandhi's adoption of homespun garb, his choice of the spinning wheel as symbol, his counterhierarchical style of leadership[11].

All this is to say that the reactive process is a highly complex dialectical one in which the categorical structures of domination may be negated or inverted—hence doubly subverted—as well as reproduced in opposition. Even where they appear to be appropriating the structures and categories and logics of colonial discourse, subaltern peoples progressively but ultimately radically transform them, in the very process of transgression and in their deployment in a counterhegemonic political struggle.[12] The Kwaio texts vividly illustrate this process.

It is worth underlining again that although in a colonial situation the cultures and politics of subalternity are inherently oppositional, structured by a "series of negations," they may be structured by "affirmations" as well: that is the classic hegemonic process, in which subalterns are deeply implicated in their own subjugation. The place of Christianity in the colonization of the Solomons and the eventual creation of a neocolonial elite affords ample illustration of this process.[13]

The discourses of Kwaio resistance provide, then, fascinating insights into the contestation of meanings, the dialectics of symbolic representation, and the categorical structures of counterhegemonic thought.

9. See Keesing and Tonkinson 1982 and a now extensive subsequent literature, and, in particular, Thomas n.d.1.

10. Sami Nair, personal communication, February 1986.

11. An example I borrow from Goldsmith n.d., who acknowledges his own debt to Cohn 1983.

12. A point for which I am indebted to Ranajit Guha.

13. See Comaroff 1985 for a brilliant exposition of the place of Methodism in the subjugation of southern Africa and the creation of a neocolonial elite, as well as further developments of this theme in Comaroff and Comaroff 1986 and 1991.

25 Why Resistance?

A final question remains, but it is one I cannot really answer. Almost all Solomon Islanders, whose grandparents were following the ways of their ancestors, have long been Christian, and are now bent on Westernization and development. How and why have the Kwaio pagans retained their commitment and maintained their resistance? Why and how did the Kwaio, who stood solidly with their "brothers" to the south and the north in the 1940s, continue to stand alone when the others were opting for new ways? How, in the face of massive temptations and massive pressures, have they retained not only a faith in their ancestors but a sense of the richness of a way of life that is materially stark and simple and physically arduous? How, especially now there is another world they can see, with its cars and videos, can these diehard traditionalists still value the old? One cannot answer these questions simply by toting up the facts of geography—a relative remoteness and isolation, the lack of coastal land for cash cropping, the lack of road and sea connections. These affect the delicate balances of choice, but they do not tip them decisively.

There is, I think, no simple answer. It certainly will not do to use the old anthropological strategy of invoking vague cultural essences to explain a proclivity to conservatism or to change. In these respects, I think, all Malaita peoples shared the same broad cultural tradition; and we cannot selectively invoke elements of "it" to "explain" conservatism in one part of the island, and openness to change in other parts.

Perhaps there were, in pre-European Malaita, some contrasts between language groups in orientations to one another and to speakers of other languages.[1] Coastal and lagoon peoples seem to have been more open to outside ideas, through trade, exchange, and mobility. Their cultural traditions were more elaborated in some areas of cosmology and myth, and they were more hierarchically organized politically. Inland peoples, perhaps most notably the Kwaio speakers, were characterized by sociological fragmentation, the absence of marked political hierarchy, an elaboration of violence, and a kind of cultural involution and closure the exact nature and degree of which is difficult to characterize. These diffuse qualities and contrasts, heightened by the circumstances of geography and economics during the Labor Trade and early mission period, may

1. This possibility was explored by William Davenport in discussion of a lecture on Kwaio resistance presented to the Philadelphia Anthropological Society in February 1991.

have created preconditions conducive to the events that were to follow.

The events of early colonial history are crucial here. Bell might have been killed at any of a dozen passages around Malaita, although even in the 1920s the Kwaio were perhaps the toughest of the island's tough guys. But once they had done the deed, and the government had responded with heavy-handed outrage rather than remediation and reconciliation, an oppositional future for the Kwaio was virtually inevitable. The massacre had set the Kwaio into a position as everyone's villains, as ruffians in the Devil's clutches, to be punished in perpetuity by the colonial state and to be the symbol of unregenerate heathenism vis-à-vis the missions. This "outlaw" situation set a powerful dynamic of opposition and defiance into motion. Kwaio pagans have known that they were condemned to dangerous marginality, isolated from the patronage of the colonial government,[2] forever to be persecuted and despised. They have perceived that in the world of plantations (and now, of town) this gives them a mystique of danger and defiance, and considerable power. There is an element of self-fulfilling prophecy here. Young Kwaio men who may be quiet and innocuous at home assume a swagger of arrogance as they hunt in packs far from home. The politics of resistance relies heavily on threat, intimidation, and the mystique of ancestrally supported violence, where what is in the eye of the beholder guides the strategy of the actor. Had the Kwaio been less marginalized and mindlessly persecuted after the 1927 massacre, the dramatic events sixty years later would never have occurred.

There are other special historical circumstances, some with origins far beyond the Solomons, that have contributed to this Kwaio stance of resistance. Had World War II not intruded, bringing both visible evidence of the vulnerability of a British colonial rule that in the 1930s had seemed all-powerful and monolithic and new visions of political possibility, the Kwaio pagans would probably have become Christians, as so many other Malaitans had. Yet other Malaitans with similar wartime experiences and similar stances of resistance in Maasina Rule have chosen paths to "development," not the ways of the ancestors.

It is worth reflecting that a stance of resistance vis-à-vis Westernization and development, although singular at the onset of the 1990s, is not

2. Recall that in 1977, on the eve of independence, the last Governor of the British Solomon Islands Protectorate confided to me that for fifty years, since the Bell massacre, it had been the unwritten policy of the colonial government to leave the Kwaio interior forever undeveloped as a reservoir of cheap unskilled labor. If so, the British bear a heavy responsibility for Kwaio hostility and defiance since independence.

unique. We might think of the Kayapo of central Brazil or the Yanomami or the Penan, who are now finding advocates for their commitment to ancestral ways among environmentalists and cultural nationalists, and finding arenas for their resistance in international conferences and worldwide media. There is a set of interesting contradictions here. The technology of mass communication and jet travel has tied remote corners of the earth into worldwide networks and has enormously increased the accessibility of previously remote pockets. (This same technology has provided dramatic new material temptations.) At the same time, a Western cultural tradition that was absolutely confident of its ascendancy and superiority, in an earlier imperialist and expansionist phase, is now riven with internal contradiction, criticism, and self-doubt. Countercultural critiques, environmentalist politics, and senses of the alienation of contemporary mass society have led to a romanticization and idealization of primitivity and a search for alternatives. The Kwaio have had little direct contact with Western ideologies idealizing primitivity. They are surprised when I tell them that there are anthropology students and others reading my books around the world who praise and value their struggles, their cultural conservatism, their nakedness, and the material simplicity of their lives. But indirectly, I think, and partly from the debates that rage around the contemporary Solomons about the perceived environmental, social, and cultural costs of logging and cash cropping, the Kwaio perceive that Christianity and Westernization are not the irresistible juggernauts they once seemed to be. These factors cannot account for the decades of resistance against colonial rule and Christian ascendancy; but the pagans who have resisted so long now find support and sympathy from unexpected quarters, and encounter doubts where once there were certainties, despite the mounting material temptations.

The slow trickle to the mission villages continues, and perhaps the ancestral ways will disappear as the trickle turns to a stream. But perhaps, the resistance and the pride that fuels it will endure into the twenty-first century.

Works Cited

Abu-Lughod, L.
1990   "the Romance of Resistance: Tracing Transformations of Power through Bed-
        ouin Women." *American Ethnologist* 17(1):41–55.
Allan, C. H.
1957   *Customary Land Tenure in the British Solomon Islands Protectorate*. Report of the
        Special Lands Commission. Honiara: Western Pacific High Commission.
Anderson, G. M.
n.d.   Green Acres under Smoke. Unpublished Ms.
Bennett, J.
1987   *Wealth of the Solomons: A History of a Pacific Archipelago, 1800–1978*. Pacific
        Islands Monograph Series, No. 3. Honolulu: Univ. of Hawaii Press.
Boutilier, J.
1984   "European Women in the Solomon Islands, 1900–1942." In D. O'Brien and S.
        Tiffany, eds., *Rethinking Women's Roles: Perspectives from the Pacific*. Berkeley:
        Univ. of California Press, 173–99.
Brewster, A. B.
1938   *King of the Cannibal Isles*. London: Robert Hale.
Burt, B.
1982   "Kastom and the First Ancestor of the Kwara'ae." In R. M. Keesing and R.
        Tonkinson, eds., *Reinventing Traditional Culture: The Politics of Kastom in Island
        Melanesia. Mankind*, special issue 13(4).
Comaroff, Jean
1985   *Body of Power, Spirit of Resistance: The Culture and History of a South African
        People*. Chicago: Univ. of Chicago Press.
Comaroff, Jean and John L.
1986   "Christianity and Colonialism in South Africa." *American Ethnologist* 13:1–20.
1991   *Of Revelation and Revolution: Christianity, Colonialism, and Consciousness in
        South Africa*. Vol. 1. Chicago: Univ. of Chicago Press.
Cooper, F., and A. Stoler
1989   "Tensions of Empire: Colonial Control and Visions of Rule." *American Ethnolo-
        gist* 16(4):609–21.
Coppet, D. de
1977   "First Exchange, Double Illusion." *Journal of the Cultural Association of the Sol-
        omon Islands* 5:23–39.
Coppet, D. de, and H. Zemp
1978   'Are'are: Un Peuple mélanésien et sa musique. Paris: Seuil.
Corris, P.
1973   *Passage, Port and Plantation: A History of Solomon Islands Labour Migration,
        1870–1914*. Melbourne: Univ. of Melbourne Press.
Cromar, J.
1935   *Jock of the Islands: Early Days in the South Seas*. London: Faber and Faber.

Deck, N.

1910   "Across Malaita." South Sea Evangelical Mission Pastoral Letter, March 1910.

Eyerdam, W. J.

n.d.   Journals of the Whitney South Seas Expedition. American Museum of Natural History, New York (unpublished manuscript, 1930).

1933   "Among the Mountain Bushmen of Malaita." *Natural History* 33:430–38.

Fanon, F.

1963   *The Wretched of the Earth*. Trans. C. Farrington. New York: Grove Press.

1965   *A Dying Colonialism*. New York: Grove Press.

1967   *Black Skin, White Masks*. Trans. C. L. Markmann. New York: Grove Press.

Fatnowna, O. N.

1989   *Fragments of a Lost Heritage*. Ed. R. M. Keesing. Sydney: Angus and Robertson.

Fifi'i, J.

1989   *From Pig-Theft to Parliament: My Life Between Two Worlds*. Ed. and trans. by R. M. Keesing. Honiara: University of the South Pacific and Solomon Is. College of Higher Education.

Firth, R.

1979   "A Comment on 'Killing the Government' [by J. A. Boutilier]." In M. Rodman and M. Cooper, eds., *The Pacification of Melanesia*. Ann Arbor: Univ. of Michigan Press.

Friedlaender, J., et al.

1987   *The Solomon Islands Project: A Long-Term Study of Health, Human Biology, and Culture Change*. Oxford: Clarendon Press.

Genovese, E.

1974   *Roll, Jordan, Roll: The World the Slaves Made*. New York: Pantheon.

Goldsmith, M.

n.d.   "The Tradition of Invention." Forthcoming in proceedings of annual meetings of New Zealand Association of Social Anthropologists.

Gramsci, A.

1971   *Selections from the Prison Notebooks*. Ed. and trans. Q. Hoare and G. N. Smith. London: Lawrence and Wishart.

Great Britain

1887   *Papers Relating to the Recent Operations of HMS Opal against Natives of the Solomon Islands*. British Colonial Office. London: Henry Hansard and Sons.

Guha, R.

1983   *Elementary Aspects of Peasant Insurgency in Colonial India*. New Delhi: Oxford University Press.

1984   "The Prose of Counter-Insurgency." In R. Guha, ed., *Subaltern Studies II: Writings on South Asian History and Society*. New Delhi: Oxford University Press.

Hau'ofa, E.

1987   "The New South Pacific Society: Integration and Independence." In A. Hooper et al., *Class and Culture in the South Pacific*. Auckland: Centre for Pacific Studies; Suva: Institute of Pacific Studies, Univ. of the South Pacific.

Hobsbawm, E., and T. Ranger, eds.

1982   *The Invention of Tradition*. Cambridge: Cambridge University Press.

Huessler, R.
1963   *Yesterday's Rulers: The Making of the British Colonial Service.* Syracuse: Syracuse Univ. Press
Janmohamed, A. R.
1986   "The Economy of Manichean Allegory: The Function of Racial Difference in Colonialist Literature." In H. L. Gates, ed., *"Race," Writing, and Difference.* Chicago: Univ. of Chicago Press.
Keesing, R. M.
1967a   "Statistical Models and Decision Models of Social Structure: A Kwaio Case." *Ethnology* 6(1):1–16.
1967b   "Christians and Pagans in Kwaio, Malaita." *Journal of the Polynesian Society* 76:82–100.1
1968a   "Chiefs in a Chiefless Society: The Ideology of Modern Kwaio Politics." *Oceania* 38:276–80.
1968b   "Nonunilineal Descent and Contextual Definition of Status: The Kwaio Evidence." *American Anthropologist* 70:82–84.
1970a   "Shrines, Ancestors and Cognatic Descent: The Kwaio and Tallensi." *American Anthropologist* 72:755–75.
1970b   "Kwaio Fosterage." *American Anthropologist* 72:991–1019.
1970c   "Toward a Model of Role Analysis." In R. Cohen and R. Naroll, eds., *A Handbook of Method in Cultural Anthropology.* Garden City, N.Y.: Natural History Press.
1971   "Descent, Residence and Cultural Codes." In L. Hiatt and J. Jayawardena, eds., *Anthropology in Oceania.* Sydney: Angus and Robertson.
1978a   "Politico-Religious Movements and Anti-Colonialism on Malaita: Maasina Rule in Historical Perspective." *Oceania* 48:241–61; 49:46–73.
1978b   *'Elota's Story: The Life and Times of a Solomon Islands Big Man.* St. Lucia: Univ. of Queensland Press (reprinted 1983, New York: Holt, Rinehart and Winston).
1980   "Further Notes on Maasina Rule." *Journal of Pacific History* 13:102–107.
1981   "Still Further Notes on Maasina Rule." *Journal of the Anthropological Society of Oxford* 12:130–33.
1982a   *Kwaio Religion: The Living and the Dead in a Solomon Island Society.* New York: Columbia Univ. Press.
1982b   "Kastom and Anticolonialism on Malaita: 'Culture' as Political Symbol." In R. M. Keesing and R. Tonkinson, eds., *Reinventing Traditional Culture: The Politics of Kastom in Island Melanesia. Mankind,* special issue 13(4):297–301.
1985a   "Kwaio Women Speak: The Micropolitics of Autobiography in a Solomon Islands Society." *American Anthropologist* 87:27–39.
1985b   "Killers, Big Men and Priests on Malaita: Reflections on a Melanesian Troika System." *Ethnology* 24:237–52.
1986a   "The Young Dick Attack: Oral and Documentary History on the Colonial Frontier." *Ethnohistory* 33:268–92.
1986b   "Experiments in Grassroots Development: Malaita, Solomon Islands." *Quality of Work Life* (Chandigarh, India) 2:279–90.

1987a   "Anthropology as Interpretive Quest." *Current Anthropology* 28:161–76.
1987b   "African Models in the Malaita Highlands." *Man* 22:431–52.
1987c   "Ta'a Geni: Women's Perspectives on Kwaio Society." In M. Strathern, ed.,
         Dealing with Inequality. Cambridge: Cambridge University Press.
1987d   "Pijin Calquing on Kwaio: A Test Case." In D. Laycock and W. Winter, eds.,
         A World of Language: Festschrift for Prof. S. A. Wurm. Pacific Linguistics,
         C-100:335–60.
1988   *Melanesian Pidgin and the Oceanic Substrate.* Stanford, CA: Stanford University
         Press.
1989a   "Exotic Readings of Cultural Texts." *Current Anthropology* 30(43):459–77.
1989b   "Creating the Past: Custom and Identity in the Contemporary Pacific." *The
         Contemporary Pacific* 1(1):16–35.
1989c   "Sins of a Mission: Christian Life as Traditionalist Ideology." In M. Jolly and
         M. Macintyre, eds., *Family and Gender in the Pacific: Domestic Contradictions
         and Colonial Impact.* Cambridge: Cambridge Univ. Press.
1989d   "Social Structure as Process: Longitudinal Perspectives on Kwaio Society." In
         M. Marshall and J. Caughey, eds., *Culture, Kin and Cognition in Oceania: Essays
         in Honor of Ward H. Goodenough.* American Anthropological Association Spe-
         cial Publications 25:107–118.
1990   "Colonial History as Contested Ground: The Bell Massacre in the Solomons."
         History and Anthropology 4:279–301.
1991   "Not a Real Fish: The Ethnographer as Inside Outsider." In P. DeVita, ed., *The
         Naked Anthropologist.* Wadsworth Publishing Company.
n.d.1   "'Earth' and 'Path' as Complex Categories: Semantics and Symbolism in Kwaio
         Culture." Forthcoming in P. Boyer, ed., *Cognitive Aspects of Religious Symbol-
         ism.* Cambridge: Cambridge Univ. Press.
n.d.2   "The Uses of Knowledge in Kwaio Society." Forthcoming in A. Pawley, ed.,
         Man and a Half: Essays in Honour of Ralph Bulmer. Auckland: Auckland Univ.
         Press.
n.d.3   "Colonial and Counter-colonial Discourse in Melanesia." *History and An-
         thropology* (in press).
n.d.4   "Murder on Mount Austen: Kwaio Framing of an Act of Violence." Forthcom-
         ing in G. Bibeau and E. Corin, eds., *The Order of the Text: Asceticism and Vio-
         lence in Interpretation.* Berkeley: Univ. of California Press.
n.d.5   "Foraging in the Urban Jungle: Notes from the Kwaio Underground." Paper
         presented in symposium on urban culture in the Pacific, Association for Social
         Anthropology in Oceania, Kauai, March 1990.
n.d.6   "Kwaisulia as Culture Hero." Forthcoming in J. Carrier, ed., *History and Tradi-
         tion in Melanesian Anthropology.* Berkeley: University of California Press.
n.d.7   "Colonial Discourse and Codes of Discrimination in the Pacific." Forthcoming
         in volume from UNESCO Division of Human Rights and Peace.
Keesing, R. M., and P. Corris
1980   *Lightning Meets the West Wind: The Malaita Massacre.* Melbourne: Oxford Uni-
         versity Press.

Keesing, R. M., and F. M. Keesing
1976   *New Perspectives in Cultural Anthropology.* New York: Holt, Rinehart and Winston, Inc.
Keesing, R. M., and R. Tonkinson, eds.
1982   *Reinventing Traditional Culture: The Politics of Kastom in Island Melanesia. Mankind,* special issue 13(4).
Lakoff, G.
1987   *Women, Fire, and Dangerous Things: What Categories Reveal about the Mind.* Chicago: University of Chicago Press.
1990   "The Invariance Hypothesis: Is Abstract Reason Based on Image-Schemas?" *Cognitive Linguistics* 1(1):39–74.
1991   "The Internal Structure of the English System of Metaphors." Plenary address, 2nd annual conference of the International Cognitive Linguistics Association, Santa Cruz, Cal., July 31, 1991.
Laracy, H.
1983   *Pacific Protest: The Maasina Rule Movement.* Suva: Institute of Pacific Studies, Univ. of the South Pacific.
Mann, W. T.
1948   *Ant Hill Odyssey.* Boston: Little, Brown and Co.
Mannoni, O.
1956   *Prospero and Caliban: The Psychology of Colonization.* Trans. P. Powesland. London: Methuen.
Marx, K.
1852   *The Eighteenth Brumaire of Louis Bonaparte* (reprinted in K. Marx and F. Engels, *Selected Works.* 2 Vols. Moscow: Foreign Languages Publishing House).
Moore, C.
1986   *Kanaka: A History of Melanesian Mackay.* Port Moresby: Institute of Papua New Guinea Studies.
Mytinger, C.
1942   *Headhunting in the Solomon Islands around the Coral Sea.* New York: Macmillan.
Nash, J.
1979   *We Eat the Mines and the Mines Eat Us.* New York: Columbia Univ. Press.
Ong, A.
1987   *Spirits of Resistance and Capitalist Discipline: Factory Women in Malaysia.* Albany: State Univ. of New York Press.
Ross, H. M.
1973   *Baegu: Social and Ecological Organization in Malaita, Solomon Islands.* Illinois Studies in Social Anthropology 8. Urbana: Univ. of Illinois Press.
Sahlins, M.
1981   *Historical Metaphors and Mythical Realities: Structure in the Early History of the Sandwich Island Kingdom.* Ann Arbor: University of Michigan Press (Association for Social Anthropology in Oceania Monograph).
1985   *Islands of History.* Chicago: University of Chicago Press.

Saunders, K.
1976   "The Pacific Islander Hospitals in Colonial Queensland." *Journal of Pacific History* 11(1):28–50.
Scarr, D.
1970   "Recruits and Recruiters: A Portrait of the Labour Trade." In J. W. Davidson, ed., *Pacific Islands Portraits*. Canberra: Australian National University Press.
Scott, J. C.
1984   *Everyday Forms of Peasant Resistance*. New Haven: Yale Univ. Press.
1986   "Everyday Forms of Peasant Resistance." In J. C. Scott and B. J. Trea Kerkvliet, eds., *Everyday Forms of Peasant Resistance in South-East Asia*. London: Frank Cass.
1990   *Domination and the Arts of Resistance: Hidden Transcripts*. New Haven: Yale Univ. Press.
Stoler, A.
1985   *Capitalism and Confrontation in Sumatra's Plantation Belt*. New Haven: Yale University Press.
1989   "Making Empire Respectable: The Politics of Race and Sexual Morality in 20th Century Colonial Cultures." *American Ethnologist* 16(4):634–60.
Talmy, L.
1978   "Relation of Grammar to Cognition." in D. Walz, ed., *Proceedings of TIN-LAP-2* (Theoretical Issues in Natural Language Processing). Champaign IL: Coordinated Science Laboratory, University of Illinois.
1988a   "The Relation of Grammar to Cognition." in B. Rudzka-Ostyn, ed., *Topics in Cognitive Linguistics*. Amsterdam: John Benjamins, pp. 165–205.
1988b   "Force Dynamics in Language and Cognition." *Cognitive Science* 12(1):49–100.
n.d.   "Fictive Motion in Language and Perception." Plenary Address, 2nd annual conference of the International Cognitive Linguistics Association, Santa Cruz, Cal., July 30, 1991.
Taussig, M.
1980   *The Devil and Commodity Fetishism in Latin America*. Chapel Hill: Univ. of North Carolina Press.
Thomas, N.
n.d.1   "Substantivization and Anthropological Discourse: The Transformation of Practices into Institutions in Neotraditional Societies." Forthcoming in J. Carrier, ed., *History and Tradition in Melanesian Anthropology*. Berkeley: Univ. of California Press.
n.d.2   "The Inversion of Tradition." *American Ethnologist* (in press).
White, G.; D. Gegeo; D. Akin; and K. Watson-Gegeo, eds.
1988   *The Big Death/Bikfala Faet: Islanders Remember World War II*. Honiara: Univ. of the South Pacific and Solomon Is. College of Higher Education.
Williams, F. E.
1976   *"The Vailala Madness" and Other Essays*. Ed. with introduction by E. Schwimmer. St. Lucia: University of Queensland Press.

Willis, P.
1977   *Learning to Labour: How Working Class Kids Get Working Class Jobs.* New York:
          Columbia Univ. Press.
Woodford, C. M.
1890   *A Naturalist among the Headhunters.* London: George Philip and Son.
Young, F.
1926   *Pearls from the Pacific.* London, Edinburgh: Marshall Bros.

Index